David Constantine was for thirty years a university teacher of German language and literature. He has published several volumes of poetry, most recently *Nine Fathom Deep*; also a novel, *Davies*, and three collections of short stories, the latest being *The Shieling*. He is a translator and editor of Hölderlin, Goethe, Kleist and Brecht. His translation of Goethe's *Faust* was published by Penguin. With his wife Helen he edits *Modern Poetry in Translation*.

'In his excellent study, David Constantine traces the course of Europe's discovery of Greece in the seventeenth and eighteenth centuries. He not only captures the pioneering excitement but makes an interesting contribution to the history of ideas. A worthy and delightful celebration of the Hellenic Ideal in its many guises.'

William St Clair, *Times Literary Supplement*

'Fulfils an important function in establishing the interconnection of early travel publications and the development of the sentimental admiration and idealisation of Greek antiquity.'   *The Greek Gazette*

'An eloquent defense of the ideal to which the travellers bore witness: "Accurate knowledge is not detrimental to true love ... A single column is like a basic unit of aesthetic pleasure ... why should not the imagination love precision?"'   *Christian Science Monitor*

'Constantine's lucid account is to be praised not only for its informative quality but also for effectively capturing the spirit of the various undertakings and shifts in response to the classical world.'

Modern Language Studies

Tauris Parke Paperbacks is an imprint of I.B.Tauris. It is dedicated to publishing books in accessible paperback editions for the serious general reader within a wide range of categories, including biography, history, travel and the ancient world. The list includes select, critically acclaimed works of top quality writing by distinguished authors that continue to challenge, to inform and to inspire. These are books that possess those subtle but intrinsic elements that mark them out as something exceptional.

The Colophon of Tauris Parke Paperbacks is a representation of the ancient Egyptian ibis, sacred to the god Thoth, who was himself often depicted in the form of this most elegant of birds. Thoth was credited in antiquity as the scribe of the ancient Egyptian gods and as the inventor of writing and was associated with many aspects of wisdom and learning.

IN THE FOOTSTEPS OF THE GODS

Travellers to Greece and the Quest for the Hellenic Ideal

David Constantine

TAURIS PARKE
PAPERBACKS

Revised paperback edition published in 2011 by Tauris Parke Paperbacks
An imprint of I.B.Tauris and Co Ltd
6 Salem Road, London W2 4BU
175 Fifth Avenue, New York NY 10010
www.ibtauris.com

Distributed in the United States and Canada Exclusively by Palgrave Macmillan
175 Fifth Avenue, New York NY 10010

First published in 1984 by Cambridge University Press as *Early Greek Travellers and the Hellenic Ideal*

Cover image: *Grand Tourists at the Monument of Philopappos, Greece, 1821* (ink and w/c) by Cassas, Louis Francois (1756–1827) Private Collection / Photograph © Bonhams, London, UK / The Bridgeman Art Library

ISBN: 978 1 84885 545 8

A full CIP record for this book is available from the British Library
A full CIP record is available from the Library of Congress

Library of Congress Catalog Card Number: available

Printed and bound in Sweden by Scandbook

CONTENTS

ILLUSTRATIONS

ACKNOWLEDGEMENTS

During the work on this book I was able to spend time in Greece and Germany thanks to the generosity of the British Academy, Durham University Sabbatical Leave Fund and the German Academic Exchange Service. I am grateful to Mr Roger Norris of the Dean and Chapter Library, Durham, for advice and practical assistance in my study of George Wheler; to the Librarian of Wadham College, Oxford, for permission to quote from Gilbert Bouchery's manuscript memoir of Samuel Lisle; and to several colleagues in Durham and Oxford who took an interest in what I was doing and gave me useful hints. The book I owe most to, though his topic was not mine, is Terence Spencer's *Fair Greece Sad Relic*.

NOTE

Where possible I have supplied a translation from the English edition of the work; otherwise the translations are my own.

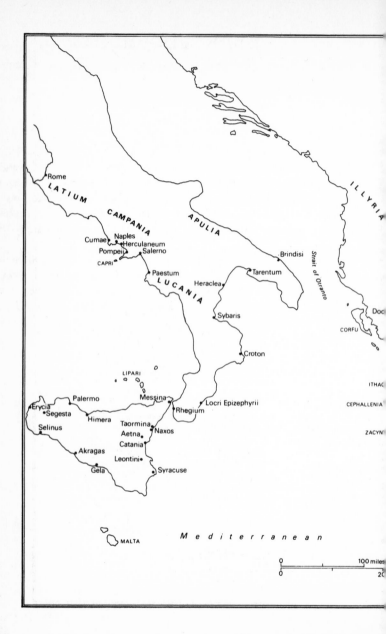

Rome

LATIUM

CAMPANIA

APULIA

ILLYRIA

Cumae
Naples
Herculaneum
Pompeii
Salerno
CAPRI
Paestum

Brindisi

Strait of Otranto

Heraclea
Tarentum

LUCANIA

Sybaris

Dod

CORFU

Croton

ITHAC

CEPHALLENIA

LIPARI

Messina
Locri Epizephyrii
Rhegium

ZACYN

Palermo
Erycia
Segesta
Himera
Selinus

Taormina
Aetna
Naxos
Catania
Akragas
Leontini
Gela
Syracuse

MALTA

Mediterranean

0   100 miles
0   2(

CHRONOLOGY OF TRAVELLERS

Traveller	Journey	Publications
Sandys	1610	*Relation*, 1627
des Hayes	1621	*Voiage de Levant*, 1624
Duloir	1639–41	*Voyages*, 1654
Thévenot	1655	*Relation*, 1665
Smith	1671	*Remarks*, 1678
Babin	1671–2	*Relation*, 1674
Randolph	1671–9	*State of the Morea*, 1686, and *Archipelago*, 1687
Cornelio Magni	1673–4	*Relazione*, 1688
Vernon	1675–6	letter of 1676
Spon	1675–6	*Voyage*, 1678
Wheler	1675–6	*Journey into Greece*, 1682
Chishull	1698–1702	*Antiquitates*, 1728, and *Travels*, 1747
Tournefort	1700–2	*Voyage du Levant*, 1717
Lady Montagu	1717–18	*Letters*, 1763
Pococke	1739–40	*Description*, 1743–5
Wood	1742–3. 1749–51	*Essay*, 1769 and 1775
Guys	from 1748	*Voyage littéraire*, 1771
Stuart and Revett	1751–5	*Antiquities of Athens*, 1762, 1787 and 1794
Leroy	1754	*Ruines*, 1758
Chandler	1764–6	*Asia Minor*, 1775, and *Greece*, 1776
Riedesel	1767. 1768	*Reise*, 1771, and *Remarques*, 1773
van Krienen	1770–1	*Breve Descrizione*, 1773
Choiseul-Gouffier	1776–9	*Voyage pittoresque*, 1782
Lechevalier	1785–6	*Plain of Troy*, 1791

PREFACE

I wrote this book not out of an antiquarian interest but for love of the travellers, scholars and poets who, in their various ways, discovered, described and celebrated Greece and took the land and the idea and ideal of it into their own lives. I've gone back to that land, to more and more places in it, many times since, most recently a year ago, to Thasos and Samothrace. The premise of my experience is in essence what it was for the characters in my book: that Ancient Greece matters. That premise is less of a commonplace now than it was in the eighteenth century; indeed, it may by now have become eccentric or even unintelligible. The relativization of the Ideal of Greece was already well under way – through contacts with other cultures in the South Seas, the Americas and along the coast of Africa – in the century that so extolled it; and the process has accelerated and widened since. Today Greece is, so to speak, just one possibility among thousands.

The chief components of the experience of Greece – then and still – are severance (or discrepancy) and continuity. What continues? The language, for one thing. The landscape and real places in it, for another. Homer and Ritsos share a language, they are far closer to one another in their speech, though much further apart in time, than are the author of *Beowulf* and his translator Heaney. And no one steeped in the poetry, myth and history of Ancient Greece ever quite gets over the fact that Delphi, Olympus, Thebes, Sparta, the Eurotas, Parnassus and countless other such celebrated places are there on a modern map and can be visited. You can better understand the battles of Marathon and Thermopylae by going where they were fought. The physical structure of Greece – the sea, the archipelago, the mountains, the severe hinterland, the flowery well-watered valleys – this is all still very apparent. Early travellers and the poets dwelled on that vast survival. Some included the people too – still there, in that place, after so many centuries. But just as strong, or in the more elegiacally minded even stronger, was the sense of loss, severance, discrepancy. The people were not the same, they had been under Turkish rule for three hundred years, they were Christian, not heathen, they were mixed, they were ignorant of the arts and sciences of their own illustrious ancestors. The remnants of the great cities and cult places, where they could be discovered, were in ruins – against which (this was especially the case in Athens) most modern building looked like slums and shanties. Discrepancy between what had been and what was, stared the travellers, and the poets reading them, in the face. Some then took all the consolation they could in the continuing earth and sky, the mountains, the islands and the sea. The place survived, the locus of a once and – some hoped – a future humane civilization.

And nowadays? There are more visible survivals than the eighteenth century every dreamed of, more and more beautiful things in museums, more sites opened, ever more coming to light – in Greek Macedonia, for example – as proofs of what was. Bestir yourself a little, work out the buses and the boats, and throughout the length and breadth of Greece (and along the coast of what was Asia Minor too) you can see spectacular locations, colossal and homely remains and fine and beautiful works of art. There is little point here in drawing attention to the loss. It is manifest. Parts of Greece have been and are still being trashed just as fast and thoroughly as money permits. Anyone haunted by Periclean Athens, the grove at Colonus, the Sacred Way to Eleusis will feel distressed. The landscape itself, the very sea, the forests, the fresh water places, in some areas now cannot serve as images of survival and continuity. Modernity (not just in Greece) sits ill with most ideals of Nature and Culture located in the far-away past.

Samos, when we got there, was host to a convention of 5000 bikers. They circled the island endlessly, on its one road. A little inland, in a watery lap of the mountains, early morning in the Sanctuary of the Great Gods, we had the place to ourselves but for a girl doing t'ai chi in what remains of the Hieron. The old city walls of Thasos run through the back gardens of the modern houses – one such garden has a Gate of the Charites in it. Up the coast on a spit of land the bars and tavernas face one bay, a Sanctuary of the Dioscuri faces the other. In the old Acropolis, among pine trees not recovered from drought, disease and fire, we found a bas-relief of Pan embossed on the rockface like a trilobite. The early travellers to Greece were forever coming across such amusing, poignant and desolating contiguities. The land is littered with images.

David Constantine
January 2011

INTRODUCTION

My aim in this book is twofold: to introduce the most important and interesting of those men who, during the first century of revived European interest in Greece, went there and wrote accounts; and to define and discuss the Idea of Greece held by the travellers themselves and by certain contemporary men of letters who never made the journey. I pursue those two interests – early travel in Greece and European Hellenism – as one topic.

All the travellers with whom I am principally concerned (except Riedesel) were English and French; but the scholars and poets to whom I look for the expression of the Hellenic Ideal were German. This is not an arbitrary arrangement, and not one dictated by my own predilections. No German of any real consequence travelled in Greece during the period here treated; and yet, towards the end of and immediately after that century of travel, Germans were the most passionate believers in the Idea of Hellas and German writers were Europe's best exponents of it. There is not in the literatures of eighteenth-century France or England any Hellenist poet like Hölderlin or any critic of Greek art like Winckelmann. That, in my view, justifies the disposition of my interest in Greece among the three nations.

Why Germans during the years of their Hellenist obsession never did go to Greece is an intriguing question. One reason may be that Germany lacked sources of enlightened patronage. The French Crown sent Tournefort and Fourmont to Greece; the Society of Dilettanti sent Chandler. No such sponsorship was possible in Germany, or at least none ever came about. Nor was there an aristocracy cultured, self-confident and adventurous enough to extend the customary Grand Tour as far as Greece. And classical scholarship in Germany, until the end of the eighteenth century, was backward by comparison with that in France and England; the best editions, the finest publications on classical matters came into Germany from abroad. There was in

England and France a long tradition – not broken by anything so devastating as the Thirty Years War – of classical scholarship and foreign educational travel, and out of this tradition the exploration of Greece (using commercial contacts not available to Germany) easily grew. Then finally, often asserted but not capable of conclusive proof: Germans by their very temperament shied away from ever seeing with their own eyes the ideal land itself. 'Nur aus der Ferne', Humboldt said, 'nur von allem Gemeinen getrennt, nur als vergangen muß das Altertum uns erscheinen' ('at a distance, in the past, and removed from its everyday reality – only thus should the Ancient World appear to us'). No doubt there is something in this pronouncement. Goethe quotes it in his essay on Winckelmann – who was curiously reluctant to avail himself of real opportunities to visit Greece; and, in Hölderlin's poetry, longing, inevitably unfulfilled, is the main motivating force.

Be that as it may, for one reason or another eighteenth-century Germans did not go to Greece, but the French and the English did. And in Germany Hellenism was more variously and passionately expressed than anywhere else.

Though I make this distinction between the nations it is not my wish to separate travellers in Greece from writers at home, as though the former were only purveyors and the latter only recipients of information and influence. Influence of that sort can, of course, often be proved: Goethe read Lechevalier when he worked on his *Achilleis*, Hölderlin read Chandler and Choiseul-Gouffier and took from them topographical details for his novel and images for his poems. That is interesting enough (and becomes more so the more closely one studies the poetic transmutation of received factual information); but the travellers themselves were the receivers and carriers of current literary, aesthetic and cultural ideas, they travelled with these and saw Greece accordingly. Guys and Riedesel had read – indeed they were disciples of – Winckelmann; Robert Wood, in the view of Homer which he formulated as he travelled through Greece, was in tune with the literary enthusiasms of his age, and then himself, especially in Germany, contributed to the current debates.

The Idea and Ideal of Greece, in the travellers who went there and in the scholars, poets, critics and philosophers who did not, was not a monolithic thing; and I have tried to indicate the variety of its facets and possibilities. I have tried in the case of each traveller to define what his particular predisposition was; in the first place, whether his interest in Greece was Hellenist at all, and if so to what degree. Spon and Wheler, for example, may be distinguished one from the other, by the quality and degree of their enthusiasm for Hellas; Tournefort, though he added notably to Europe's factual knowledge of Greece, was first and foremost a botanist. Riedesel went as a *philosophe*, economist and diplomat, a reader of Rousseau and Montesquieu as well as of Winckelmann. And although the German exponents of Hellenism shared a belief in the Ideal, their individual interests and emphases were very different. Hellas, as an ideal, had philosophical, cultural and political potential. It was the state before the Fall, or after the Revolution. For Winckelmann and Heinse, concerned with aesthetic, personal and sexual values, Hellas was the natural sunny condition of man before the shadow of Christianity came over it.

I have attempted then, chapter by chapter, to make clear various facets of and – perhaps most important – shifts in the Hellenic Ideal. I like especially those occasions when it may be said with some confidence that an adjustment, an expansion of taste, has occurred: Goethe at Paestum is one such, Pars in Athens drawing the Parthenon frieze is another.

Such moments are of course part of a process of change, an adjustment, that was taking place throughout the period and to which all the figures I have dealt with more or less, and more or less consciously, contributed. I mean the turning-away from Rome, the distinguishing and raising-up of Greece. When Rome conquered Ancient Greece, the centre of the classical world shifted to the west. Artists migrated to work for patrons in Italy; works of art were seized and shipped from east to west. It was in Rome, then, that the earliest rediscoveries of classical art were made in the Renaissance; one thinks of the marvellous coming to light of the Laocoön group, for example, and its immediate effect on Michelangelo's work. For most eighteenth-century classicists, because of the ever-increasing wealth of ancient art there and because it was so much more accessible than Greece, Rome was quite simply the centre of the classical world; and to spend time in Rome was enough and more than enough. Winckelmann, a passionate Hellenist, was never fully persuaded that he needed to go further east than Rome. But even those who did went figuratively and in most cases literally to Greece via Rome. Their expectations were conditioned by what they had seen, with their own eyes or in engravings, of sculpture and architecture in Rome; and their reception of true Greek forms was sometimes halting and uncertain. But in the 1670s attention and enthusiasm began to turn towards Greece. Stuart and Revett, in the

1750s, worked quite deliberately to conclude that process; and it was against a rearguard of the old school, against Sir William Chambers' preference for Rome, that their editor, Willey Reveley, addressed himself in the third volume of the *Antiquities of Athens*. That was in 1794, and by then 'Grecian principles', *gusto greco*, were truly ascendant.

The sentimental accompaniment of this focussing on Greece was nostalgia. Though it was possible to recover, clarify and substantiate the Hellenic Ideal, that ideal remained, as an ideal, unrealizable, lost. Visiting the land itself, recovering the sites and the works of art, enhances the sense of loss, in that one sees more clearly what once was. There were sentimental journeys to Greece and lament over the passing of her ideal culture in Roman times. Cicero's sentiments on the debased condition of Athens so matched those of seventeenth- and eighteenth-century travellers that they could quote him at the appropriate point in their accounts. Troy was another focus of nostalgia. With the vision of Greece the modern travellers recovered simultaneously the late Ancient World's nostalgia for its own glorious past: for Periclean Athens or Homeric Troy.

The substantiation of the Ideal (and thus the material images of nostalgia) is what the travellers, as early and amateur archaeologists, brought back. The relationship between collected facts and the Ideal is an interesting one. It is almost the old question of Letter and Spirit, or how shall scholarship and imagination mix and what will ensure the triumph of the latter? That perennial concern runs more or less obviously throughout my book. It surfaces clearly in the configuration Winckelmann–Heyne, but the discussion of imitation in the chapters on Wood and Guys is equally a part of it. The travellers themselves, whether as their main purpose or incidentally, supplied information. Always with some hardship and often at considerable risk they increased the stock of facts about Greece – through the identification and description of sites, through the publication of inscriptions, drawings and views. There is in all of them, supremely in Stuart and Revett, the wish to be accurate; and I have charted their progress as exactly as I could. Of course, in early archaeology things established as facts one year are overturned the next and that is why, in the travellers themselves, it is important to capture the enthusiasm that is the spirit of their enterprise. As we follow Tournefort on his rather puzzled and erratic tour of Delos it will be obvious, I think, wherein his lasting value as a traveller lies. For I do not think it matters that one man's findings are qualified or contradicted by his successor. The process itself by which that correction occurs is valuable and sometimes poignant. The discovery had as its impetus an enthusiasm that is not essentially harmed when the established facts fall away. Archaeology at this early stage could scarcely be called a science; it was an amateur passion, more or less scholarly. Still, its devotees were concerned to get things right, and they corrected one another vigorously.

I´have therefore made it a main purpose of my book to describe the transmission of facts and enthusiasm among the travellers and from them to those who did not travel. Embarking on a century of travel-literature one soon grows to love the sense of tradition and community among those who had been in Greece, their sense of predecessors, companions and successors; and wherever I have been able to I have reconstructed such dealings in some detail and have been throughout attentive to connections.

The order of the book is chronological, from Spon and Wheler at the outset to Choiseul-Gouffier and Chandler at the end; in all a century, the German Hellenists coming in the last quarter or in the immediate aftermath. In abiding by that chronology I have, I hope, preserved the feeling of tradition and made evident both the gradual gathering of information and some shifts in the formulation of the Ideal. I should say that I have not attempted to be exhaustive. Several travellers worthy of attention and some important German Hellenists have scarcely been mentioned. My choices were determined by the wish to present distinct facets of the Idea of Hellas and the dealings of its exponents with one another. Thus each chapter is, within the chronology, a dwelling upon those constellations of people and ideas which seemed to me most capable of significant illumination. Or, it may be, a dwelling on certain places. Because occasionally I have interrupted the chronology in order to assemble around a particular monument or locality several accounts, both back and forwards in time, again the better to illuminate some shift or trend. Thus, in chapter 2, with the island of Delos and the Gate of the Persecution at Ephesus.

The men who travelled in Greece were botanists and clerics, Oxford scholars, aristocratic dilettanti, ambassadors, merchants and adventurers. They knew their Bible, their Homer, Herodotus, Strabo and Pausanias, or Montesquieu, Rousseau, Spence, Winckelmann and Webb. Their purposes and attitudes were very various. But being in Greece they were necessarily travellers, and it would do their enterprises less than justice were one to discuss their ideas and their contributions to scholarship and disregard the practical matters of their journeying. I have given considerable attention, then, to the journeys themselves, though not so much to dates and itineraries as to whatever details might best convey the excitement of the real undertaking.

The journey to Greece and travel in Greece were strenuous and dangerous. The travellers risked capture and robbery by pirates at sea, by brigands on land; as well as plague, harassment by the Turks and a thousand casual accidents. Eastcourt and Bouverie fell sick on the road and died; Vernon and Bocher were murdered, and James Stuart two or three times came close to the same fate. All feared for their lives more than once in bad weather at sea. For some – Wheler, Chishull, Chandler – the journey to Greece was by far the boldest undertaking in their lives; others, like Vernon, Transfeldt and Randolph, were by nature adventurous and restless men. Hardship and risk heightened the pleasure of the travellers when they were successful, and against these tribulations the strength of their wish to learn sustained them. It is a pity that their books are only in libraries and often difficult of access, for many of them write well and have a good story to tell.

I hope, then, that an interest in these people will not be thought merely antiquarian. We can see in the poets what a brilliant image Greece became. Enthusiasm survives, and is communicable, even when some of its forms have tarnished or passed away. The Ideal of Hellas – that is, the admiration of, the longing for those values which the eighteenth century sited in Ancient Greece – survives today. And we seem, despite our greater factual knowledge, yet further on in the inexorable process of loss.

1

THE 1670s. SPON AND WHELER

Substantial contributions to classical studies and the enthusiasm for Hellas were made during the seventeenth century by Europeans travelling or resident in Greece; but nearly all these men – purveyors of information and works of art – were in the country primarily for some other purpose. All more or less admiring of the Greek Ideal, they were, in their professional capacities, diplomats, churchmen or merchants; and what they did for Hellenism was done on the side and often at the instigation of wealthy dilettanti in France or England. Jacob Spon and George – later, after the dedication of his book to Charles II, *Sir* George – Wheler were the first to travel Greece in the primary intention of identifying and describing her classical monuments, and the accounts they wrote founded the modern tradition of Greek travel-literature. They take up from Pausanias, after a gap of 1500 years and with modern sentiments. This chapter will concentrate on Spon and Wheler, because their accounts are by far the most important in their day, and also because it is through them – not exclusively but most conveniently – that we may learn what others did.

Earlier in the century the English Ambassador to the Porte, Sir Thomas Roe, serving two masters, Lord Arundel and the Duke of Buckingham, had his agents all over Greece with instructions to lay their hands on whatever movable antiquities they could. Through his efforts, and more through those of the extremely resourceful William Petty, the famous Arundel Marbles – later bequeathed to Oxford, where Wheler and Tournefort saw them – were collected. And, like Roe, the French Ambassador des Hayes exerted himself on behalf of patrons at home. The spoliation of certain sites, like Delos, was well under way within the first decades of the century. The scavenging must have been pretty thorough, particularly by Roe and Petty in Asia Minor, for at the end of the century Edmund Chishull wrote: 'The scarcity of antiquities now to be found in *Smyrna* arises from hence, that it furnished the greatest

7

part of the *Marmora Arundeliana*.'[1] The Provençal scholar Peiresc, whom both Spon and Tournefort praise as a predecessor, was, through his agent Samson, prominent among these early collectors. In fact it was from Samson, when he was imprisoned at Smyrna and his collection confiscated, that Petty acquired the famous *Marmor Parium* for Arundel. Peiresc was admirably generous about the publication later in Oxford of marbles that he had himself collected with much labour.

The activities of these early scholars, patrons and agents have been well described elsewhere.[2] For my purposes here, two or three important factors emerge. The first is that by the 1670s it was well established that Western Europe needed classical Greece as a main ingredient in her culture. Secondly, as a part of that realization, there were the beginnings of an ability to distinguish Greece from Rome. Thirdly, it was becoming more generally feasible, though still difficult, to visit the land itself; and it was already thought right and proper that travellers should take ('rescue') all they could of classical remains from the Turks and the Greeks. The Greeks, in their hopeless apathy and ignorance, and the Turks, taught by a barbarous religion to detest all representation of the human form, were not fit keepers of a great heritage. Peacham, in his *Compleat Gentleman* of 1634, praises the achievement of patrons and agents in transplanting 'old Greece into England', into civilized safekeeping. Since self-congratulation will often be heard in the European travellers' accounts it might be as well, in anticipation, to broach the issue of Barbarism and Civilization now. Of course the Turks, with their unsympathetic persuasions, were unsuitable inheritors of the works of the Greeks, for whom the depiction of human beauty was a religious act; and there are many instances of their barbarity so appalling or amusing that I shall not be able to refrain from quoting them when the time comes. But Christianity in its orthodox line – that is, when not overridden by an essentially heretical love of art – was not more sympathetic. Who lopped the phalluses on Delos (and burned the works of 'the Tenth Muse', Sappho)? Not the Turks. The Duc de Mazarin, inheriting Richelieu's collection of antique statues, set about them with a hammer in the Palais Royal, in 1670, affronted by their nudity; and Winckelmann, of all people, had to witness the fig-leafing of the Belvedere statues, by order of the Pope in 1759. Christians had a horror of the body, and not just of its depiction in art. And Babin, in 1674, records a destruction done for another, Church–political, purpose: the statue of a mother and child, wrongly supposed to be a

Virgin and Christ, was smashed by the Greek Orthodox Archbishop of Athens, in whose precinct it was found, apparently so that no one should think it a sign from heaven in favour of his rivals the Catholics.[3]

Moreover, there remained in Greek Orthodoxy, despite the defeat of Iconoclasm in the ninth century, a strong antipathy towards statuary or carving in relief. Several travellers note this. Chishull, for example: 'they abhor all imagery in *relievo*, and look upon it as inclining to heathenism and idolatry'.[4] Although, properly speaking, it concerned only the images in their own Church, the Orthodox Greeks' dislike of reliefs and statues naturally extended to all such work; most were in any case ignorant of their country's pre-Christian past and thus maltreated whatever carvings they came across without distinction.

Worse still perhaps, in that they degraded their aims, were the acts of vandalism committed by the collectors and amateurs themselves. Fourmont with an army of labourers in Sparta, going with brutal single-mindedness after inscriptions (like Schliemann at Troy, after Priam's city), did terrific damage to whatever else of ancient remains got in his way. It is also said of him, though let us hope this is not true, that he smashed the inscriptions once he had copied them, in order to put his own authority beyond dispute.[5] What is left of the colossal statue of Apollo on Delos, a part of the trunk and a part of the thighs, will serve for all time as an indictment of crude European acquisitiveness. Works were chopped and sawn unmercifully to be transported; dealers broke them to sell piecemeal at greater profit; restorers cobbled bits together with a brutal tastelessness – what monsters Winckelmann saw (and admired) in the gallery at Dresden!

Travellers in Greece were for ever coming across small details of the highest symbolic value – sarcophagi used as cisterns, altars used for grinding corn – and the more sentimental, like Choiseul-Gouffier, make great pathos of these. Throughout the eighteenth century, until it was finally rescued by Lord Elgin, successive travellers lamented the vile use which the ignorant inhabitants of Sigeum had found for their famous Sigean Stone. It was believed to have powers against the ague and the celebrated *boustrophedon* inscription,[6] which European visitors in turn had copied more or less accurately, was being slowly but surely obliterated by the backs of the credulous natives rolling, writhing and being dragged to and fro upon it. Chandler was a witness of its sorry condition in 1764. Poor Sigean Stone – it was, he wrote, 'destitute of a patron to rescue it from barbarism, and obtain its removal into the safer custody of some private museum; or, which is rather to be desired, some public repository'. In a footnote he added this proposal or appeal:

It is to be wished that a premium were offered, and the undertaking recommended to commanders of ships in the Levant trade. They have commonly interpreters to negotiate for them, with men, leavers, ropes, and the other requisites; besides instruments or tools, by which the stone might be broken, if necessary. By a proper application of all-prevailing gold, it is believed they might gain the permission or connivance of the papas and persons concerned. It should be done with secresy. The experiment is easily made, when they are at Tenedos, or wind-bound near the mouth of the Hellespont. (*Travels in Asia Minor*, p. 39)

But often the objects bought and stolen from degenerate Greek and barbarian Turk would have been better off left lying where they were. Charles I's collection was destroyed by fire in 1698. The Earl of Arundel's was dispersed at his death and much of it subjected to a scandalous neglect. A half of the priceless *Marmor Parium*, for example, was lost for years up a chimney in Arundel House; Mr James Theobald took the drum of an antique pillar down to his seat in Berkshire, for use as a roller on his bowling green; and as late as 1960 a fragment of the frieze from Pergamum, another of Arundel's treasures, was removed from the wall of a cottage near Worksop and offered to a monumental mason to be broken up for cemetery chippings. (The mason refused it, and this fragment of the south side of the Pergamum Gigantomachy frieze is now in the Worksop Museum.)

In the 1670s the process of learning about Greece suddenly accelerated. One cause, after a war that had lasted twenty-five years, was the final defeat of the Venetians at the Siege of Candia in 1669 and the consequent establishment of Ottoman supremacy throughout the Archipelago. Though there was still piracy to contend with (and would be during all the period of our interest), the cessation of hostilities did make sailing in Greek waters easier and safer. The war resumed in 1685, when Morosini invaded the Morea, and the years of Spon and Wheler and their immediate predecessors were thus a fortunate interlude. Improved conditions for commerce were another important factor. Good trade connections were extremely useful to foreigners travelling in Greece. Travellers arriving at Zante, Patras, Corinth, Athens, Smyrna or on any of the larger islands, would invariably avail themselves of the local consuls for hospitality, guidance or the provision of money. Where possible they would travel in the company of merchants, who knew the routes and the particular difficulties and dangers. Thus, wherever trade was well established, there the business of travelling was very much facilitated.

Before the arrival of Spon and Wheler in the Levant, the two rival trading nations, France and England, both improved their relations with the Porte and secured important freedoms for their merchants. France at first enjoyed the greater influence and prestige, largely due to their extravagant ambassador, Charles-François Olier, Marquis de Nointel. At a time when his British counterpart, Sir John Finch,[7] was denied the sultan's permission to travel, Nointel, having captured valuable concessions for his country, set off on a tour of Greece to assert the prestige of his master the Sun King, and to follow his own passion for wonders of Nature and classical sites. Nointel was ambassador for nine years and spent five of them travelling. He travelled with as much ostentation as possible, thinking that modesty ill-became the representative of the King of France. In the long competition between French and English ambassadors Nointel was a star on the French side. He was soon legendary wherever he passed. Tournefort, covering some of the same ground nearly thirty years later, found the ambassador's fame still flourishing. He did much to maintain it into our day, for it is in Tournefort's book that we have the best account of the Christmas Mass that Nointel caused to be celebrated, with all possible pomp, deep underground in the grotto of Antiparos. He spent three days down there

... accompagné de plus de 500 personnes, soit de sa maison, soit marchands, corsaires, ou gens du pays qui l'avoient suivi. Cent grosses torches de cire jaune, & 400 lampes qui brûloient jour & nuit étoient si bien disposées, qu'il y faisoit aussi clair que dans l'eglise la mieux illuminée. On avoit posté des gens d'espace en espace dans tous les précipices, depuis l'autel jusques à l'ouverture de la caverne: ils se firent le signal avec leurs mouchoirs, lorsqu'on éleva le corps de J.C. A ce signal on mît le feu à 24 boëtes & à plusieurs pierriers qui étoient à l'entrée de la caverne: les trompettes, les hautbois, les fifres, les violons rendirent cette consecration plus magnifique. L'Ambassadeur coucha presque vis à vis de l'autel, dans un cabinet long de sept ou huit pas, taillé naturellement dans une de ces grosses tours dont on vient de parler. (*Voyage du Levant*, I, 193)

... accompany'd by above five hundred Persons, as well as his own Domesticks, as Merchants, Corsairs, or Natives, that were curious to follow him. A hundred large Torches of yellow Wax, and four hundred Lamps that burnt night and day were so well placed, that no Church was ever better illuminated. Men were posted from space to space, in every Precipice from the Altar to the opening of the Cavern, who gave the signal with their Handkerchiefs, when the body of J.C. was lifted up; at this signal fire was put to 24 Drakes, and to several Patereroes that were at the Entrance of the Cavern: the Trumpets, Hautbois, Fifes, and Violins, made the Consecration yet more magnificent. The Ambassador lay in the night almost opposite to the Altar, in a Cabinet seven or eight foot long, naturally cut in one of those large Spires which we mention'd before. (Eng. ed., I, 150–1)

On Naxos Tournefort searched diligently for a certain rock on which Nointel had carved the coat of arms of the King of France; but the guide informed him that it had been destroyed by lightning.

If Nointel wrote an account of his travels it has been lost. There are some dispatches, the one from Athens of the 17 December 1674 being the most interesting. His admiration is genuine and perceptive. He praises in the Parthenon frieze 'un si bel ordre et une disposition si vivante et une expression de tant de passions différentes' ('great harmony and naturalness in the arrangement of the figures and their wide variety of emotional expression'). And he adds, anticipating Lord Elgin in the wish if not the act:

Tout ce que l'on peut dire de plus eslevé de ces originaux, c'est qu'ils méritteroient d'estre placés dans les cabinets ou galleries de Sa Majesté, où ils jouiroient de la protection que ce grand monarque donne aux arts et aux sciences qui les ont produits; ils y seroient mis à l'abri de l'injure et des affronts qui leur sont faits par les Turcs, qui, pour éviter une idolâtrie imaginaire, croyent faire une oeuvre méritoire en leur arrachant le nez ou quelque autre partie.[8]

(The highest praise we can accord these original works is to say that they would be worthy of a place in His Majesty's collections or galleries, where they would enjoy the protection extended by that great monarch to the arts and sciences which have produced them. There they would be safe from the insults and injuries done to them by the Turks, who, in their horror of what they call idolatry, deem it a worthy act to break off a nose or some other part.)

Nointel had with him, so Tournefort records (I, 194), 'trois ou quatre maçons avec les outils necessaires pour détacher & pour enlever les marbres les plus lourds. Jamais Ambassadeur n'est revenu du levant avec tant de belles choses' ('three or four Masons with Utensils that would loosen and lift away the most lumbersome pieces of Marble. Never did Ambassador return from the *Levant* with so many fine things' (Eng. ed., I, 151)). But in France he fell from favour and had to sell his finds to make ends meet.

Nointel, if little of his own survives, did also instigate scholarly activity in other people, and three or four in his entourage contributed notably to the study of Greece. One was Antoine Galland, who travelled as the ambassador's personal antiquary and in that capacity took measurements and copied inscriptions. (In another capacity, serving his master's religious and political ends, he was to document exactly the nature of the Greek Orthodox Church.) Galland's journal of 1672–3 describing life in Constantinople and, unfortunately, only the beginning of the ambassador's tour, was published in 1881. Spon cites him frequently, under the title 'Antiquaire du Roi', on such erudite matters as the leaf-mouldings of antique columns and the darkness inside Greek temples, and recalls that they discussed this latter point at their meeting in Constantinople.

Cornelio Magni, with Nointel throughout, published an account of Asia Minor, the Archipelago and Athens (in two parts, 1679 and 1688) deriving from the famous expedition. He says in his preface that three years before publishing he went to visit Spon in Lyons to check with him that he had got his observations right; a good instance, at the start of the tradition, of collaboration and concern for accuracy. Spon by then, when Magni visited him, was in a state of extreme penury and poor health. In fact he had only a few months to live, and the revival of the happiest period of his life, when he toured Greece and wrote his excellent account, must have affected him deeply.

Jean Giraud, first French then English Consul in Athens, who played cicerone to a succession of travellers for fifteen years or more, was almost certainly inspired or even commissioned by Nointel to work on his description of Attica and the Peloponnese, which latter part Spon saw 'ébauchée entre ses mains' ('in draft form') (*Voyage* II, 100). It was, apparently, the ambassador's wish to make a general survey of Greece (his ambassadorial domain) with particular but not exclusive reference to classical remains; and he seems to have engaged men on the spot like Giraud for this end. Spon and Wheler found Giraud invaluable:

...nous luy avons l'obligation des antiquitez qu'il nous fit voir à Athenes, que nous n'aurions pas découvertes dans six mois de sejour, sans un secours semblable. Il nous mena luy-même voir ce qu'il avoit observé dans la Ville & dans la Citadelle. (*Voyage* II, 100)

(...we are obliged to him for showing us ancient remains in Athens which without such help we should not have discovered ourselves had we stayed six months. He showed us personally the things he had observed in the city and on the Acropolis.)

In 1687 he was still showing travellers round 'mais avec beaucoup de peine, étant incommodé aux pieds' ('but with considerable difficulty, being bad on his feet').[9] He saw his beloved Parthenon vandalized by that champion of the civilized West, Morosini.

Nointel, arriving in Athens in 1674, gave one of his attendant artists

1   Portrait of Spon

the job of sketching the entire frieze, and thus secured, before the bomb landed, at least a poor after-image of the marvellous work. The draughtsman, Spon says, 'y travailla deux mois, & faillit à s'y crever les yeux, parce qu'il failloit tout tirer de bas en haut' ('was two months working on them and almost lost his eyesight since everything had to be drawn from below by looking up') (*Voyage* II, 113). The 400 drawings, now in the Bibliothèque Nationale, were always ascribed to the Tours artist Jacques Carrey, and still often are; though Albert Vandal, eighty years ago, argued conclusively that a young Flemish painter, attached to Nointel's suite, did the work and remained, to posterity, anonymous and overlooked.[10] The drawings survived; they were the best until William Pars did his, in better conditions, under the direction of Richard Chandler, in 1765; and, of course, they are evidence of what the bombardment in 1687 destroyed. Spon and Wheler, arriving in Constantinople about a year after Nointel's return, were shown these drawings and were thus prepared for their first sight, three or four months later, of the Parthenon.

It is not hard to imagine what that meeting in October 1675 must have meant to the enthusiastic men who had just come from the fabulous places and to those who were going there. Nointel, whom Spon describes as 'extrémement curieux' ('of very lively curiosity' – high approbation), showed them not only his drawings of the Parthenon frieze but also 'environ trente marbres ou Inscriptions antiques' ('about thirty marbles or ancient inscriptions') from Athens and the islands. He allowed them to copy what inscriptions they liked, showed them his collection of antique coins, and, inviting them several times to his table, entertained them with accounts of '[les] belles choses qu'il avoit veuës dans son voyage' ('the beautiful things he had seen on his travels') (*Voyage*, 1, 199–200). There were besides conversations with the antiquary Galland and, in the English camp, with the Ambassador Finch 'un Gentilhomme sçavant, & de beaucoup de merite' ('a learned and very worthy gentleman') (*ibid.* 1, 166) and his chaplain John Covel. The excitement of these early travellers passes from person to person; at their meetings what they exchange is of a potent novelty.

Another man in Nointel's entourage, the abbé Pecoil of Lyons, meeting the Jesuit Jacques-Paul Babin in Constantinople, urged him to write an account of the state of Athens, which he had five times visited from Negrepont, where he was stationed. Babin obliged and, from Smyrna, sent his *Relation de l'état présent de la ville d'Athènes* to Pecoil, who was back in Lyons. Here is the seed of Spon's journey to Greece. For to Spon, a doctor of medicine but already neglecting his practice for classical studies, Pecoil passed on Babin's account and it was he who edited and published it in 1674.

This book, very rare in the original but re-edited by Ludwig Ross in 1846 and by Laborde in 1854, was timely rather than accurate or full. It was written in Smyrna by a man whose acquaintance with Athens, in five separate visits, was in all five weeks. Still, such was the oblivion into which the city had fallen that almost any factual information would be novel and interesting. Indeed, Babin could start from the premise that Athens was widely believed among European scholars to have vanished from the face of the earth. It came as a revelation then to learn that beautiful buildings from the time of Pericles still stood. Though scanty, inexact and often quite mistaken, Babin's account is curiously exciting, even moving; for here is a man waking to what is around him. Beautiful buildings, fragments of beauty, in the squalor and servitude of the forgotten city:

... des maisons sans aucune magnificence, faites des ruines anciennes, ayans pour tout ornement quelques pieces de colomnes de marbre mises dans les murailles sans ordre, & à la façon des autres pierres.

(... houses quite without grandeur, made of the ruins of ancient buildings, their sole ornaments being a few pieces of marble column set into the walls according to no pattern and in the manner of the other stones.)

There is also, more important than the accuracy or inaccuracy of his observations, the note of admiration:

Pour moy je vous avoüe que d'aussi loin que je la découvris de dessus la mer avec des lunettes de longue vûe, & que je vis quantité de grandes colomnes de marbre, qui paroissent de loin, & rendent témoinage de son ancienne magnificence, je me sentis touché de quelque respect pour elle.[11]

(For myself I must confess that even at a distance, looking through a telescope from the sea, I was moved to feel some respect for the city of Athens when I saw so many tall marble columns which, visible from afar, are proof of her former glory.)

That will have touched the antiquary Jacob Spon.

The volume, as it appeared, is more Spon than Babin. He provides a preface, explaining how he came by the manuscript; then follows Babin's account, occupying sixty-one pages in the original edition. The remainder of the book, twice as much again in length, is an *Abbregé de l'histoire d'Athenes* put together by Spon using the ancient authors and inscriptions, some from Gruterus, some passed on to him by his friend the King's numismatist, Jean-Foi Vaillant, who had collected them in Greece some years before. The *Abbregé* is interesting only as an example of a manner of composition – compilation out of the ancient authors and modern travellers – which remains to a greater or lesser degree characteristic of the genre, the travel-book, throughout the succeeding century. The third, and later the chief element, namely personal experience, Spon at that stage could not supply. Babin's account, dated Smyrna 8 October 1672, came out in 1674. In that year Spon began his journey to Greece.

The Revᵈ Sir Geo Wheler Knᵗ STP
Preb of Durham
died Janʸ 15 1724
aged 74

Presented by
The Revᵈ Charles Granville
Wheler M.A.

2   Portrait of Wheler

It is not certain that he intended from the start to go so far. He was working on a collection of inscriptions, a supplement to Gruterus, and Vaillant, passing through Lyons in 1674, suggested that he should accompany him to Rome. Spon agreed, but, rather fortunately, failed to make the rendezvous in Marseilles. Vaillant sailed without him, and was captured by pirates. He spent four and a half months imprisoned in Algeria. He was released then in an exchange of prisoners, Algerian for French, and his valuables, among them a collection of twenty gold coins, were returned to him. These Vaillant swallowed as a desperate and, in the event, unnecessary precaution when, on the voyage home, his ship was again threatened by pirates. Finally, having been blown in a gale down the coast of Spain, he stepped ashore near the Bouches-du-Rhône with his hoard in his gut. The two doctors he consulted were divided in their advice, the first prescribing an emetic, the second a purge. Vaillant wisely let Nature run her course, aiding her only with a diet of spinach, and one by one his treasures came to light. In Lyons he sold several not yet emerged to a friend and fellow-collector M. Dufour, who had to bide his time before being able to claim what he had paid for.

Spon was in Rome, collecting inscriptions and visiting the usual classical sites and the famous galleries, for five months. And in Rome he met George Wheler who, since October 1673, had been touring Europe, for the first part, as far as Marseilles, with his Oxford tutor George Hickes. Spon, when they met, was twenty-eight, Wheler twenty-five; they were both of the Protestant Church. Wheler knew Vaillant too, having been his pupil. As Spon says, 'la passion de voyager croît en marchant' ('the passion for travel increases en route'). In Rome he and Wheler between them decided to push on to Greece, to Athens at least; in the event, they went further. Wheler, who had recently come into a substantial inheritance, undertook to pay his companion's expenses. Still, Spon came back from his travels very badly off.

The party for Greece met in Venice. They were, beside Spon and Wheler, two other English gentlemen, Sir Giles Eastcourt and Francis Vernon. Vernon, who knew the Italian Ambassador to the Porte, arranged their passage with him on a ship bound for Constantinople. When they sailed, on 20 June 1675, they took with them a book just published in France and sent to Spon in Venice. It was their reading matter on the voyage.

The book, a *succès de scandale* in its day, was entitled *Athènes ancienne et nouvelle*. Its author was one Guillet de Saint-George, but it was published under the name of the author's brother, la Guilletière. It purported to be a description, at first hand, of the city of Athens, by a man, 'the brother', who had escaped thither after four years in Turkish captivity. In fact 'the brother' was an invention. The author, Guillet de Saint-George, had never left his study: his account was a work of scholarship, fiction and research at a distance (through French priests resident in Athens). But at first, on the boat from Venice to Zante, Spon and his companions would have had no reason to doubt the book's authenticity. The fiction – capture by pirates – was *vraisemblable* enough (it happened to Vernon twice), as the writers of contemporary comedy knew very well. Not long after the fictional and soon notorious la Guilletière was supposed to be in Athens gratefully enjoying his freedom and surveying the monuments, the real but unheard-of Georg Transfeldt was in fact there and actually doing just that.[12]

When the party reached Zante there was some disagreement and they split up, Spon and Wheler continuing by boat to Constantinople, Eastcourt and Vernon making their way directly to Athens. These two had Guillet's book with them and, arriving in the city, they began to check its descriptions against the reality. They found them, in Vernon's words, 'wide from truth'. In a letter written to the Royal Society from Smyrna on 10 January 1676 he warned the learned world against *Athènes ancienne et nouvelle*, which by that time was in its third edition and was about to appear in English. Spon and Wheler, when they arrived in Athens, retrieved their copy and continued the demolition of its claims to accuracy. They discovered, by meeting the French priests with whom Guillet had corresponded, that 'the brother', la Guilletière, was a fiction and that the true author of the book had never left France. Spon's account of his own travels, published in 1678, charged Guillet with numerous inaccuracies, and a sharp polemic ensued. Guillet stuck to his fiction, and even suggested that Spon himself had never been to Greece; Spon replied indignantly, with a long index of Guillet's aberrations. (Guillet meanwhile had produced a similar book on Sparta, again through the medium of the fictitious brother.)[13]

Spon's anger was not entirely appropriate. By his own scholarship, using the ancient authors, and through the researches of others – French Capucine priests – on the spot, Guillet had compiled a respectable and informative (and very timely) book, and had made it more readable by means of an unexceptionable fiction. His own scholarship he freely confesses: how could 'the brother' possibly have access to the necessary works? 'Il luy manquoit en ce pays là des Livres que j'ay consultez à Paris; & j'avouë de bonne foy que mon plus grand secours m'est venu des Volumes de Meursius' ('in that country he lacked books – which I have consulted in Paris; and I readily admit that my greatest help has come from Meursius').[14] What Spon revealed as evidence of Guillet's subterfuge – namely, that he had corresponded with Capucine priests – was in fact the book's prime strength: that was where its contemporary picture came from, and if there were inaccuracies that might be expected (there were such in Babin too), and obviously a scholar like Spon, being there himself, would soon detect them. The fiction, had Guillet freely admitted it, need not have been a stumbling-block, since under its agreeable guise he was making a serious contribution to the study of Athens. Myself, I find in both *Athènes ancienne et nouvelle* and in the polemical *Lettres* of 1679 an irony, or at least an unseriousness with regard to the fiction, which Spon in his indignation overlooked. Being a generous soul he was incensed at Guillet's quite gratuitous slandering of Consul Giraud. Giraud was from Lyons, Spon's home town. Over a trivial incident he had been dismissed from the French consulship, and had accepted the English instead. Guillet's sources passed on this scandal, and added reports of drunkenness and love of gambling for good measure. Spon gave over several pages of his book to refuting these stories and rehabilitating his fellow-citizen's good name. In his anger he could see no merit at all in Guillet's work.

Yet a hundred years later, out of exactly the same ingredients – scholarship, local accounts and an agreeable fiction – the abbé Barthélemy composed his monumental and enormously successful *Voyage du jeune Anacharsis*. Guillet is a not wholly unworthy predecessor in that particular field; in fact, Barthélemy uses him as an authoritative source. He has, for example, or at least he affects, the proper sentiments. In this passage 'the brother' is approaching Athens:

Icy, je veux vous avoüer ma foiblesse, nommez la folie, si vous voulez. A l'aspect de cette memorable Ville, frappé d'un sentiment de veneration, pour les miracles de l'Antiquité, je tressaillis; un long fremissement me courut par tout le corps. J'appre-hendois, que nos Voyageurs ne me vissent, & ne se moquassent de moy; mais je n'estois pas seul dans cette agitation; nous ouvrions tous, les yeux sans rien voir, à force de les trop ouvrir, tant chacun de nous se remplit alors l'imagination des grands Hommes, que cette Ville a produits, comme si a chaque pas nous eussions rencontré Thesée, Socrate, Alcibiade, ou quelqu'autre de cette force. Je ne pûs alors m'empescher de m'écrier, *Adsunt Athenae, unde humanitas.*

And here I cannot but acknowledge my own weakness, you may call it folly if you please: At the first sight of this Famous Town (struck as it were with a sentiment of Veneration for those Miracles of Antiquity which were Recorded of it) I started immediately, and was taken with an universal shivering all over my Body. Nor was I singular in my Commotion, we all of us stared, but could see nothing, our imaginations were too full of the Great Men which that City had produced. We fancied every step we made, that we met either *Theseus*, or *Socrates*, *Alcibiades*, or some other of those Reverend Persons: I could not contain my self, but cryed out, *Adsunt Athenae, unde Humanitas.*

And he concludes, after a long quotation, 'Vous vous souviendrez bien que cela est de Ciceron' ('You may remember it in *Tully*').[15]

Neither Eastcourt nor Vernon survived. Leaving their companions at Zante they made for Athens via Patras and Domvrena. It seems possible that at one or other of these places they met Giraud and the adventurer Bernard Randolph, for Randolph claims – in the index of his *Present State of the Islands in the Archipelago* (1687) – that all four of them were together at Thespiae. (He gives a date, 1674, which cannot be right. From Vernon's journal, in the library of the Royal Society, B. D. Meritt concludes that if they were indeed there together it could only have been on 24 August 1675.[16]) On 25 August Eastcourt and Vernon reached Athens. Their names, with Randolph's, are carved, all in one hand I think, and still faintly to be seen, on the south wall of the Theseum. They stayed only a week in Athens, beginning a tour of the Peloponnese on 2 September. Their route was: Eleusis, Megara, Corinth, Argos, Mistra. Vernon copied inscriptions into his journal. At Mistra Sir Giles bought 'a peice of brass' as a souvenir. They continued to Calamata and up the west coast to Patras; they crossed the Gulf to Naupactus (Lepanto). Here Sir Giles fell ill. Randolph gives this account:

About Fifteen Miles from hence [Lepanto], upon the same side of the Gulph, stands a small Village called *Vitrenizza*, near unto which Sir *Giles Eastcourt* was Buried, travelling in Company with Mr. *Francis Vernon*; and in his way towards Mount *Parnassus*, Sir *Giles* complained in the Morning, but would not be persuaded to tarry at *Lepanto*, hoping it would pass: he called to his man to help him down, and in less than half an hour he Dyed, and was Buried with the assistance of *Greek* Priests, who live in *Vitrenizza*.[17]

Vernon noted in his journal that Sir Giles died at four of the afternoon and was buried by nine. Vernon continued alone to Salona and Delphi, where he copied some important inscriptions (more accurately than Wheler four months later). He was back in Athens on 3 October.

He stayed two months and busied himself during that time with the monuments, copying inscriptions and taking measurements and bearings. He visited the Parthenon three times – 'it is as entire as the *Rotunda* [in Rome]', he wrote. He took the dimensions as exactly as he could 'but it is difficult, because the Castle of *Athens*, in which it stands, is a garrison, and the *Turks* are jealous, and brutishly barbarous, if they take notice that any measures it'.[18] This is a factor worth remembering, when considering the accuracy of the early travellers' accounts: fear of the Turks, who could see no sense in looking at ancient buildings and who assumed therefore that the tourists must be spies. Duloir, in Athens in 1641, was not even allowed into the Acropolis: 'ils [the Turks] la deffendent absolument aux estrangers' ('they absolutely forbid foreigners to enter it'),[19] he says. The Acropolis of Corinth was similarly difficult of access to tourists because of its military importance. Sketching was felt by the Turks to be a particularly suspicious activity. Spon tells us that Nointel's artists were always under the surveillance of two janissaries whilst they sketched. Had it not been for the great personal prestige of the ambassador the work could scarcely have proceeded at all. Early archaeological exploration had very often to be pursued surreptitiously, in fear and trembling; which in part explains the crudeness of the maps, diagrams and pictures in the earliest travel-books. The first rough maps of Athens, drawn by the Capucines, were circulated in secret among Western visitors. Vernon himself got into serious trouble in the Theatre of Dionysus, below the Acropolis:

... le sieur Vernhum Anglois prenant toutes les mesures de ce theâtre à son aise, fut aperceu par les soldats de la garnison, qui en murmurent fort, & voulurent tirer sur luy, sans la consideration du Consul Giraud qui les appaisa.[20]

(... the Englishman Mr Vernon, taking the measurements of this theatre at his leisure, was noticed by the soldiers of the garrison who objected strongly and would have fired on him but for Consul Giraud, who managed to appease them.)

Before leaving Athens, Vernon wrote a short account of his tour of Greece to James Crawford Esq., the English Resident at Venice. He had, he said,

... well examined the ruins of the temple of Delphi and all that was remarkable at Thebes, Corinth, Sparta, Athens &c and had clambered up most of the mountains celebrated by the antients, as Helicon, Parnassus, &c. That he had spent some time on the banks of the river Alpheus, where he searched with much diligence for the Stadium Olympium, but could not find any vestiges of it.[21]

Then in the new year he wrote at greater length from Smyrna – where he arrived plundered by pirates – and his letter, published in the *Philosophical Transactions of the Royal Society*, XXIV (24 April 1676), is one of the very earliest English accounts of Greece, and certainly the best to date. Had he lived he could have written a better book than Wheler's. 'I have Memorials by me of all I saw; which one day, if it please God, I may shew you.' Spon translated the letter to the Royal Society and printed it in his polemics against Guillet, as an authority against a charlatan. More than a century later it was reprinted, in the third volume of Stuart and Revett's *Antiquities of Athens*, and its author praised as a 'most earnest and diligent enquirer'. He was an energetic and talented man: 'Astronome & bon Mathematicien', Spon says, '& qui parloit sept ou huit Langues' ('an astronomer and a good mathematician, master of seven or eight languages')(*Voyage*, 1, 116 and 117). He had done a good deal of travelling, sometimes on diplomatic business but mostly for his own amusement. Spon and Wheler both cite him with respect, as does Chandler, for his exact measurements and topography. Spon seems to have felt real admiration and affection for him. Vernon reached Constantinople, where he was noted thus in the diary of the chaplain to the ambassador, the Rev. John Covel: 'Here is now one Mr. Vernon (lately Secretary to Mr. Montague in France), who is mightily eager after all such things [antiquities], and is going for Persia.'[22] In Persia, near Isphaham, in the spring of 1677, he was murdered in a quarrel with some Arabs 'concerning an English pen-knife, that Mr. Vernon had with him; who shewing himself cross and peevish in not communicating it to them, they fell upon him and hack'd him to death'.[23] 'Voilà les risques à quoy s'exposent les voyageurs' ('such are the risks that travellers run') says Spon (*Voyage*, 1, 118). Pushing east twenty-five years later Tournefort found hospitality in Erzeron at the house of the English Consul Mr Prescott:

Nous demandâmes un jour à Mr Prescott, où étoit mort Mr *Vernon* sçavant Mathematicien Anglois qui avoit fait de belles observations astronomiques en Levant & dont Mrs *Wheler* & *Spon* parlent avec eloge; le Consul nous assûra qu'il lui avoit prédit souvent qu'il seroit malheureux avec toute sa science, s'il ne se modéroit. Mr Vernon étoit d'une vivacité admirable mais il s'emportoit trop facilement. En effet Mr Prescott fut prophete, & nôtre Mathematicien mourut à Hispaham des blessures qu'il avoit reçeües à la teste dans une querelle qu'il eut avec un Persan en sortant de table. Mr Vernon accusa le Mahometan de lui avoir volé un fort bon couteau à l'angloise; le Persan ne fit qu'en rire, soit qu'il eut pris le couteau ou non; l'Anglois en fut encore plus offensé. On s'échauffa la-dessus, on en vint aux mains, & le Persan frappa si rudement Mr Vernon sur la teste, qu'on fut obligé de l'attacher sur son cheval pour le conduire à Hispaham où il mourut quelques jours aprés sans secours, car il n'y avoit pas encore des Anglois établis en cette ville. (II, 280–1)

We one day enquir'd of Mr. *Prescot*, in what Parts died Mr. *Vernon* a learned *English* Mathematician, that had made very fine Astronomical Observations in the *Levant*, and who is honourably mention'd by *Wheeler* and *Spon*: the Consul inform'd us he had often told him he would come to some ill end with all his Knowledge, if he did not learn to keep his Temper. Mr. *Vernon* was a Man of admirable Vivacity, but he was too cholerick. In short, Mr. *Prescot* prov'd a true Prophet, and our Mathematician died at *Hispahan* of the Wounds he receiv'd in the Head, in a Quarrel he had with a *Persian* one day after dinner. Mr. *Vernon* accus'd the *Mahometan* of having robb'd him of a very good Knife, *English*-make; the *Persian* only laugh'd at him, whether he had taken the Knife or no; the *Englishman* was provok'd more at this than t'other. The Dispute grew warm; from Words they came to Blows, and the *Persian* wounded Mr. *Vernon* so dangerously in the Head, that they were forc'd to tie him upon his Horse, and carry him to *Hispahan*, where he died some days afterwards wanting Assistance, for the *English* were not then settled in that City. (Eng. ed., II, 210)

If the two accounts do not tally in their details they do agree on the grimness of Vernon's end.

Spon and Wheler were nearly seven weeks sailing from Zante to Constantinople. They put in at several islands on the way, most notably Delos, and went ashore for a day at Alexandrian Troy. They stayed three weeks in Constantinople, consorting with the two ambassadors, Finch and Nointel; and by the latter they were given not only inspiration for their further journeys – in the form of the drawings of the Parthenon frieze – but also practical assistance, in the form of a passport, so that they travelled thereafter, the Englishman and his French companion, under the protection of the King of France. (Finch was less influential with the Porte than Nointel was.)

Deterred by plague from travelling through Thrace they went instead to Smyrna. They were accompanied on that journey by Chaplain Covel (who shared Wheler's botanical interests), by an English Doctor Pickering ('sçavant & curieux' – 'a learned man, of inquiring mind' – in Spon's phrase) and by two English merchants, one of whom died on the way. Of Pickering we shall hear more later, in connection with Richard Chandler. He was so well liked and esteemed in Smyrna that when he and his party arrived there about fifty of the English community came out to meet them. In Smyrna Spon and Wheler were received by the English Consul, Sir Paul Rycaut. He had been in Turkey since 1661, first as secretary in Winchelsea's embassy, then as consul to the Levant Company, and was the author of an important work, *The*

Present State of the Ottoman Empire (1668). He was the ideal man to advise and encourage the travellers; 'il nous fit mille civilitez', Spon says, ' & voulut que nous mangeassions souvent avec luy' ('he showed us every courtesy, and often invited us to eat with him') (*Voyage*, 1, 235).

From Smyrna it was customary to visit Ephesus and others of the Seven Churches. At Pickering's instigation, Spon and Wheler had seen Thyatira as they came from Constantinople. They saw Ephesus also, in an excursion from Smyrna; and used the accounts of Rycaut and Pickering to describe the present condition of Laodicea and Pergamum. The tradition of an autumn visit to these Christian sites had established itself among the English in Smyrna about ten years before. Every chaplain of the Turkey Company went at least once during his term of office. They would make up a party of a dozen or so, with armed guards to keep off robbers. The tour of all seven churches took nearly three weeks. Educated at Oxford and Cambridge for the ministry, the chaplains knew their classical authors and busily searched out inscriptions and remains of famous cities along that extraordinarily rich and, so to speak, ambiguous coastline. There is always, in their accounts, some general sentiment over what Wheler calls 'the Instability of humane things', and some lament for the passing of the particular glories of the pagan Greeks; but in Asia Minor, more easily than elsewhere, this heretical nostalgia, an aberration inherent in their schooling, is overwhelmed by the more proper pathos of the fall of the Christian places. Their text is Revelations; they see with their own eyes how the very direst warnings have been fulfilled: the remnants of Christianity are housed in brutish ignorance among the ruins of their once-flourishing cities; elsewhere they have been quite extirpated, and the only inhabitants are wolves and jackals. It makes for some strong rhetoric, the author's prose fusing with that of the Authorized Version from which he quotes. There is an exact repetition of sentiment – Thomas Smith's in 1671, Wheler's in 1676 – and not much variation in expression. Spon is just as strong in the same vein. But the English, post-Restoration, had a peculiar slant on Pergamum, Ephesus and Laodicea. Safely back in Oxford, when they wrote up their accounts, they offered the sites they had visited as examples of what England had narrowly escaped: the English cathedrals themselves, Smith says, might soon have been 'laid wast and levelled with the ground, and turned into confused heaps of stone and rubbish, like Ephesus or Laodicea'. Smith and Wheler equally, when the occasion arises, warn against sedition, schism and fanatical principles. If readers knew what it was like to live among the Turks they would 'the more thankfully and seriously reflect upon that most blessed and merciful providence, which [had] cast [their] lot in *Christendom*, and in a Country especially, where the *Christian Doctrine* is profest in its primitive purity and integrity'.[24] Wheler concludes his *Journey into Greece* with thanks to God:

That he had placed the Lot of mine Inheritance in a Land that he had blessed, and hedged about for himself... and rendered me into the Bosom of a Church, that I had often heard, but now knew, to be the most refined, pure, and Orthodox Church in the World; freed from Slavery, Errour and Superstition, and without Novelty or Confusion, established in Purity of Doctrine, Decency and Order.[25]

Those sentiments derive principally from Ephesus; they are no more than one would expect and they do not mean that he was unmoved by what he saw, of classical remains, in the rest of Greece; but they constitute his particular bent. He was a Royalist, a Protestant, an Englishman. Fulfilling a vow made before he ventured into foreign parts he took holy orders in 1683: his book was out, and in that year, as though to finish with Greece, he gave his antique marbles to Oxford. His other published works are exclusively Christian and devotional. But even as a young man travelling, and even in his first book, the account of his journey, there is never a chance that his admiration for the classical past will divert him from the Church of England, not even in those places, like Delos, Delphi or the Acropolis of Athens, where no Christian achievement competes with the classical. He is careful throughout to refer to ancient Greek religion as superstition; in his own copy of *A Journey into Greece* (in the Cathedral Library at Durham) he altered the word 'sacred' to the pejorative 'enthusiastic' in a sentence describing Parnassus: 'On this Top of the Mountain, *Pausanias* saith, it was, that the *Thyades* sacrificed to *Bacchus* and *Apollo*, inspired with a sacred Rage' (p. 317). Of the darkness inside the Parthenon – he was there before the explosion that let in the light – he comments:

And that the Heathens loved Obscurity in their Religious Rites and Customs, many Reasons may be given; especially, because by that means the Pomps they exposed to the People, had much advantage by it; and the Defects of them, with all their juggling and cheating, were less exposed to view. (p. 363)

In Spon, whose description of the temple Wheler translates, the equivalent comment has no such disparaging tone: 'ils s'imaginoient sans doute que l'obscurité avoit quelque chose de plus majestueux, & qui imprimoit plus de respect à ceux qui entroient dans ces Temples' ('doubtless they thought darkness more impressive, and more likely to excite respect in the people who entered these temples') (*Voyage* ii, 118). At Delphi Spon was inspired to compose two couplets in demotic Greek, though he was mainly ignorant of that language and no versifier either, he says. Wheler on the other hand seems to have been most affected not by the ancient sites but by those rare occasions when, amidst bigotry and ignorance, he came across the Christian life being lived in piety and simplicity – by the monks below Mt Helicon, for example.

It was natural that Wheler should wish to assert his faith; both for his own conscience, and as the representative of a kind of Christianity still relatively young. Other Protestant churchmen went to Greece in the seventeenth century, for reasons wholly religious. Isaac Basire was one of them. Forced abroad, like Wheler's parents, after the Royalist defeat, he made himself an apostle of Anglicanism in Greece and the Levant. He was in Zante, the Peloponnese, Smyrna and Constantinople twenty-five years before Wheler. What Protestants hoped for was an alliance with the Greek Orthodox Church, against the Roman Catholic. Both Spon and Wheler were sympathetic to such a *rapprochement*, as was their acquaintance in Constantinople, John Covel. On the other side Nointel was doing *his* best to bring about a 'reunion' of Catholic and Greek under the protection of His Majesty Louis XIV. (The Anglicans had a less energetic champion in Sir John Finch, the ambassador of a king, Charles II, who was himself in the matter of religion highly untrustworthy.) One crux in all the discussions was the doctrine of Transubstantiation. Did the Greeks, or did they not, believe Christ to be literally present in the bread and the wine? The Catholics claimed that they did, the Protestants that they did not. Spon gives a detailed and balanced account of the rituals and ceremonies of Greek Orthodoxy towards the end of his book (*Voyage*, ii, 269–81).

In his overwhelming Anglicanism Wheler is distinct, at the outset, in the line of early travellers. He is not elegiac, and why should he be? He lives in Restoration England, a far better place than Periclean Athens. When he becomes rhetorical and sentimental, as he does in Asia Minor, then it is over the fate of wretched Christians under the infidel Turk: 'When I had seen, and considered all this Desolation, How could I chuse but lament the Ruin of this Glorious Church! To see their Candlestick, and Them removed, and their whole Light utterly extinguished!' (p. 259). At Ephesus he found the Church of St John 'now sacrilegiously turned into a *Mahumetan Mosque*' (p. 256), and the 'fair

Pillars' of the Cathedral Church at Pergamum 'adorning the Graves, and rotten Carkasses of its Destroyers, the *Turks*' (p. 262). Christians under Infidels – but for later travellers the centre of pathos lay in the sufferings of *Greeks*, descendants of Pericles and Themistocles, under the tyranny of Barbarians; and wherever a site or an incident brought this to mind there they were aroused to greatest passion.

Spon and Wheler left Smyrna for Zante at the end of November 1675; it was a fearful crossing, lasting thirty-seven days. From Zante they made their way to Athens by the route Vernon and Eastcourt had followed the previous September. Perhaps they would have learned of Eastcourt's death when they came through Lepanto. They arrived in Athens at the end of January and lodged with Giraud. They were in the city for about a month, had Giraud as their guide and Guillet's book, left them by Vernon, as a starting-point or incentive to the accurate survey of Athens.

What they wrote on Athens, partial, inexact and mistaken though it was in places, remained authoritative for a hundred years, until Stuart and Revett surveyed the buildings in the 1750s and produced their volumes, the *Antiquities of Athens*, the first in 1762. Indeed, it is remarkable how cautiously and respectfully Stuart sets about the correction of his predecessors' work:

Now if we reflect on the shortness of the Days in February, and how unfavourable that Season of the Year must have proved to their researches; that much of their time was employed in other places, and that neither of them appear to have made much proficiency in the Arts of Design, we shall readily excuse any mistakes they have made concerning the Sculpture and Architecture of Athens. Indeed whoever considers all the circumstances attending their Voyage, will find himself obliged to admire their diligence, their sagacity, and the genuine truth of their relations: and will rather praise them greatly for what they have performed, than censure them for what they have left to the future diligence of those, who, informed and excited by their valuable writings, might undertake this journey after them.[26]

Their description of the Parthenon, though they were wrong in the dating and interpretation of the frieze, is particularly valuable because they were the last (and among the first) to see the building intact. They improve on Babin in fullness and accuracy at every turn; with great energy, in quite a short time, they comprehended and superseded the sketchy knowledge made available to them by the Capucine priests; doubtless they owed a good deal to the consul, Giraud, so that they become the publishers of his years of observation and scholarship. Like Vernon a few months before them, they were impressed by the beauty, variety and quantity of the works still to be seen in this all-but-forgotten city. In them, as in Vernon, the shift from Rome was beginning. Vernon wrote: 'In *Athens* I have spent two months. Next to *Rome* I judge it the most worthy to be seen for *Antiquities* of any I have yet been at.' And Wheler: 'As to the eminent Monuments of Antiquity, yet remaining at *Athens*, I dare prefer them before any Place in the World, *Rome* only excepted' (p. 357). (Nointel actually asserted the all-important preference: 'l'on peut dire d'icelles qui se voyent dans le chasteau, autour du temple de Minerve [the Parthenon], qu'elles surmontent ce qu'il y a de plus beau dans les reliefs et les statues de Rome' ('it may be said of those which are to be seen in the citadel around the Temple of Minerva that they exceed in beauty the best of the reliefs and statues in Rome').[27]

In both accounts – in Spon's more than in Wheler's – there is the excitement of discovery. For it was not only that they were confronted by works of great beauty, a powerful enough experience; theirs was also the privilege and excitement of making these things known. Spon says of the Parthenon (*Voyage*, II, 109):

Sa veuë nous imprima certain respect, & nous demeurâmes long-tems à le considerer, sans lasser nos yeux. Je souhaiterois que vous eussiez autant de plaisir à lire sa description, comme j'en ay eu à voir toutes ses beautez.

(It was an impressive sight, and we stood for a long time in unwearying contemplation of the building's beauties. I wish my description of them might give you as much pleasure as the sight of them gave me.)

Europeans of any education who had been in Athens were few and far between; Spon and Wheler are at the start of the appropriation of the place into the culture of the West.

From Athens, accompanied by Giraud, they made excursions around, the longest to Eleusis, Megara and Corinth. Here they are picnicking among the ruins of Eleusis:

Faute de logis & de couvert pour nous recevoir, nous étions venus mettre pied-à-terre dans les debris du Temple de Ceres: & comme la curiosité se rafroidiroit fort, si l'on n'avoit rien à manger, nous faisions boüillir une marmite de ris à l'ombre de ces superbes marbres, sans respect de Ceres, ni de Proserpine, pour lesquelles le tems n'en a point eu. (*Voyage*, II, 214)

(For want of a lodging-place and eating-house we had made our camp among the ruins of the Temple of Ceres: and since our curiosity would have been markedly cooler had we gone hungry we boiled our pot of rice in the shade of those superb columns, showing no more respect towards Ceres and Proserpine than Time itself has shown.)

They crossed to Salamis; but used material offered them by Giraud to give a fuller account of the Saronic Gulf than their own observations would have permitted.

They left Athens at the end of February, intending to visit Athos and travel northwards home overland. They saw Marathon and Rhamnus, but after ten days, just beyond Livadia, they heard that their further route was blocked by snow. They parted company. Spon reached Zante and embarked for Venice. Wheler was unwilling to put to sea so early in the year and so soon after the bad crossing from Smyrna: he made his way slowly back to Athens and finally sailed about the middle of April. He was home by November, three or four months after Spon.

Spon was the first to get his account of the tour into print. His *Voyage d'Italie, de Dalmatie, de Grèce et du Levant* was published in Lyons in 1678 in three volumes. A two-volume edition came out the following year, in Amsterdam. There were reprints in 1680, 1689 and 1724; and translations into Italian (1681), Dutch (1689) and German (1690). Wheler was arranging his own material when Spon's account appeared. Spon sent him a copy. This, and the rumour that a translation into English was planned, encouraged Wheler to finish, and his *Journey into Greece* was published in 1682.

Laborde, comparing the two accounts, dismisses Wheler thus: 'n'ayant rien en propre, il copie tout simplement l'ouvrage de Spon, et quand il se permet des additions, ce sont des erreurs' ('having nothing of his own he simply copies Spon's work, and when he allows himself to add things, they are wrong').[28] This is a bit harsh, but perhaps not wholly unfair. Laborde was upset by the pre-eminence that Wheler's account soon gained over Spon's. (Stuart, for example, in his polemics against Leroy, quotes Wheler in French, rather than Spon.) It is obvious that in the composition of his own book Wheler had his friend's to hand. Laborde says: 'il le copia tout entier' ('he copied him entire'); and the different arrangement was merely to disguise that fact. Certainly, long passages are copied/translated verbatim; but it can hardly be that Wheler was attempting any deceit. There is some evidence, I think, in Spon's *Réponse* to Guillet,[29] that it was from the first agreed that Wheler would translate Spon's account when it appeared and thus give it circulation in England. Then doubtless he thought he had done enough over and above translation to call the book his own. He added, of his own, what he himself calls, rather disarmingly, 'insipid descriptions of Weeds'; also 'Divine Reflections on the various events of things, and Phaenomena of Nature',[30] that is, Anglican sentiments; and both contributions, it might be argued, we could well have done without. But the sentiments were understandable, and the descriptions and pictures of plants were useful in their day (he brought back more than 1000 specimens). Whatever Wheler himself may have thought, and it is true that his tone tends towards the self-satisfied and the condescending, in the matter of classical scholarship and enthusiasm for Ancient Greece he was a poor second to Spon. In the nicest way possible, again in the *Réponse*, Spon says as much: throughout the tour he was Wheler's tutor in classical knowledge.[31]

Spon was the better traveller, more open, less self-conscious; Wheler appears just a little pompous by his side: 'here walking in the streets, we were dashed out of Countenance by the Children; who flocked after Monsieur Spon, making a noise we understood not: which I believe was, by reason Monsieur Spon had put on a pair of Turkish Slippers to his French Sute; which I confess made but a ridiculous show' (p. 78). On the journey home Spon wore Armenian dress as far as Zurich. His tolerance of foreigners was rather larger. One tiny instance: he writes of their hosts at the Dardanelles that they were 'tous deux Juifs de Religion, & fort civils' (*Voyage*, I, 158). Wheler translates: 'both Jews, but very civil persons' (p. 74).

In his enthusiasm for Greece Spon was certainly the freer of the two. Often in his book admiration for the Greek achievement is frankly expressed, without any of the anxious hedgings or intrusions of orthodox impertinence which characterize Wheler's account. Full of admiration, he is, naturally, at times nostalgic too. Thus at Delphi:

Il nous en falut tenir là, & nous contenter de ce que les Livres nous pouvoeient apprendre des richesses & des ornemens de ce lieu-là; car il n'y a plus que de la misere, & tout son éclat a passé comme un songe. (*Voyage*, II, 51)

(We were obliged to halt there and content ourselves with what we could learn from books of the riches and ornaments of the place; for nothing remains now but wretched poverty and all its glory has passed like a dream.)

The business he and Wheler were engaged in – to locate and identify, after hundreds of years of obscurity, the western world's most famous sites – itself seemed to him curious and lamentable:

Ce que je trouvois de plus bizarre, que le lieu le plus celebre du monde eût eu un tel revers de fortune, que nous fussions obligez de chercher Delphes dans Delphes même, & de demander où étoit donc ce Temple [of Apollo], lorsque nous étions sur ses fondemens. (*Voyage*, II, 45)

(What I found stranger still was that the most famous place in the world should have suffered such a reversal of fortune that we were obliged to look for Delphi in Delphi itself and inquire after the whereabouts of Apollo's Temple even as we stood on its foundations.)

Or again, looking for Plato's Academy:

Au fonds il faut avoüer que c'est une chose étonnante, qu'on soit reduit à faire de grandes reflexions, & à deviner pour ainsi dire, où étoit ce lieu si celebre par tout le monde. (*Ibid.* II, 150)[32]

(It is after all surely astonishing that one should be reduced to lengthy pondering and to little more than guesswork as to the location of a site so universally renowned.)

His academic knowledge (out of which he had composed the *Abrégé* for Babin's book) made him acutely aware of what in the course of centuries had been lost. He concludes his account of Athens with a list of famous buildings no longer to be seen or even located, and comments: 'Le temps est venu à bout, de ce que les guerres avoient épargné' ('time has completed the destruction of what war has spared') (*Voyages*, II, 236–7). He would have been amazed at what modern archaeology has uncovered, in Athens or on Delos.

It was a consequential step Spon took when he continued to Greece, even if, when leaving home, he had no intention of going so far. His work to date, particularly his editing of Babin, demanded it, and, unlike most, he had the courage to go.[33] There is not the same necessity in Wheler's journey.

On his return to Lyons Spon continued in his passion. He was not able to recover enough of his medical practice ever to put his finances to rights. Late in 1685, in ill health and poverty and under the threat of religious persecution after the Revocation of the Edict of Nantes, he set off for Switzerland with his friend Sylvester Dufour (the man to whom Vaillant had sold his swallowed gold coins). Spon's father had taken citizenship in Geneva in the fear that exile might become necessary. But the son and his friend only reached Vevey, and there they collapsed, and died in the public hospital, Dufour first and Spon a week after him.

Spon is perhaps to be counted among the earliest victims of the passion for Greece. Wheler was in the Church by 1685. He lived to be seventy-three and had eighteen children. He founded and endowed a school for girls. He is buried in the Galilee Chapel of Durham, and has a handsome monument erected by his one surviving son. Evelyn, who heard him preach, thought him 'a very worthy person, a little formal and particular, but exceedingly devout'.[34]

Spon and Wheler were the founders of modern Greek travel-literature. Their importance will continually be indicated in the following chapters. They offer a basis of factual information on which subsequent travellers, through the proper process of correction, qualification and corroboration, were able to build. And it will be clear, I hope, that they themselves built upon others, on contemporaries and immediate predecessors, in compiling their accounts. Their method of compilation was that most commonly adopted throughout the hundred years I am dealing with. Chandler's books, at the end of this period, are a final perfect example.

Spon and Wheler are important in another respect. It will be my intention to define in the case of each succeeding traveller what idea of Greece he travelled with, what his characteristic emphasis or predisposition was. It happens that the first two in the tradition, travelling together, are pleasingly distinct. Spon and Wheler were unlike in character and unlike also in the degrees of their Hellenism. Spon, though a man of wide interests and curiosity, knew what he wanted primarily in Greece.

... c'est seulement l'amour de l'Antiquité, qui m'a fait entreprendre le voyage ... Mes plus grandes recherches ont eu pour but la connoissance des Monumens antiques ... & que ç'a été là ma plus forte inclination. (*Préface*)

(... it was only my love of the Ancient World that made me undertake the journey ... My studies were for the most part directed towards the knowledge of ancient monuments ... and there my strongest inclinations lay.)

He went there with his admiration for the Greek achievement already well established and what he saw in Greece answered his passion and increased it. Wheler, the Anglican and amateur botanist, responded to pre-Christian Greece less wholeheartedly. He was in the country as an extension of his educational tour in France and Italy. He certainly enjoyed himself there, profited from the visit, and contributed to the knowledge of Greece among his fellow-Europeans. But since the essence of my concern throughout will be to assess the part that enthusiasm for Hellas plays in a man's whole life, here, at the outset, without denigration of Wheler, his travelling-companion may appropriately be distinguished. The irony is, as I have already indicated, that it was Wheler's book, in English and in French, that had the wider circulation.

2

CHISHULL AND TOURNEFORT

I have moved on in this chapter twenty-five years to the turn of the century, 1699–1701, and have put together two travellers, the Englishman Edmund Chishull and the Frenchman Joseph Pitton de Tournefort. There were European visitors to Greece and Turkey after Spon and Wheler and before these two, but few of importance. Besides, my wish is not to be exhaustive but to choose vantage points from which observations in several directions may be made. Tournefort and Chishull suit that purpose admirably. They met briefly in Smyrna in the winter of 1701 and exchanged information on antiquarian matters; and they had acquaintances in common, as well as interests and places. But they are very different, both in character and in the nature and scope of their journeys, Tournefort's enterprise being incomparably the more important. Each is, in his individual manner, a typical figure, and as such serves a major aim of my inquiry, which is to illustrate a variety of attitudes and emphases in the early journeys to Greece.

I have also included in this chapter, at the risk of creating some disunity, surveys of two places, Ephesus and Delos. My excuse is that Chishull was at the former and Tournefort at them both; but what I hope to achieve by interrupting the narrative with these two accounts (extending before and after 1700) is, again, observation from a point of vantage. Both places exerted an extraordinary pull on travellers in the seventeenth and eighteenth centuries, and by assembling several individual responses I hope to highlight certain interesting facets of the enthusiasm for Greece and especially, in the case of Ephesus, a certain conclusive shift.

Edmund Chishull, born of a good family in March 1671 at Eyworth in Bedfordshire and educated at Winchester and Corpus Christi College, Oxford, went out to Smyrna in November 1698 as chaplain to the factory of the Turkey Company. Like other chaplains before and after

him in Smyrna, Aleppo or Constantinople, he took time off from his
clerical duties to pursue his hobby, pagan antiquities.

He kept a diary account of his travels in Asia Minor and of his journey
home which, edited by his son and by his friend and collaborator in
classical studies, Richard Mead, was published in 1747, fourteen years
after his death. Less than half of that book, *Travels in Turkey and back
to England*, has to do with places of the old Greek world, only the first
three sections in fact (pp. 1–71), which recount an excursion to Ephesus
in April 1699, a visit to Constantinople between March and June 1701
and the journey to Adrianople in the spring of 1702, which was the start
of his long overland return to England. Still, there are several evocative
and interesting passages among those carefully edited diary entries.

Chishull appended to his earlier publication, the *Antiquitates Asiaticae*,
some Latin verses entitled 'Iter Asiae Poeticum A.D. 1701'. They are
addressed to his former schoolmaster, Jonathan Horn. Since they
characterize rather well the spirit in which Chishull and others of his
nationality, class, education and profession went into Ancient parts at
the start of the Hellenist eighteenth century, these ninety-eight uninspired hexameters might be worth looking at before we turn to the
more serious *Travels*. It was from Horn at Winchester that Chishull first
heard the names of the fabulous places he was to travel through and
the tribute of a poem is thus an appropriate one:

> Dum tu vimineum dextro moderamine sceptrum
> Dirigis, Horne pater, ludi ter amande magister;
> Me pia Musa comes duxit per avita locorum,
> Et faciem ostendit, famamque & nomina rerum,
> Quæ tu victuris, nitidæ prope mœnia Ventæ,
> Concelebras chartis; & carmine Diva retractat
> Wiccama, Grajugenûm felicia somnia vatum.

> (Whilst you, father Horn, our thrice beloved master,
> Continued skilfully wielding the cane,
> I was conducted by the blessed Muse through the ancient places
> And shown their appearance and the fame and the names of the things
> Which you, in the illustrious city of Winchester,
> Have published abroad in your writings; in Wykehamist verses
> We take up again the Greek poets' happy dreams.)

The poem describes the voyage out of Smyrna[1] and the most memorable
localities visited from there. All the places are evoked in entirely
traditional style, using epithets and descriptive phrases lifted from the
Latin poets. Thus the author proceeds through the Pillars of Hercules,

through Scylla and Charybdis (the Straits of Messina) and rounding Cape Matapan crosses to Smyrna through the Cyclades. Smyrna, as Homer's supposed birthplace, gets eight lines in a style both learned and facetious:

> Smyrnâ non certior ulla disertos
> Jactat Nympha lares, & cive superbit Homero.
> Credite, Wiccamidæ! nemorosâ in valle legebam
> Ingentem Iliada, & resonantis ad antra Meletis
> Somnia carpebam, cùm protinus alma verendi
> Ante oculos stetit umbra senis, litemque diremit
> Urbibus, & dixit, Sacras cave molliter herbas
> Lædere, Smyrnæi quondam incunabula vatis.

> (No Nymph can claim to dwell in any place more learned
> Than Smyrna and none can claim with more right
> Homer for her native son. Believe me,
> Wykehamists: I was reading the *Iliad*, that mighty work,
> In a wooded valley and fell asleep by the cave of the echoing Meles
> When suddenly there stood the shade of a venerable old man before my eyes
> Who put an end to the quarrel among the cities, saying: take care
> Not to do any harm to the sacred things that grow hereabouts
> For among them the former poet of Smyrna was born.)

Smyrna was a favourite among those cities contending for the honour of being Homer's birthplace. His mother Critheis, pregnant either by a god or by some person unknown or by one Maeon (hence his occasional surname Maeonides), gave birth on the banks of the Meles outside Smyrna, making that river, as Tournefort puts it 'le plus noble ruisseau du monde, dans la Republique des Lettres' (II, 510). In the cave at the source of the Meles, here the setting for Chishull's vision, Homer was said to have composed his verses. The scrupulous Chandler found it to be 'about four feet wide, the roof a huge rock cracked and slanting, the sides and bottom sandy'. The entrance, at which he 'crept in' was low and narrow; but, he continues, 'there is another avenue, wider and higher, about three feet from the ground, and almost concealed with brambles. It may be entered also from above where the earth has fallen in' (*Asia Minor*, p. 74). Hölderlin read Chandler, but for his novel *Hyperion* needed something more spacious and agreeable than the reality of 'Homer's Grotto'. Hyperion and his friends gather for a quasi-religious celebration of the blind Bard's life and works:

> So kamen wir an die Grotte Homers.
> Stille traurende Akkorde empfiengen uns vom Felsen herab, unter den wir traten; die Saitenspiele ergossen sich über mein Innres, wie über die todte Erde ein warmer

Regen im Frühlinge. Innen, im magischen Dämmerlichte der Grotte, das durch die verschiedenen Öffnungen des Felsens, durch Blätter und Zweige hereinbricht, stand eine Marmorbüste des göttlichen Sängers, und lächelten gegen die frommen Enkel.

Wir saßen um sie herum, wie die Unmündigen um ihren Vater, und lasen uns einzelne Rhapsodien der Ilias, wie sie jedes nach seinem Sinne sich auswählte; denn alle waren wir vertraut mit ihr.

Eine Nänie, die mein Innerstes erschütterte, sangen wir drauf dem Schatten des lieben blinden Mannes, und seinen Zeiten. (III, 177–8)

(So we came to Homer's Grotto.

As we went in, a soft and melancholy music came down to us from the rocks above; the music of lutes bathed my soul as warm rain bathes the dead earth in spring. Inside, in the magical twilight that entered through openings in the rock and through leaves and branches, stood a marble bust of divine Homer smiling upon us, his descendants, piously gathered there.

We sat in a circle around the pedestal, like children around their father, and read aloud from the *Iliad*, choosing whatever passages we liked, for we all knew the poem well.

Then we sang a hymn in loving memory of that blind bard and the times he lived in. The singing shook me in my innermost soul.)

The cave is a place like several in the novel, and in Heinse's *Ardinghello* too, which excite nostalgia, reverence, heroic fervour and sexuality in a curious mixture. Personal relationships – here between Hyperion and the heroine, later (at the supposed tomb of Achilles and Patroclus) between Hyperion and his warrior friend – are intensified by the power of the famous place. After an emotional paroxysm Hyperion returns to the cave:

Die Grotte war erleuchtet. Wolken von Weihrauch stiegen aus dem Innern des Felsens, und mit majestätischem Jubel brach die Musik nach kurzen Dissonanzen hervor.

Wir sangen heilige Gesänge ... (III, 180)

(The grotto was illuminated. Clouds of incense rose from within the rock and the music issued forth from its preliminary discords with a joyful majesty.

We sang sacred hymns ...)

The setting has become more like the grotto on Antiparos in which M. de Nointel celebrated Christmas Mass than the inconvenient hole described by Chandler.

Sharing that celebrated locality Chishull's Latin hexameters and Hölderlin's novel, a century apart, are at opposite poles on any scale of enthusiasm and commitment. The frivolous Chishull, the tragically serious Hölderlin and the reality of the place itself form one of Hellenism's most intriguing juxtapositions.

Chishull's poem continues with the excursion of April 1699 to Mt

Tmolus, Sardes and the golden River Pactolus, the Niobe rock at Sipylus, Ephesus and the River Cayster. Each of these evocations, resonant enough in its classical borrowings, is undermined by reference back to Horn, Winchester and the Home Counties. Thus, in jocular tone, Niobe is comforted for the loss of her 7 children by the thought of 700 young Wykehamists; and if Homer's swans have gone from the Cayster they have flocked instead to the Thames. Worse still, some lines later a competent conjuring-up of the Trojan Plain is annihilated by heavy tributes to Horn and Winchester: Troy, Chishull suggests, is sensible of Horn's classical labours; the Homeric city and its famous Mt Ida are transcended by Winchester and its chalk hills.

It would be foolish to make too much of Chishull's 'Poetic Journey', but two or three generally useful points suggest themselves. First, he need never have taken any journey at all to write it; having really been in those localities adds nothing whatsoever to the lines. Secondly, there is the display of learning – perfectly ordinary learning, simply what he got at school and university, but on display. The places have their proper associations, as established in the classical writers with whom Chishull's education had made him familiar. Those associations are presented in their original, not Chishull's, formulations. All that Chishull can or does add of his own is what used to be called wit, in the form of the connections he makes between the exotic places and his own bit of England. The connections are made in a tone of sustained facetiousness, and that fundamental unseriousness in the evocation of Greek places is of some interest here as a contrast with what was to follow in poets, scholars and other travellers.

The wit or facetiousness is lacking in *Travels in Turkey*, and many of the diary entries read very well. Chishull writes lucidly and with that elegance which gentlemen of his day seem almost to have had as a birthright. Still, though he was without any doubt truly affected by certain of the localities he visited, an underlying mechanicalness in his account is very apparent. I do not mean that altogether disparagingly, since the mechanism in question is an appropriate one that, on occasion, when skilfully employed, will produce something expressive and satisfying. The technique is to ornament the description of the places visited with quotations from the ancient authors. It is the old rhetorical exercise of *inventio*, of invention not in a modern Romantic sense (implying individual genius), but in the sense simply of finding, as in the phrase 'The Invention of the True Cross'. An author composing in this way needs not what we call 'inventiveness' but knowledge of where his illustrative instances are to be found; and that knowledge is erudition. *Nutrix inventionis eruditio est* was still the writer's and orator's watchword in Chishull's age. Like any other learned author, then, the compiler of a travel-account goes for his illustrative and decorative instances to the *loci* of his classical education. There is an amusing aptness in searching out these *loci*, *topoi*, commonplaces, for the evocation of famous localities. That is the mechanism of the Latin verses we looked at, and also of the *Travels*; but in the *Travels* everywhere the traveller's real firsthand observations predominate and the classical authors only supplement the modern observer's own words. Thus in each passage there is the place itself, Chishull's experience of it, and its appearance in Homer, Virgil, Ovid or Horace. That is a simple mixture, but an effective one; of those three ingredients, with their different levels of time and reality, a good deal can be made.

There is nothing extraordinary in this working method, it is one that would offer itself naturally to any traveller of education; and clearly the charlatan or the man with no mind or language of his own might reach for it very readily to cobble a book together. But it can be used to good effect. It is the characteristic method of the seventeenth-century traveller George Sandys (he sailed through the Archipelago in 1610) and in his account works particularly well since he happened also to be a firstrate translator and a poet. Thus he brings to each famous locality his own observation, a classical locus and his own English version. Here he is passing Corfu, which he identifies very confidently with Homer's Phaeacia:

Corfu, the first Iland of note that we past by, lyeth in the *Ionian* sea; stretching East and West in forme of a bow: 54 miles long, 24 broad; and distant about 12 from the maine of *Epirus*. Called formerly *Corcyra*, of *Corcyra* the daughter of *Æsopus* there buried: but more anciently *Phæacia*. Celebrated by *Homer* for the shipwracke of *Vlysses*, and orchards of *Alcinous*.

> *These at no time doe their rare fruits forgoe:*
> *Stil breathing Zephyrus makes some to grow,*
> *Others to ripen. Growing fruits supply*
> *The gathered: and succeed so orderly.* [Odyssey, VII. 117–19]

Ex iis fructus numquam perit, neque deficit.
Hyeme, neque æstare; toto anno durant sed sane semper,
Zephyrus spirans haec crescere facit aliáque maturescere.
Pirum post pirum senescit, pomum post pomum.
Porro post uvam uva, ficus post ficum.[2]

Chishull composes his passages similarly. In fact his antiquary friend and editor Richard Mead did some of the work when preparing the diary for publication, since he 'had often left the places cited from antient authors to be supplied out of their own works' (*Travels in Turkey*, p. iv). It fell to Mead to 'fill up the quotations'. Between them, especially in the book's first section, the excursion to Ephesus, they produced several passages that are excellent of their kind – on the Niobe rock, for example; on the vestiges of Sardes by the Pactolus; on the crossing of Mt Tmolus with the view of the Hermes and the Gygean Lake. But the richest is perhaps the entry for 29 April, when Chishull and his party were heading for Thyatira across the plain of the Cayster:

April xxix

We continued our journey by four a clock this morning thro the *Caÿstrian* plain for *Tyria*, and had the satisfaction of fording that celebrated river about three hours from our *conáck*. Not far from hence we found a stone bridge of three considerable arches, built directly along the bank of the river; and therefore now serving to no other purpose, but only to witness that the stream had changed its chanel. Our way lay from hence near the course of the *Caÿster*, thro a fertile and well cultivated champain; a place inexpressibly delicious, and which can be equalled by nothing, but the sweetness of that immortal verse:

$$'A\sigma i\omega\ \dot{\epsilon}\nu\ \lambda\epsilon\iota\mu\hat{\omega}\nu\iota\ K\alpha\ddot{\upsilon}\sigma\tau\rho i\varsigma\ \dot{\alpha}\mu\phi\dot{\iota}\ \dot{\rho}\dot{\epsilon}\epsilon\theta\rho\alpha$$

Iliad B.v.461

Or those of *Virgil*

Pelagi volucres, et quae Asia circum
Dulcibus in stagnis rimantur prata Cäystri

Geor. i.384

It is inhabited by frequent villages, and enclosed on both sides with two high and snowy mountains, namely *Tmolus* on the right hand, and on the left what *Strabo* calls $M\epsilon\sigma o\gamma\epsilon\iota\acute{o}\tau\eta\varsigma$, or the *Midland hills*. (*Travels*, p. 19)

The chief effect of this manner of compiling an account, when it is successful, is a strong sense of continuity. The landscape continues into the present, in unlessened beauty. There has been some alteration of the river's course (as at Troy, in the course of the Scamander), but essentially the locality survives. The survival and continuity of landscape is perhaps the single most important discovery made by the early travellers to Greece. But rather than expand upon it here, with reference to Chishull, who perhaps did not fully realize what he was discovering, I should prefer to let its importance emerge gradually, with reference to authors such as Wood, Riedesel and Guys in whom Hellenism was far more developed and to whom it mattered more that something of Ancient Greece should survive. Still, it *is* there in Chishull, a simple observation capable of powerful expansion.

Like the landscape, poetry itself lasts; it is continued from poet to poet and from one age of readers to the next. The lines in the *Georgics*, quoted by Chishull to embellish his description, derive in literary tradition from that in the *Iliad*, which he uses first. His association of poetry and landscape is, whether he knows it or not, peculiarly apt. In Sandys, himself a poet, the connection of landscape and verse is all the more alive in that he is able to complement his own new view of the place with a new version in his own language of the appropriate ancient text. Again, more and better instances of this re-creative process will come to light as we go further into the eighteenth century. At its most serious, in Hölderlin and Goethe, the re-creation of Greek landscape in poetry is the attempt to recover or re-create the ideals previously rooted in those places; the poet's own version, in his own language, being the attempt to appropriate the past ideal for modern times.

It should be obvious, I think, that a great deal is *implied* in the activity and writing of the early travellers in Greece that they themselves, bound by other personal and cultural interests, did not fully realize or exploit. Thus in this short passage from Chishull's diary: the physical continuation of landscape, the continuation of landscape in poetry, the wished-for and even attempted revival of an ideal in its former locality. And we might add, with reference to the bridge made useless by the river's change of course, the travellers' perhaps unconscious highlighting of details that are, so to speak, themselves naturally symbolic. I do not suppose that Chishull himself intended any symbolism with his observation, but in his brief and lucid notes the topographical detail stands out in a nearly poetic prominence and clarity, and any reader disposed to brood on such matters as the passage of time and the works of man might well, I think, give the superseded bridge by the Cayster more than a glance. As the predisposition of the travellers became more decidedly Hellenist so they tended to highlight or discover a pathos or symbolism in the details they observed. And if they themselves remained neutral in their observations, their Hellenist readers were not able to resist quarrying their accounts for telling instances. When Hölderlin composed his novel *Hyperion* he read Chandler and Choiseul-Gouffier in a mood of Hellenist nostalgia, and took from them for his own tendentious purposes such details as the migration of cranes, the howling of jackals or, analogous to Chishull's bridge, the Arch of Hadrian in Athens which, being a gateway nobody now enters or leaves by, stands as something superseded and as a remnant of better times. Goethe, when he composed his *Achilleis*, made his focal point the barrows above the Hellespont described by Chandler and Lechevalier. Reading the travellers one soon gets an eye for these things: the unfinished sculptures in the marble quarries on Naxos come to mind.

The way from Smyrna to Ephesus and back was rich in famous and beautiful localities. I shall have occasion later, in the chapter on Richard Chandler, to mention Chishull's camp-site at Sardes and his ascent of Mt Tmolus, but I want now to concentrate on the goal of his excursion, Ephesus.

Of all the Seven Churches Ephesus was the most obviously ambiguous in its significance. The Christian community, to which Paul addressed his epistles and John his threats, was established where the Temple of Diana, one of the Seven Wonders of the Ancient World, had formerly stood. The earliest travellers, most of them churchmen, searched diligently but inconclusively for the ruins of the temple. The bolder ones groped their way through a subterranean labyrinth ('dark and noisome', Chishull calls it (*Travels*, p. 27)) in the belief that these passages, in fact the foundations of Roman baths, were what remained of Ephesian Artemis' colossal home. (The site was not exactly located until 1869, by the professional J. T. Wood.) There is always in the early accounts more or less expansive lament for the condition of the surviving Christians. I gave examples in the previous chapter. And that sentiment coexists or fuses with some pathos over the passing of the Ionian Greeks. It is instructive in the case of each traveller to note where his archaeological interest and sentimental emphasis lie. Smith in 1671, though he assiduously copied pagan inscriptions and urged others to do likewise, was effusive in sentiment only over the lot of Christianity or, like the preacher in Ecclesiastes, over the vanity of all things. Choiseul-Gouffier in 1776 disregards Christian Ephesus completely. Between those two there are fluctuations in emphasis according to each visitor's character and interests, but the trend towards a predominant or exclusive Hellenism is unmistakable.

Chishull sorts the remains at Ephesus into three categories: Turkish, Christian and Heathen. He has very little to say about the first, and since, as a rational man, he was unwilling to countenance such dubious

42

monuments as the Cave of the Seven Sleepers, St John's Font and St Peter's Prison, he has very little to say about the second either. Most of the detail and all the rhetoric and pathos of his account concerns the heathen remains. He begins with this general view:

THE once glorious and renowned *Ephesus* was seated in a fruitful vale, encompassed almost round with mountains, at a small distance from the *Caÿster*, and about five miles eastward from cape *Trogilium*; where, at the common charge of all *Ionia*, the *Panionia*, or *common councils of Ionia*, were formerly celebrated. This vale rises advantagiously in the middle with two or three little hills, on which the several parts of the antient city lay extended. The same spot of ground is still covered with the rich remains of its former glory. Such are the massy walls, the portals, the arches, the aqueducts, the marble chests, together with the dejected cornishes, shafts, and capitals of many lofty pillars. But the face of the whole yeilds a melancholy and disagreable prospect, being overrun with an incredible quantity of rank and luxuriant weeds, which serve only to corrupt the air, and to conceal the curiosities of the place. This we found to be a disadvantagous circumstance, and such as doubled the labour of this day in compassing the circuit of the city, and tracing the uncertain footsteps of so many valuable antiquities. (*Travels*, p. 23)

The former glory of the Temple of Diana is conveyed *per negativum*, by the absence of considerable ruins. He found nothing 'lofty and beautiful enough to bespeak it the remains of that famous structure', only some 'dejected pillars of beautiful and splendid marble' and nothing besides but 'venerable heaps of rubbish, and uncertain traces of foundations'. He concludes: 'the traveler ... must be forced to supply his curiosity with considering, that this was the place, where once stood and flourished that renowned wonder of the world' (*Travels*, p. 27).

One monument at Ephesus resumes in itself the whole ambiguity of the site and successive travellers' depictions of it are of considerable interest here. It is the so-called Gate of the Persecution, through which the road enters Ayasoluk. Tourists admired three marble reliefs set in the arch of the gate. The gate itself is thought to be work of the sixth century A.D.; the reliefs, though, originally panels of sarcophagi, are much older: Michaelis, in his *Ancient Marbles in Great Britain*, says they are Greek, a modern guide-book published by the Austrian Archaeological Institute says they are Roman. The important thing is not their age but that they depict – by common (modern) consent – scenes from the life of Achilles, and most notably the death of Patroclus and the dragging and ransoming of Hector. But the Christian builder of the gateway either wilfully or in ignorance overlooked the fact, and set the reliefs across his arch as the depiction of the persecution of a Christian martyr; and in that traditional sense local people and the earliest travellers looked at them. Smith writes as follows:

Northward of the Church [of St John] on the gate leading up to the new Castle are very curious figures engraven, representing several, who seem to be haled and dragged away, as if perchance the design had been to shew how the poor Christians were formerly seized upon and treated by their heathen persecutors.[3]

Tournefort and Chishull, who were at Ephesus within a couple of years of one another, each give a description of the reliefs. Tournefort's is brief and of little interest (unless as an indication of his small enthusiasm for Christian remains). He says merely that the gate is 'de fort bon goût' ('of a very good Taste' (II, 388)), and of the three marbles he distinguishes only the one on the left, which shows 'une Bacchanale d'enfans qui se roulent sur des pampres de vigne' (II, 513–14) ('a Bacchanal of Children, who roll upon Vine-Branches' (II, 388)). But he does provide an illustration, a very indifferent drawing of the reliefs in a line across the arch, which is useful for my purposes here. Chishull (pp. 25–6) writes at some length and with more enthusiasm about them (among his 'heathen antiquities'). He is least interested in the Bacchanal; it has been 'somewhat injured by time'. But on the second he writes:

THE second marble is a military piece, consisting of many intire figures, all cut in postures very bold and masterly, and such as undoubtedly are the work of some noble hand. It designs a warlike horse surprized by an enemy, with his rider lying at his feet; near which several persons are carried captive by Roman soldiers. The chieftain stands by, and is supplicated by a woman in a large loose mantle, whose intercession seems to intercept the action. This has been by some refered to the *destruction of Troy*, and by others to a Christian persecution; but with greater probability it may be thought to represent the event of some Roman victory. (*Travels*, p. 26)

This is both admiring and, in its interpretation, modest and tentative. As works of Antiquity, irrespective of date, irrespective of subject, the reliefs receive their due of perhaps conventional admiration. Chishull completes his description thus:

THE third marble is a sepulchral monument, and represents a dead person extended, from his knees upwards, on a funeral bed; the chief mourner sitting, and five other persons standing in a melancholy posture, and lamenting over him. These likewise are very lively figures, and cut with an inimitable perfection. (p. 26)

The early travellers, being the first Europeans to see classical works *in situ*, do tend to think most of them of an 'inimitable perfection'. Tournefort on Delos, among the scattered remains, is very generous in his praises; and it is interesting to see his verdicts qualified or flatly contradicted by the highly professional Ludwig Ross in the 1830s. Admiration exists so to speak latently or platonically in the Hellenist traveller and wants for its expression not so much a fit object as a not wholly unfit occasion. Those German enthusiasts who never left Germany and who saw no more of original classical works than poor plaster casts were not checked in their excitement by the real inferiority of what they were looking at.

Richard Chandler came to Ephesus in the summer of 1765. He had with him in his party the painter William Pars. This is Chandler's description of the marbles in the Gate of the Persecution (what Tournefort and Chishull saw as one piece, in the centre, he sees as two):

Over the arch are four pieces of antient sculpture. Two in the middle are in alto relievo, of most exquisite workmanship, and parts of the same design; representing the death of Patroclus, and the bringing of his body to Achilles. A third is in basso relievo. The figures on it are a man leading away a little boy, a corpse extended, two women lamenting, and soldiers bearing forth the armour and weapons of the deceased, to decorate his funeral pile. This, if it be not the sequel of that transaction, may be referred to the story of Hector. The fourth is carved with boys and vine-branches, much injured. (*Asia Minor*, pp. 115–16)

In that interpretation – that the marbles depict scenes in Homer's *Iliad* – and with an unambiguously Hellenist enthusiasm Pars drew the two pictures that appeared as engravings in Robert Wood's *Essay on the Original Genius and Writings of Homer* in 1775.[4] Putting side by side the illustration of the gate in Tournefort and those done by Pars in Wood, one can see at a glance what Hellenism means. It is not just that Pars is the better draughtsman; full of Homer, he has *composed* upon the dubious original. His pictures are *creative* copies, compositions in their own right, in the Greek spirit as the eighteenth century understood Greece, and very appropriately are they placed there before and after the text of Wood's book. Pars began by making sense of what he saw. He ascribed a meaning to the figures, and lent them coherence in that light, grouping them, reducing their number, leaving none unconnected, inconclusive or peripheral. (Much in the Tournefort drawing is evidently copied quite uncomprehendingly.) Thus arranged, simplified and enhanced, and careful attention being given to their gestures and to the folds of their garments, the figures compose a scene that is coherent in sense and in emotion. The true original is not the reliefs at Ephesus but the last books of Homer's *Iliad*, and Pars has recreated at least some of their dignity and pathos in his drawings. In the end

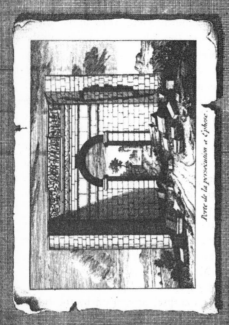

Porte de la persécution à Éphèse.

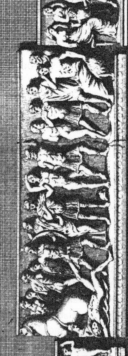

Bas reliefs qui se voyent sur la Porte d'Éphèse.

it matters precious little what the marbles themselves in fact depict: their sculptor thought one thing, the builder of the gate another; nor of what date or quality they are: the experts disagree. On Pars they worked creatively, as numerous poor remains did upon travellers, scholars and poets throughout that century of creative enthusiasts.

A few months later Chandler's party came to Athens and there Pars set to work drawing what was left of the Parthenon frieze. Excellence in the original will not pass automatically into the copy; imitation, such as Homer's 'Imitation of Nature', or Winckelmann's evocation of the Apollo Belvedere, or Pars' drawings of the Parthenon frieze, is a creative act. His drawings were not published until 1816, in the fourth volume of the *Antiquities of Athens* (by which time many of the sculptures were in London). Set them side by side with those done by Nointel's Flemish artist in 1674 and again it will be obvious what Hellenism is. Without disrespect to the early draughtsman, who worked in conditions far less favourable than those enjoyed by Pars, and whose sketches, wooden though they be, are quite invaluable, not as art but as documents – still it must be said that only Pars, child of the eighteenth century, was at one in spirit with what he drew. It is, after all, not a matter of photographic reproduction but of attempting to transfer from one medium to another, from stone to pencil line, a passionate idea and its material realization; and that transference is a creative act in which skill and sympathy are equally necessary.

The reliefs at Ephesus remained where the Christian architect had set them, in the Gate of the Persecution, until 1819. Then they were removed for John Russell, the sixth Earl of Bedford, and transported, badly damaged, via Smyrna and Malta to his seat at Woburn Abb. The 'Bacchanale d'enfans' was left in place and is, apparently, there stil a large fragment, showing Hector's corpse, broken off by the Earl': clumsy agents, was left lying where it fell below the gate. Woburn Abbey, now a safari park, still houses the rest.

In 1701 Chishull took another journey. To be exact 'a voyage from *Smyrna* to *Constantinople*, and a journey back from thence to *Smyrna*' (*Travels*, p. 32). He sailed on 26 March and returned on 28 June. In Constantinople he waited on the ambassador, Lord Paget.

Travellers by ship to Constantinople saw the Troad and the ruins of Alexandrian Troy more or less well according to how quickly they could advance against the strong current of the Hellespont. Chishull's ship made very slow headway and for the space of three days, he writes, 'I viewed ... the whole *Trojan* shore ... at a convenient distance in calm and serene weather from the poop of the ship, feeding my eyes and mind with an eager and boundless curiosity' (*ibid.* p. 34). Though they anchored one evening under the Sigean headland, he did not go ashore. Those early travellers who did, like Des Hayes and Sandys, were always in fear of being stranded and dared not go far inland. It required a determined expedition, like Robert Wood's in 1750, to make any progress at all towards Priam's city. Chishull's short account is simply a delineation of the Troad using Strabo. Characteristically he dismisses as 'vain ... the accounts of our modern *journalists*, who pretend to have seen the walls, the gates, or other ruins of *Troy*'. What they saw was the debris of Alexandrian Troas, on the coast. Of ancient Troy itself as long ago as the reign of Tiberius, so we are assured by Strabo, 'there remained not the least footstep ... to satisfy the curiosity of the most searching traveler' (*ibid.* p. 35). What sentiment Chishull felt at Troy he put into his Latin verses, and there destroyed it with heavy flippancy, as we have seen; his prose account is plain and rather sceptical.

Back in Smyrna, Chishull was visited by Tournefort who, coming from Prusa, arrived there on 18 December 1701. Tournefort had been travelling for eighteen months. Evidently he got on well with Chishull – 'C'est un galant homme, habile Antiquaire' (II, 501) ('He is a pretty Gentleman, and a good Antiquary' (II, 378)) – for he passed on to him inscriptions he had copied at Ancyra two months before. Chief among them was the *Monumentum Ancyranum*: the record of Augustus' life and deeds inscribed on the walls of his temple at Ancyra. This document, discovered by Busbecq in 1555, had already been published and commented on several times; but in 1728, in his *Antiquitates Asiaticae*, Chishull published it again, in Tournefort's version, with fulsome tributes to his learning and generosity, including also the drawing of the *pronaos* (that is, the hall or first room of the temple, around which the inscription was cut) done by Tournefort's artist and his description of it in French. There was clearly much discussion of their common interests and a friendly exchange of information. Tournefort writes: 'Pour le Temple d'Apollon [in Smyrna] il ne devoit pas être bien loin de là, & le Chapelain de M^r le Consul d'Angleterre m'asseûra qu'il en avoit découvert les ruines' (II, 501) ('As for the Temple of *Apollo*, it can't be far off, and the *English* Consul's Chaplain assured me he had discover'd the Ruins of it' (II, 378)). (This discovery is noted in Chishull's sketchy account of Smyrna included in the preface to his

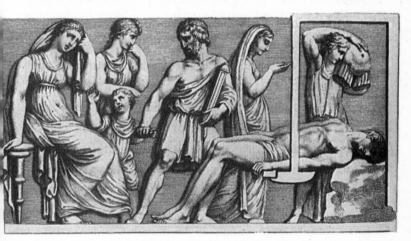

4   Pars' drawings of the Gate of the Persecution

Travels, p. v.) He continues: 'Nous devions à mon retour d'Ephèse avoir une conference sur nos recherches, mais il partit pendant mon absence... ainsi je n'ay pas appris d'autres nouvelles du Temple d'Apollon' ('We were at my Return from *Ephesus* to have had some Conversations upon our Discoveries, but during my absence he went to *Constantinople*...so that I learnt nothing more of the Temple of *Apollo*' (II, 378–9)). Chishull, resigning his chaplaincy, had gone to Adrianople (his journey there, between 10 February and 4 April 1702, is described in his *Travels*, pp. 55–71) to join the departing ambassador and to proceed homewards with him through Bulgaria, Hungary, Germany and Holland (which journey, 8 April 1702 – 14 May 1703, forms the last and longest part of his book). Tournefort, visiting Ephesus, Samos and Patmos, was back in Smyrna on 27 March 1702, missing Chishull by six weeks or so. He sailed home himself on 13 April.

The consul to whom Chishull was chaplain was one William Raye; his successor, arriving the year after Chishull and Tournefort had left, was the botanist and antiquary William Sherard. Sherard had studied botany under Tournefort in Paris from 1686 to 1688; and in 1689, hiding his identity behind the letters S.W.A., he had published Tournefort's *Schola Botanica*. Knowing of his appointment to the post in Smyrna, Tournefort writes: 'J'espere que Mr *Sherard*... nous éclaircira de toutes les Antiquitez de Smyrna & des environs; car c'est un tres sçavant homme, de mes bons amis, & tout plein de zéle pour la perfection des Sciences' (II, 501) ('I hope Mr. *Sherrard*...will inform us of all the Antiquities of *Smyrna*, and the places adjacent; for he is a very learned Man, and full of Zeal for the Perfection of the Sciences' (II, 379 – omits 'de mes bons amis')).

Established in Smyrna, Sherard did a good deal of work both as a botanist and as an antiquary. He visited the Seven Churches in 1705, accompanied by the Rev. John Tisser, Chishull's successor, and Antonio Picenini, a Swiss scholar and physician, a friend of Leibniz.[5] There were other expeditions in 1709 and 1716, the latter in the company of Dr Samuel Lisle. Lisle is perhaps worth resurrecting briefly, being so perfectly representative of his kind. He became Warden of Wadham College, Oxford. The college library has a manuscript memoir of him by his former curate, the Rev. Gilbert Bouchery. He was chaplain in Smyrna from 1710 until 1716, 'during which time when the affairs of his Cure would give Him Leisure, he gratified his Curiosity by visiting Constantinople, and making journeys through most Part of Ionia and

Caria viewing the Situation and Antiquities of the famous Cities in that part of Asia'. In 1716 he swapped places with his colleague in Aleppo, and from there saw Balbec and the Holy Land. He came back to England in 1719 and rose through the Church thereafter. The memoir concludes:

He left behind Him several Notes and Observations made in his Travels, especially in Asia Minor, Syria and the Holy Land, the Publication of these would have been very acceptable to the Learned World, for his Classical Tast and Knowledge were eminent, but by an express Clause in his Will He appointed *all his Compositions of what sort soever to be committed to the Fire by the Hands of his Executor, not permitting them in any manner or by any form whatsoever to be printed, transcribed, or perused by any Body but Himself* – This was faithfully though reluctantly executed.

Perhaps his travels seemed to him vanity at the end. There is always *some* suggestion of bad conscience in these churchmen journeying through heathen places.

Tournefort died in 1708, but in the years before then, whilst he was preparing his book, he corresponded with Sherard. They were friends of long standing, with botany, Antiquity and a knowledge of the Ionian sites in common. Writing up his own account, Tournefort gratefully made use of whatever information Sherard, on the spot, could send him; and it goes without saying that the assistance was always courteously acknowledged: 'il m'a communiqué quelques lumieres pour la situation de *Clazomene* & de ses Isles' (II, 501) ('he has given me some light into the Situation of *Clazomene*, and its Islands' (II, 379)). Political relations between France and England were on the whole unfriendly throughout this early period of the exploration of Greece; and thereafter, in Napoleonic times, archaeology itself became another battle-ground; but generosity far more than chauvinism or self-interest characterizes the dealings of the early travellers and scholars among themselves. Selden and Peiresc, Vernon, Spon and Wheler, sharing an enthusiasm, dealt with one another impartially across the frontiers. When Chishull and Tournefort met in Smyrna in the winter of 1701–2, their nations were close to war; but, as we have seen, the two antiquaries co-operated on the best of terms.

Sherard, from Smyrna, must have corresponded with Chishull too, keeping him abreast of the latest discoveries. Certainly, when he returned to England in the winter of 1717, he and Chishull collaborated. For the *Antiquitates Asiaticae* contains not only Tournefort's contributions from Ancyra and Delos but also several important inscriptions collected by Sherard, Picenini and Lisle in the Troad, at Teos, Aphrodisias, Stratonicea, Miletus and Larnaka. This scholarly, and collective, work appeared in 1728, the year of Sherard's death, and is dedicated to him. When Chandler compiled and published the *Ionian Antiquities* for the Society of Dilettanti in 1769, he included and acknowledged the researches done by Chishull, Sherard and the others in Asia Minor half a century before.

After his return from Turkey, Chishull did not leave England again. He married, resigned his Oxford fellowship and was instituted to the living first of Walthamstow then of Southchurch in Essex. His publications apart from the *Antiquitates* and the *Travels* were some notes on the Sigean inscription and on numismatics, several sermons, and some Latin verses on George III's victory at La Hogue and on the death of Queen Mary, as well as an abusive attack upon one Mr Dodwell for supposed heresy (which caused the antiquary Hearne, a friend of Dodwell's, to call him 'a confident, opiniative little writer'). Through his book of commentated inscriptions and the posthumously published diary of his travels he contributed something to Hellenic studies and to the enthusiasm for the ancient places themselves. He is an instance of the happy combination of Classics and the Anglican Church. He had scholarship and a proper, untroublesome love of the Greek and Latin authors and the localities they allude to and evoke. As chaplain to the Worshipful Turkey Company he camped by the golden Pactolus, close to the ruins of a temple of Cybele, climbed Mt Tmolus, sacred to Dionysus, and searched at Ephesus for vestiges of the Temple of Artemis of the Many Breasts; as Vicar of Walthamstow he focussed his learning on the retrieved inscriptions. Greece, for Chishull, was only the customary cleric's sideline. He would be worth our attention for his exemplariness; and, in addition to that, he writes well and had moments of vision.

Tournefort's journey (March 1700–June 1702) was instigated and financed by the French Crown. His brief, presented to the Académie des Sciences on 16 February 1700, was, he writes, as follows:

...d'aller dans la Gréce, aux Isles de l'Archipel, & en Asie, pour y faire des recherches touchant l'Histoire naturelle; pour m'instruire des maladies & des remedes que l'on y employe; pour y comparer l'ancienne Geographie avec la moderne...(1, 3)

...to go into *Greece*, to the Islands of the *Archipelago*, and into *Asia*; to make diligent Search after things relating to Natural History; to inform my self touching the several Distempers and Medicaments in those Countries; to compare the Antient Geography with the Modern...(Eng. ed., 1, 3)

He was to have with him two assistants, of his own choosing. They were Claude Aubriet (1665–1715), the Royal miniaturist (who did botanical illustrations for both Tournefort and Sébastien Vaillant[6]), and Andreas Gundelsheimer (1668–1715), a German doctor of medicine who had already made a name for himself in Paris. (Leaving Tournefort in Constantinople, he went to Berlin, where he became physician at the Court of Brandenburg.) Tournefort himself was already well known as a botanist and had travelled widely in Europe at Louis XIV's command, collecting plants for the royal garden. He was in Oxford in 1688, and maintained cordial relations with scholars there.

Tournefort's expedition was a professional and scientific one, like Chandler's sixty-five years later; but, unlike Chandler's, its aims were still not predominantly the exploration and description of classical sites. He was not a Hellenist. Neither in the eulogy of Tournefort that prefaces the account of his travels, nor in the *Life* added to the third French edition and to the English editions, is there any significant mention of his classical learning and his contribution to classical studies. All three travellers, even Gundelsheimer, were botanists. Tournefort proposed, as the author of the *Life* puts it, 'to examine upon the spot whether what *Theophrastus*, *Dioscorides*, *Matthiolus*, and several other Authors, have written concerning Plants, were conformable to Truth. His Exactness strongly inclined him to inquire whether they had not impos'd upon Nature, or whether Nature herself had not degenerated since their Observations' (Eng. ed. p. xvii). And in the same spirit, respectful but not submissive to the classical authors, he wished to study the geography of the Ancient World, comparing the past, as it appears in Strabo, Pausanias, Herodotus and the poets, with the present as he saw it himself, and rectifying or clarifying the picture as he could. It was in pursuing this intention that Tournefort contributed most to the factual basis of European Hellenism. In 1700, aged forty-four, already well-travelled and enormously erudite, botanist, physician and classical scholar, he was 'the properest Man in the world' for the king's commission. He was so thoroughly prepared by his reading for the countries he would visit 'that when he came there he found himself as it were naturalized in each by his Learning' (p. xviii).

Tournefort and his companions set off from Versailles on 9 March 1700 and on 23 April sailed from Marseilles. Their route was through the Greek islands, calling first at Crete, then among the Cyclades and along the coast of Asia Minor as far north as Tenedos. They passed then through the Dardanelles to Constantinople and, after a stay there, continued into the Black Sea and along its southern coast into Armenia and Georgia, as far as Teflis. They returned via Erzeron, Tocat, Ancyra and Prusa to Smyrna, and from there completed their tour in Asia Minor with visits to Ephesus and the islands of Samos and Patmos. On their way home to Marseilles they were blown in at Scyros.

Tournefort's account of his journey, *Relation d'un voyage du Levant fait par ordre du roy*, came out in two volumes in 1717, nine years after his death. In an *Avertissement* prefixing the work it is reported that Tournefort himself oversaw the printing of the first volume, and that he left his manuscripts in good order for the second. He was to have written his own preface, but the eulogy delivered by Fontenelle at the Académie des Sciences on 10 April 1709 served instead. The book was translated into English in 1718, reissued in 1741, and into German in 1776–7. It is in the form of letters, twenty-two in all, addressed to the Comte de Pontchartrain, Secretary of State to Louis XIV and the man who first suggested the enterprise.

Voyage du Levant is a long and engrossing book, wearing all its great learning very lightly. Tournefort had the curiosity, tolerance and versatility of the good traveller; 'une curiosité fort étenduë... & un certain don de bien voir' ('a most extensive curiosity... & a certain Gift of Clearsightedness' (Eng. ed., p. xxxix)), as the author of the *Eloge* puts it. Among the islands and in the hinterland of Asia Minor he did not keep to the best-known and safest routes but went with his party wherever he thought it would be interesting or amusing to go. Thus he risked all the usual perils and a few unusual ones beside. Landing after dark on Thermia (ancient Cyanthus) he and his companions were mistaken for pirates by the inhabitants and almost lynched. On Joura, spending the night (as they often did) in a dilapidated chapel, they lay awake in fear of having their ears bitten by mice. Frequently in their keenness to botanize they marooned themselves for days on inhospitable unpeopled islands in cruel weather. Such discomforts must have reminded Tournefort of his early days climbing after plants in the Pyrenees, when he was robbed so often that he went in rags and hid what little money he had in a hunk of black bread, his only rations, which his assailants, desperately poor though they were, disdained to take; and once he was buried under a collapsing shack. This hardened and adventurous man finally met his death when he was knocked down by a cart in a Paris street, on his way to the Académie des Sciences.

His characteristic tone of voice in the *Voyage* is lightly ironic. Towards the natives, Turkish and Greek, he has the Frenchman's sense of superiority: 'Presque toute leur vie se passe dans l'oisiveté: manger du ris, boire de l'eau, fumer, prendre du caffé: voilà la vie des Musulmans' (I, 19) ('Almost their whole Life is spent in Idleness: to eat Rice, drink Water, smoke Tobacco, sip Coffee, is the Life of a *Musselman*' (Eng. ed. 1, 15)). The modern Greeks, he notes, descendants of the greatest architects the world has known, are incapable of building a stairway in their houses and mount to the upper storey via a ladder propped outside; they are 'naturellement chicaneurs' (I, 282) ('naturally litigious' (I, 218)), 'ils ne peuvent pas s'empêcher de tromper' (I, 279) ('can't forbear playing their tricks' (I, 215)), 'ils ne sont curieux que de piastres, & tous voleurs de profession' (I, 252) ('the Inhabitants have no notion of anything but the Pence; they are all Thieves by Profession' (I, 195–6)). But his remarks are never *too* harsh; there is none of that bitter disappointment that characterizes the accounts of later, more sentimental travellers. He is generally sceptical, but humane. And he is quite without self-importance. The book contains delightful pictures of himself and his companions: climbing Mount Ararat, for example, stalked by tigers. Warned that there would be no water until they reached the snow, they bloated themselves like camels before setting off. Of the descent he writes:

Je laisse à deviner de quelle voiture Noé se servit pour descendre, lui qui pouvoit monter sur tant de sortes d'animaux puisqu'il les avoit tous à sa suite. (II, 369)

I leave it to be guess'd what method *Noah* made use of to descend from this Place, who might have rid upon so many Sorts of Animals which were all at his command. (II, 275)

For their part, they came down the lower grassy slopes on their backsides, legs in the air. There is no conceit in his impressive display of learning. In the following passage, for example, when he is marooned on Macronisi, the academic question and the erudition are nicely ironized:

Nous couchâmes dans une caverne auprés de la cale; mais nous eûmes belle peur dans la nuit: quelques Veaux marins, qui s'étoient retirez dans une caverne voisine, firent des cris si épouventables que nous ne sçavions si c'étoient des animaux d'un autre monde; nos matelots ne faisoient qu'en rire, & cela nous rassura: je ne sçai si ces veaux crient en veillant ou en dormant, c'est une grande dispute parmi les commentateurs de Pline: Hermolaus Barbarus croit que c'est pendant leur sommeil, son sentiment n'est pas favorisé par les anciens manuscrits de Pline; d'ailleurs on lui oppose un texte d'Aristote conforme à ces manuscrits; sans entrer dans cette dissertation, je crois qu'il vaut mieux s'en tenir à ce que nous en dirent nos matelots, qui nous assurerent que ces Veaux faisoient l'amour à leur aise dans ce temps-là: à la pointe du jour on les vit sortir de leur caverne, & ils se plongerent si vite dans la mer, qu'on n'eut pas le temps de tirer dessus. (1, 343)

We lay in a Cavern near the Creek: but we were heartily scared in the Night: some Sea-Calves, which had taken up their quarters in the next Cavern to ours, set up such hideous Cries, that we thought 'em some Fiends from the other World; our Mariners laughing, put us into heart again. Whether these Creatures make this noise waking or sleeping, I know not; it is a great dispute among the Commentators of *Pliny*: *Hermolaus Barbarus* thinks it is the latter, but he is not back'd by the old Manuscripts of *Pliny*; besides, they oppose to him a Text of *Aristotle* conformable to these *Manuscripts*: without entering into this Dissertation, it is better abiding by what our Mariners told us of the matter, namely, That these Calves were at that time making love, or catterwawling. At Day-break they quitted their Cavern, and dived so swift into the Sea, there was no catching 'em (1, 262 – omits the nice phrase 'à leur aise')

Much of Tournefort's attention is given to matters of natural history. In the grotto on Antiparos, where Nointel had celebrated Mass in 1673, he pursued his theory of the 'vegetation of stones'. Noting that the concentric rings of growth in a section of stalagmite closely resembled those of a tree, he concludes: 'il semble que ces troncs de marbre vegetent' (1, 191) ('these Stems of Marble must certainly vegetate' (1, 149)); other calcareous excrescences looked so like 'les pieds, les branches, & les têtes des choux fleurs, qu'il semble que la nature nous ait voulu montrer par là comment elle s'y prend pour la vegetation des pierres' (1, 191) ('the Roots, Branches, and Heads of Colly-Flowers, that one would think Nature meant by this to shew us how she operates in the Vegetation of Stones' (1, 148)). In the Elogium this eccentric notion, an extension of Tournefort's botany into the inanimate world, is expounded at length and with great respect. Volcanic Thera fascinated him. He was able to incorporate into his account news reaching him shortly before his death of the emergence, in 1707, of a new island out of the sea. It rose with 'un effroyable mugissement' (1, 268) ('terrible Noises under ground' (1, 207)).[7]

Tournefort was a great collector, in the seventeenth-century manner, a collector of stones and minerals, weapons, costumes and musical instruments. His *cabinet* was renowned. He is the very type of the curious traveller. He had the sort of curiosity that takes in all things of interest impartially: limestone formations, crocodile-lizards, the costumes of the island women. He spends some pages describing execution by impalement, or the equally hideous ganch, and provides an illustration of this latter death, because such things unavoidably fell within the notice of travellers in Turkey.

Those half-dozen letters in the first volume which are given over to a description of one or more of the Aegean islands provide the best illustration of Tournefort's working method. Only in the account of Delos, and there inevitably, do classical antiquities preponderate; elsewhere they have a subordinate and sometimes a negligible part. It may be useful to indicate what other interests classical studies had to compete with. The report on each island will generally begin with a brief statement of the travellers' itinerary, a date, and perhaps a note on their accommodation. Then there is some discussion of the island's modern and ancient names, its situation and size as given by Strabo and Pliny and corroborated or corrected by Tournefort. Then follows a synopsis of local history, with mention of famous native sons and daughters, from fabulous times to the wars of the Turks and Venetians and the present day. The survey of the island's present condition will almost always include details of its administration and taxation (the degree of its oppression by the Turks or, previously perhaps, the Venetians); of its produce – silk, wine, olives, lentisk, turpentine etc. – and commerce; of its religion, whether Catholic or Orthodox or both, what power the Jesuits, Capucines or Cordeliers have there, and what are the principal churches, monasteries and chapels. These last, like the names of the villages, may be presented simply in a list. Often the letters conclude with precise and yet amused descriptions (with accompanying engravings) of local female costume. If the island has a convenient vantage point the travellers ascend it, to take compass bearings on the surrounding islands in sight. Most accounts carry an engraved plan of the island and often also a view of the port. Safe anchorages and fresh-water sources will generally be noted.

Those are the salient items in almost every account. They will be more or less full as occasion demands and available information permits. It is obvious that in their compilation of useful, interesting and curious facts the travellers proceeded in each place systematically. Where the locality had some outstanding curiosity to show – the labyrinth near Gortyn on Crete, the grotto on Antiparos, the marble quarries on Paros and Naxos – the party made a conscientious effort to do the phenomenon justice, hiring guides and mounting a small expedition. And with considerable *Schadenfreude* they put local wonders, especially those under the management of the *papas*, thoroughly to the test.

But the party's chief purposes were botanical and antiquarian, and their researches in those subjects are reported in every letter. Botany has pre-eminence. It was to go after plants that the travellers had themselves set down on uninhabited rocks devoid of archaeological interest. Botanizing, they walked miles – across Ios, for example, almost missing the boat. Their passion for plants caused them any amount of hardship. But Tournefort had suffered for years in the cause of botany. It was said of him that he was born a botanist as others are born poets; and, as the writer of the Elogium remarked, botany is not an armchair science. Its devotee Tournefort had climbed walls like a cat-burglar in his boyhood and Pyrenean mountains in his early manhood, after plants; middle-aged he was island-hopping across the Aegean and trekking up Mt Ararat. The party brought back more than 1300 specimens. The *Voyage du Levant* has scores of exact descriptions of new plants, together with engravings of them.

Very few of the book's engravings are of classical remains and those few – the Temple of Dionysus on Naxos, for example – are singularly stiff and uninspired. Still, along with the botany and perhaps most often secondary to it, the ancient remains in any locality were also Tournefort's concern. I must quote in full his party's encounter with the Bishop of Ceos. It exceeds what is required for this precise context, but is too good to cut:

Les bourgeois de Zia s'attroupent ordinairement pour filer de la soye, & s'assoyent sur les bords de leurs terrasses afin de laisser tomber le fuseau jusques au bas de la rue, qu'ils retirent ensuite en roulant le fil; nous trouvâmes l'Evêque Grec en cette posture; il demanda quelles gens nous étions; & nous fit dire que nos occupations étoient bien frivoles, si nous ne cherchions que des plantes & de vieux marbres: nous repondimes que nous serions plus édifiez de lui voir à la main les œuvres de Saint Chrysostome ou de Saint Basile, que le fuseau. (I, 337)

The Burghers of *Zia* generally get together in knots when they spin their Silk; they sit upon the very edge of their Terrass-Roofs, and let fall the spindle into the street, and then draw it up again in winding the Thred. We found the *Greek* Bishop in this posture; he ask'd who we were, at the same time giving us to understand that 'twas a sign we had not much to do, if we came thither only to hunt for Plants and Pieces of Antiquity: to which we reply'd, we should be much more edify'd to find him reading St. *Chrysostom's* or St. *Basil's* Works, than winding off Bottoms of Silk. (I, 257–8)

In fact Tournefort noted and described many things that were useful and inspiring to classical scholars and later travellers. His authority among eighteenth-century Hellenists was considerable; no traveller is cited more. I have already mentioned some of his discoveries in Asia Minor and his discussions with Chishull and Sherard. He was a supplier also of several of those instances of neglect, abuse and loss that are the very stuff of later sentimental indignation and lamenting over Greece. He tells us of the Turks on Samos bombarding the pillars of the Temple of Hera with cannon balls in the hope of discovering gold and silver concealed within; of the Turks disfiguring the famous Amazon of Smyrna with musket shots. Everywhere he notes the utterly uncomprehending incorporation of precious ancient marbles into squalid modern dwellings. And here on Polikandros he remarks, in characteristically laconic and unsentimental style:

Pour la statue ancienne dont parle Mr. Thevenot, on nous assûra qu'elle avoit été sciée & employée à des montans de porte: on y découvrit il y a quelques années le pied d'une figure de bronze, que l'on fondit pour faire des chandeliers à l'usage de la chapelle. (1, 259)

As for the old Statue spoken of by *Thevenot*, we were told it has been saw'd to pieces to help to make a Door-case of: some years ago they found the Foot of a Figure in Brass, which they melted down to make Candlesticks for the Chappel. (1, 201)

' Rien n'échappe à l'ignorance des Grecs' (1, 200) (' nothing can escape the Ignorance of the Greeks' (1, 156)), he comments, on Paros. He was by no means without reverence for the past. He had a strong sense of the long lapse through the centuries from a former glorious civilization. This is his account of Gortyn on Crete, a site very little visited but one that, even today, is almost eerily deep in the past:

Les ruines de Gortyne ne sont qu'à six milles du mont Ida, au pied des collines, à l'entrée de la plaine de la Messaria, laquelle est proprement le grenier de l'Isle. Ces ruines montrent bien quelle a été la magnificence de l'ancienne ville, mais on ne sçauroit les regarder sans quelque peine: on laboure, on séme, on fait paître des moutons parmi les débris d'une prodigieuse quantité de marbre, de jaspe, & de granit, travaillez avec beaucoup de soin: au lieu de ces grands hommes qui avoient fait élever de si beaux édifices, on ne voit que de pauvres bergers, qui n'ont pas l'esprit de prendre les liévres qui leur passent entre les jambes, ni de tuer les perdrix qui se trouvent sous leurs pieds. (1, 59)

The Ruins of *Gortyna* are not above six miles from Mount *Ida*, at the foot of low Hills, as you enter the Plain of *Messaria*, which is properly the Granary of the Island. These Ruins show indeed how magnificent a City it once was, but 'tis impossible to look on 'em without concern: they plough, sow, feed Sheep among the Wrecks of a prodigious quantity of Marble, Jasper, Granate-Stone, wrought with great curiosity: in the room of those great Men who had caused such stately Edifices to be erected, you see nothing but poor Shepherds, who are so stupid as to let the Hares run between their legs, without meddling with them; and Partridges bask under their very noses, without offering to catch 'em. (1, 46)

They found the remains of one of the city's ancient gates, its best stones removed; the stumps of a temple portico, capitals and architraves strewn everywhere around; and many beautiful columns, of granite or red and white jasper; but the Turks had taken the best. Tournefort adds:

Il y a un village à deux portées de mousquet de ces masures, dont les portes des jardins sont à deux colonnes antiques; au travers desquelles on met une claye de bois pour les fermer. (I, 60)

There's a Village within two Musket-shot of these ruinous Fragments, where the Garden-Gates are of two antique Columns, between which they place a Hurdle of Wood for a Door. (I, 46–7)

They found little statuary, the Venetians having taken their pick:

La statue qui est sur la fontaine de Candie, auprés de la Mosquée au delà du marché, a été tirée de ces ruines; la draperie en est belle, mais la figure est sans tête, les Turcs ne sçauroient souffrir sans horreur la représentation des têtes des choses animées, si ce n'est sur la monnoye, dont ils sont amoureux plus que gens du monde. En fouillant dans un champ, nous découvrîmes la moitié d'une figure de marbre bien drapée: la jambe étoit articulée avec science, & le bout du pied étoit fort beau. (I, 60–1)

The Statue which is on the Fountain of *Candia*, hard by the Mosque beyond the Market-place, was fetch'd from among these Ruins: the Drapery of it is excellent, but the Figure is without e'er a Head; the *Turks* having an abhorrence to the Representation of the Heads of things animate, unless upon Coins, which they are fond enough of, no People more. Rumaging in a By-place, we met with half a Figure in Marble well-drapery'd: the Leg was artfully jointed, and the Toes wonderful. (I, 47)

They appear, especially in that last detail, like figures in a contemporary 'Landscape with Ruins'.

Tournefort was on Delos, the very centre of the old Greek world. His account of the visit, occupying the whole of the seventh letter (I, 287–319: Eng. ed. I, 221–44), is well worth looking at, not least for its conscientious debate with his two great predecessors on the island, Spon and Wheler.

They were there twenty-five years before him, and, becoming marooned, spent an anxious time fearing they might die of hunger and thirst: 'But for the next meal we were very sollicitous, not knowing whose turn it might first be, to have his haunches cut out, to serve for Venison to the rest.' With their companions they had searched in vain 'for the River Inopus, which Strabo mentions to have been in this island' (*A Journey into Greece*, pp. 60–1). Tournefort arrived from Myconos on 24 October 1700, accompanied by the French Consul, and landed on the north-east tip. A map is provided; but the figures that, referring to the text, should help us follow his route, do not correspond. Delos, and its sister island, Rhenia, were at that time 'tout à fait abandonnez, & qui ne servent de retraite qu'à des corsaires & à des bandits' (1, 287) ('utterly deserted, and only serve for a Retreat to Pirates and Robbers' (1, 221)). Hunters came there too, after the quail and the rabbits. And among the hunters and the robbers were those instructed gentlemen of Europe who, from at least the early seventeenth century onwards, carried off from Delos all they could of its magnificent debris. Such fragments as could be thought of as works of art – odd bits of statuary (hacked off on the spot), chiselled capitals, pieces of moulding and sections of fluted column – found their way by devious routes, passing through many hands, into public and private collections. Admiral Sir Kenelm Digby scavenged there for the collection of King Charles I; Sir Thomas Roe, as agent for Arundel and Buckingham, reckoned it one of his richest sources.[8] But Delos, so conveniently situated, served as a quarry for all manner of monumental and building needs. Marble, laboriously fetched to the little granite island when it was still 'the star of the earth', was shipped off far and near, in bulk and in bits and pieces.

Tournefort, like all his successors, has a keen sense of this deprivation. He opens with a paragraph on the ancient fame of Delos as Pindar and Callimachus had celebrated it.[9] The fall from that condition is then implicit in all that follows. In the process of decline and disappearance Spon and Wheler themselves become witnesses of a better time. In the twenty-five years since their visit more has vanished and been destroyed:

A côté de cette Calanque à 170 pas de la mer dans un lieu assez plat, sont encore debout six colonnes de granit, & un pilier quarré de même pierre: il y avoit 11 colonnes debout dans le temps que Mrs Spon & Wheeler y arriverent, nous en comptâmes 25 de renversées. (1, 295)

On the side of this Calanque, within 170 paces of the Sea, in a flat Spot, are still standing six Pillars of Granate, and a square Pillar of the same Stone: there were eleven Columns standing when Messieurs *Spon* and *Wheeler* arrived there; we counted 25 thrown down. (1, 227)

Or by another testimony, concerning the marble lions that face what is now known to be the Sacred Lake:

A deux pas de la même architrave on rencontre quelques restes de lions de marbre tous en pieces; quoique plus aisez à connoitre que ceux qui sont à côté du temple d'Apollon. Le Sr Ostovichi, l'un des meilleurs bourgeois de Mycone, qui chasse tous les jours à Delos, nous assûra qu'il y en avoit veu cinq entiers il y a quelques années. (1, 300)

Two paces from the same Architrave you meet with some Remains of Lions in Marble much broken, tho more easy to discover than those which are on the side of *Apollo's* Temple. The Sieur *Ostovichi*, one of the most substantial Burghers of *Mycone*, who is every day a hunting at *Delos*, assured us that some time ago he saw five whole ones. (1, 230–1)

It will be convenient here, witnessing the spoliation of a place, to look forward half a century. Stuart and Revett were on Delos in March 1753. (Confined there for two days by storms, they slept in 'an antique cellar'.) This is their account, published in 1794:

The island, once so celebrated, the resort of multitudes, the seat of religion, religious ceremonies, and pompous processions, is now an uninhabited desert, every where strewed with ruins, so various, and so well wrought, as to evince its once populous and flourishing condition. The only animals we saw here, beside rabbets and snakes, were a few sheep brought occasionally from Mycone ... to crop the scanty herbage which the ruins will permit to grow ... The number of curious marbles here is continually diminishing, on account of a custom, the Turks have, of placing, at the heads of the graves of their deceased friends, a marble column; and the miserable sculptors of that nation come here every year, and work up the fragments for that purpose, carving the figure of a turban on the top of the monumental stone. Other pieces they carry off for lintels and window cills; so that, in a few years, it may be as naked as when it first made its appearance above the surface of the sea.

Their editor, Willey Reveley, adds this note:

In the year 1785, there were no remains but one single altar of marble, broken into pieces, with heaps of ruins of buildings, but not even a stone of any regular form, or any ornamental fragments. The antiquities, described in this chapter, are said to have been taken away by a Russian fleet, in the last war against the Turks.[10]

Fifty years later Ludwig Ross came. He writes as an inheritor of his country's classicism:

Delos ist eine völlig wüste Insel, ein großes trauriges Trümmermeer. Es hat kaum eine einzige pittoreske Ruine; Alles liegt in kleinen Scherben und Splittern übereinander, so schrecklich hat die zerstörende Hand des Menschen hier gewüthet. Die Reste des herrlichen Apollotempels liegen am Boden, zerschellt und zerhackt; was die Pfaffen auf Tenos davon für ihren modernen Orakeltempel haben gebrauchen können, das haben sie fortgeschleppt. Ganze Schiffsladungen von Marmor und Säulen sind schon vor Jahrhunderten nach Venedig und Konstantinopel gebracht worden. Sic transit gloria mundi. Nicht einmal ein Palmbaum ist auf Delos geblieben, um an die Geburtsstätte des Fernhintreffers Apollon und der jagdfrohen Artemis zu erinnern. Niedriges Gestrüpp wuchert jetzt zwischen den Trümmern und zwischen den Granitfelsen des Berges Kynthos, und einige hundert von Mykonos herübergebrachte Schafe und Ziegen mit ihren schmutzigen Hirten sind im Besitze des heiligen Eilandes und treten seine geschwundene Herrlichkeit mit Füßen.[11]

(Delos is an utterly desolate island, a vast and melancholy expanse of debris. It has scarcely one picturesque ruin; everything is broken up small and lies in confusion, such fearful destruction has been wrought here by the hand of man. The remains of the superb Temple of Apollo lie smashed and battered on the ground; what the priests on Tenos could use of it for their latter-day houses of prophecy they have dragged away. Whole shiploads of marble and columns were fetched away to Venice and Constantinople centuries ago. *Sic transit gloria mundi.* Not even a palm-tree is left on Delos to commemorate the birthplace of Apollo, the Bowman, and Artemis who loved the hunt. A low scrub flourishes among the debris and the granite rocks of Mount Cynthus, and a few hundred sheep and goats from Myconos with their dirty herdsmen are in possession of the sacred island and trample its former glory underfoot.)

In 1873 the process of deprivation was halted and reversed. For in that year the French School began the excavations that have continued ever since. Any visitor to Delos now is amazed by the abundance and beauty of the things to be seen; and the island's richness before the centuries of loss almost exceeds imagination, since so much still remains. The early travellers, coming to the better known sites, will generally have seen less and worse than their predecessors. Where monuments were accessible they were pillaged. Successive travellers chart the destruction, and it lends their accounts an elegiac tone. Obviously, there was discovery too. Stuart and Revett were systematic discoverers in Athens, and what could surpass Joachim Bocher's first sight of Bassae? But not until quite late in the nineteenth century was there any archaeological work in Greece as sustained and productive even as the bungled and random digging at Pompeii and Herculaneum and in the environs of Rome in Winckelmann's day. The great sites now which have filled the museums and which are overwhelming even in their emptiness, were not revealed then; what was below the surface the travellers themselves could only rarely bring to light, and what was above ground they saw damaged and disappearing. It is certain that some places now have a completeness and clarity unimaginable in the early eighteenth century; that is our compensation, and the early travellers had theirs.

There *is* a palm-tree now on Delos, to commemorate the goddess Leto. The Sacred Lake, identified, has a neat perimeter; five of the original nine lions, restored as well as may be, overlook it from the terrace. Tournefort, who had not a Blue Guide at his disposal but the classical geographers and the accounts of his own immediate predecessors, wandered somewhat at a loss through the glorious and baffling localities with their ruins. Relying on Strabo, Spon and Wheler failed to find the Inopus (when they were badly in need of it); preferring the authority of Pliny, Tournefort identified that elusive water, wrongly, with a *spring*, there being apparently no river on the island. (The Inopus had long since dried up, leaving only a rocky gorge; it was Ross who recognized its course for certain, in 1835.) Tournefort weighs what Strabo says, and comes to the conclusion that he must have been misinformed; always measured, always respectful, he disputes with Spon and Wheler about the location of an inscription (1, 299: Eng. ed. 1, 230), excuses their failure to find the Sacred Lake – 'ils furent mal conduits', he says (1, 296) ('they had ill Guides' (1, 228)), but does no better himself; cites them as authorities when his own opinion coincides with theirs. The fact that all these researches have long since been superseded matters not one jot. It is an enthusiasm we are admiring, the growing enthusiasm for Greek excellence, and the desire to locate and understand it better.

There on the island for all to see, noted by all travellers, with more or less pathos, to the present day, are the two remaining pieces of the colossal statue of Apollo: 'le dos est d'un côté, le ventre & les cuisses de l'autre: on ne lui a laissé ni tête, ni bras, ni jambes' (1, 301) ('the Back for one, the Belly and Thighs for the other: they have left him neither Head, nor Arms, nor Legs' (1, 231)). These vast mutilated lumps, which still have power and not just massiveness, stand about 80 yards to the north-west of the pedestal on which, intact, they belong. That is how far they were dragged, perhaps not long before Spon and Wheler were on Delos. Wheler writes:

This goodly structure is so entirely ruin'd, that it is impossible to judge of its form, and the God himself so ill handled, that he hath neither hands, feet, nor head left him; yet what is remaining appeareth still most beautiful... It stood upon his Pedestal upright, until about three years ago... an English-man who was there,... endeavoured to carry it away, but finding it impossible, he brake off its head, arms, and feet, and carried them with him. (*Journey into Greece*, p. 56)[12]

One hand is in the museum on Delos, part of a foot is in the British Museum. Tournefort copied the inscriptions on the pedestal. In Smyrna he showed them to Chishull, who published the famous archaic one: 'I am of the same marble, statue and pedestal' in his *Antiquitates Asiaticae* (pp. 15 and 43). Sharing the marble with those strange letters of the seventh century before Christ are the dates and names of early modern travellers.

Such chapters as this in Tournefort's book must have been read with great sympathy in the next generations, when the interest in Greece had become a compelling passion. The deserted island, with its quail and rabbits among the pillaged ruins, is the very stuff of a certain kind of nostalgic poetry. The details, the images, are there provided:

...on ne voit dans ces ruines que marbres cassez, piédestaux, pilastres, architraves, cintres & bazes renversées, la plupart des colonnes en ont été enlevées. (I, 293)

...you see among these Ruins nothing but broken Marbles, Pedestals, Pilasters, Architraves, wooden Moulds for Arches, and revers'd Bases; most of the Columns were carry'd off. (I, 225)

The times are barbarous:

...on casse une belle colonne, pour faire des marches d'escalier, des appuis de fenêtres, ou des linteaux de portes: on brise un piédestal pour en tirer un mortier ou une saliere. (I, 314)

...they will break to pieces a fine Column, to make Steps to a Stair-case, Jambs for Windows or Doors; they will carry away a Pedestal to turn into a Mortar or the like. (I, 241 – 'saliere' not translated: a mortar for grinding salt)

Regret is the other face of admiration. One regrets the maltreatment or the passing of what one admires. It is particularly exciting in these early travellers to see the beginnings of admiration. When Sir George Wheler, not always a sensitive soul, says of the abused Apollo: 'The beauty of it is such, that I am apt to believe, if Michael Angelo had seen it, he would have admired it as much as he did that Trunk in the Vatican at Rome' (p. 56) – then a long perspective opens up, all the more fascinating at our greater remove. And when Tournefort, rummaging among the debris on Delos, discovers mouldings 'd'un excellent goût dans leur simplicité' (I, 293), then again we can say that the admiration of Greece is beginning to clarify. In the English translation of 1718 those fragments are said to be 'of a noble simplicity' (I, 225), which term was to become a commonplace of approbation in the years following, after Winckelmann had given his authority to it. In that phrase, one might say, those drawings are anticipated which Pars did at Ephesus sixty-four years later.

3

ROBERT WOOD

This chapter begins a series dealing with the relations, often of an immediate kind, between travellers in Greece and exponents or disseminators of the Hellenic Ideal at home, especially in Germany. Robert Wood made of his journeys in Greece and the Levant something more than a travel-book. His *Essay on the Original Genius of Homer* is a literary–critical thesis drawing the material for its arguments from first-hand experience of the supposed Homeric localities; and the book, in its German version, contributed directly to certain important trends of thought in Germany at that time. Wood has his place in the history of Homeric scholarship, after Thomas Blackwell and in some respects anticipating Friedrich August Wolf; but it should be remembered that the study of Homer in the late eighteenth century was not an 'academic' matter, if by 'academic' we mean something remote from the creative mainstream of the nation's life. Herder and Goethe, the first and foremost writers of Germany's *Sturm und Drang*, had appropriated Homer for their central literary and cultural enthusiasms; and whatever scholarship could offer them to substantiate their own beliefs, they were glad to have. Wood recommended himself particularly, in that his scholarly theories on the Homeric texts and the nature of Homer's genius sprang from the land of Greece itself, from the surviving physical world in which, it was believed, Homer had lived and composed.

Not much is known about Robert Wood before the time of his famous journeys. He was born near Trim in County Meath in or about 1717 and probably educated at Oxford. His first employment seems to have been that of a travelling tutor. From very early on he had the reputation of an excellent classical scholar.

He was first in Greece in 1742–3, among the islands; also in Syria and Egypt. But the journey that made his name was begun in 1749. Then, being already in Italy, he accepted the invitation of two Oxford graduates, John Bouverie and James Dawkins, to travel east with them. His own words give something of the tone of the enterprise:

> As I had already seen most of the places they intended to visit, they did me the honour of communicating to me their thoughts upon that head, and I with great pleasure accepted their kind invitation to be of so agreeable a party.
>
> The knowledge I had of those gentlemen, in different tours through France and Italy, promised all the success we could wish from such a voyage; their strict friendship for one another, their love of antiquities and the fine arts, and their being well accustomed for several years to travelling, were circumstances very requisite to our scheme, but rarely to be met with in two persons, who with taste and leisure for such enquiries, are equal both to the expence and fatigue of them.[1]

They wrote to Borra, an Italian artist of their acquaintance, and all four spent the winter in Rome 'refreshing [their] memories with regard to the antient history and geography of the countries [they] proposed to see'.[1] In the spring they proceeded to Naples where a ship, specially chartered in London, was waiting for them furnished with necessaries: with mathematical instruments and with presents to bribe the Turks, and with 'a library, consisting chiefly of all the Greek historians and poets, some books of antiquities, and the best voyage writers'.[1] One is often curious to know exactly what the travellers took with them. Wood and his friends seem to have been particularly well provided. Theirs was a serious expedition, more like Tournefort's than that of Spon and Wheler in the degree of organization and provision, but financed privately, out of Dawkins' fortune; their philosophy and aims, however, were specifically Hellenist. Here is Wood's statement:

> Circumstances of climate and situation, otherwise trivial, become interesting from that connection with great men, and great actions, which history and poetry have given them: The life of Miltiades or Leonidas could never be read with so much pleasure, as on the plains of Marathon or at the streights of Thermopylae; the Iliad has new beauties on the banks of the Scamander, and the Odyssey is most pleasing in the countries where Ulysses travelled and Homer sung.
>
> The particular pleasure, it is true, which an imagination warmed upon the spot receives from those scenes of heroick actions, the traveller only can feel, nor is it to be communicated by description. But classical ground not only makes us always relish the poet, or historian more, but sometimes helps us to understand them better. Where we thought the present face of the country was the best comment on an antient author, we made our draftsman take a view, or make a plan of it. This sort of entertainment we extended to poetical geography, and spent a fortnight with great pleasure, in making a map of the Scamandrian plain, with Homer in our hands.[1]

They were in the Troad in July and August 1750. On 8 September Bouverie died, at Magnesia on the River Maeander, and was buried, very

4. Wood and his companions in Athens

handsomely, at Smyrna. Still, the expedition pursued its purposes. Having already, all four of them, explored much of the Archipelago, the Hellespont and Asia Minor, the survivors continued to Palmyra, reaching its stupendous ruins[2] on 14 March and those of Balbec on 1 April.

That was the limit of their journey east. They arrived in Athens about the middle of May 1751:

When we arrived at Athens, we found Mr. *Stewart* and Mr. *Revet*, two English painters, successfully employed in taking measures of all the architecture there, and making drawings of all the bas reliefs, with a view to publish them, according to a scheme they had communicated to us at Rome.

Wood and Dawkins had shown an interest in this work from the start. In Athens, finding it well under way, they furthered it with their approbation and with Dawkins' money. But for the latter's liberality, Stuart says, they would not have been able to stay in the city long enough. Back in London, Wood and Dawkins republished the *Proposals*, in which the scheme of surveying the antiquities of Athens was set out. The mention in the preface to *The Ruins of Palmyra* (quoted above) served as another advertisement. Wood subscribed for eight sets of the work, Dawkins for twenty (at 20 guineas a time). Dawkins was elected to the Society of Dilettanti in April 1755, proposed by Stuart; when he died in 1758 he left them a legacy of £500. The debt of gratitude to Wood and Dawkins was duly acknowledged by Stuart in the preface to the first volume, finally published in 1762. There is a picture, perfect of its kind, of all four of them together, in volume III (not published until 1794). It is plate 1 of chapter 5, of the Monument of Philopappos in Athens. This is Stuart's explanatory note:

On the foreground Mr. Revett and myself are introduced with our friends Mr. James Dawkins and Mr. Robert Wood; the last of whom is occupied in copying the inscription on the pilaster. Our Janizary is making coffee, which we drank here; the boy, sitting down with his hand in a basket, attends with our cups and saucers. A goatherd with his goats and dogs are also represented.

Stuart and Revett are in local costume; Wood and Dawkins, fresh from the Syrian desert, look quite amazingly English.

From Athens, for nineteen days in May and June, they did a longish tour together, which took in Marathon, Thermopylae, Delphi, Thebes and Corinth, all places certain to excite in such travellers a strong 'local emotion'. 'Castri', Stuart writes, 'the ancient Delphi, is a most romantic spot.' 'Romantic' is Chandler's word too. Eighteenth-century Hellenism, perhaps especially with respect to landscape, is not at all opposed to the sentiments of early Romanticism.

The Castalian fountain, the grotto of the nymphs, the picturesque and immense rocks on one hand; and on the other the valley diversified with variety of culture, through which the Pleistus runs towards the plain of Crissa, form a *coup d'oeil*, that I think I have not seen equalled anywhere. We discovered some remains of the temple of Apollo at Delphos, a wall of large stones filled with inscriptions, rather too large to take away.[3]

In the last sentence the archaeological has it over the picturesque.

Wood and Dawkins left Athens in the middle of June to return to England, leaving Stuart and Revett at work. Two of Wood's books, the accounts of the expedition's most sensational discoveries, were got out fairly quickly, *The Ruins of Palmyra* in 1753 and *The Ruins of Balbec* in 1757. They are magnificent volumes, which were widely read and appreciated in England and abroad. The preface to *Palmyra* tells us something of the circumstances of Wood's party in Greece, of their itinerary and of the spirit and intention in which they travelled. He wrote no other consecutive account.

For a few more years he continued to travel, though not so far afield. He was in France and Italy with the Duke of Bridgewater in 1753. In Rome his portrait was painted by Mengs, Winckelmann's friend.

In 1756 he became Pitt's Undersecretary of State, and was in public life thereafter, in various high capacities, until his death in 1771. Though he never went back to Greece he did much, in England, for classical studies. He was elected to the Society of Dilettanti on 1 May 1763 and became the first director of its archaeological ventures. It was he who instigated perhaps the best of the century's expeditions to Greece: that of Richard Chandler in 1764. He introduced Chandler to the Dilettanti, drew up those careful and helpful instructions which are reprinted in the preface to *Travels in Asia Minor*, and passed on to the Society at their regular meetings such letters and drawings as the travellers sent home. *Ionian Antiquities* (Part I), published by the Society of Dilettanti in 1769, has a preface by Wood and rests almost as much on his journey of 1750–1 as on Chandler's of 1764–5. Chandler, describing the temples at Priene and Miletus, cites his predecessor in those places. On Miletus he quotes him at length. Moreover, among the book's engravings are some done by the Italian, Borra, who was with Wood in 1750–1, just as in Wood's *Essay on Homer* there are plates drawn by Pars, who was with Chandler at Ephesus in 1764. At its best the Society worked as a community of people who had an enthusiasm and their journeys in common. Naturally,

Robert Wood

they promoted one another. Men like Wood and Dawkins made generous use of their influence or their wealth.

Wood made notes for his book on Homer as early as 1755. These were in the form of a letter to Dawkins, written in Rome. Dawkins approved the plan; but then public life intervened, for Wood, in his own words, 'had the honour of being called to a station, which, for some years, fixed [his] whole attention upon objects of so very different a nature, that it became necessary to lay Homer aside, and reserve the further consideration of [his] subject for a time of more leisure'.[4] But not quite aside: he was not among the Scythians in his high office.

In the course of that active period, the duties of my situation engaged me in an occasional attendance upon a nobleman, who, while he presided at his Majesty's councils, reserved some moments for literary amusement. His Lordship was very partial to this subject; and I seldom had the honour of receiving his commands on business, that he did not lead the conversation to Greece and Homer. (*Essay*, pp. vii–viii)

This nobleman, Lord Granville, being shown the letter to Dawkins in which the sketch of the book on Homer was contained, encouraged Wood to proceed. It was of Granville that Wood recounted the following well-known anecdote. At the end of the Seven Years War he waited upon him, then President of the Council, with the draft of the Treaty of Paris. 'I found him', Wood writes

. . . so languid, that I proposed postponing my business for another time: but he insisted that I should stay, saying, it could not prolong his life, to neglect his duty; and repeating the following passage, out of Sarpedon's speech, he dwelled with particular emphasis on the third line, which recalled to his mind the distinguishing part, he had taken in public affairs.

> Ὦ πέπον, εἰ μὲν γὰρ πόλεμον περὶ τόνδε φυγόντες
> αἰεὶ δὴ μέλλοιμεν ἀγήρω τ᾽ ἀθανάτω τε
> ἔσσεσθ᾽, ΟΥΤΕ ΚΕΝ ΑΥΤΟΣ ΕΝΓ᾽ ΠΡΩΤΟΙΣΙ ΜΑΧΟΙΜΗΝ,
> οὔτε κε σὲ στέλλοιμι μάχην ἐς κυδιάνειραν·
> νῦν δ᾽, ἔμπης γὰρ κῆρες ἐφεστᾶσιν θανάτοιο
> μυρίαι, ἃς οὐκ ἔστι φυγεῖν βροτὸν οὐδ᾽ ὑπαλύξαι,
> ἴομεν·   Il. xii. 322

Could all our care elude the gloomy grave,
Which claims no less the fearful than the brave,
For lust of fame, I should not vainly dare
In fighting fields, nor urge thy soul to war.
But since, alas! ignoble age must come,
Disease, and death's inexorable doom;
The life, which others pay, let us bestow,
And give to Fame, what we to Nature owe.

POPE'S HOM. Il. xii. 387.

His Lordship repeated the last word several times with a calm and determinate resignation: and after a serious pause of some minutes, he desired to hear the Treaty read; to which he listened with great attention: and recovered spirits enough to declare the approbation of a dying Statesman (I use his own words) on the most glorious War, and most honourable Peace, this nation ever saw. (*Essay*, p. vii)

In his essay 'On Translating Homer' Matthew Arnold retails this story with approval 'as exhibiting the English aristocracy at its very height of culture, lofty spirit, and greatness'.[5]

Still Wood could not find the time to write his book. Not until fifteen years after the journey, long after the death of his companion Dawkins, did he make the first publication of his very topical and stimulating ideas, and then only in restricted and unfinished form. For this first edition of 1767, having the title *A Comparative View of the Antient and Present State of the Troade. To which is prefixed an Essay on the Original Genius of Homer*, was printed in only seven copies, of which perhaps only two are extant, one in Cambridge, one in the British Museum, and neither complete. An enlarged version of the *Essay* alone, the more important part, was published anonymously in 1769, but still in only six or seven copies. Wood died in 1771; it was Jacob Bryant who was then prevailed upon to edit the work and to publish it complete, *Essay* and *Comparative View*, with all Wood's additions, in 1775, in quarto and octavo format. These two editions, that of 1769 and that of 1775, concern us equally here.

John Nichols in his *Literary Anecdotes* (III, 84–5) has this note on Robert Wood's book: 'Amongst other curiosities in my small Library at Canonbury is the copy which Mr Bowyer kept, enriched by his own notes; and, what may be more curious...the margin contains every addition and variation made afterwards by Mr. Wood, fairly transcribed, *jubente Bowyero*, "*manu pueri mei Johannis Nichols*".' Nichols, apprenticed to the printer Bowyer in 1757, was taken into partnership with him in 1766. That copy of the 1769 edition which he thus expanded is in the Bodleian Library. It is a nice curiosity, in that one can see at a glance what was altered or added to form the posthumous edition of 1775.

What Wood had to say of most importance is contained already in those half-dozen copies printed in 1769; his expansions clarify and enlarge his arguments, but add nothing new. This is a fact that needs to be emphasized, because it was through one of those copies of the early edition that Robert Wood's *Essay* became known in Germany. The history of that transmission is complicated, but worth sorting out.

A key figure in the business was J. D. Michaelis, Professor of Oriental Studies and Librarian in Göttingen, who had spent some time in England as a young man and maintained many academic contacts there. Important new English publications, works by Robert Lowth and Thomas Percy for instance, were sent to him very promptly, and by review and translation he saw to it that they became known in Germany.

Wood got to know of Michaelis via a mutual friend, John Pringle: and it was Pringle who, writing to Michaelis on 16 November 1769, announced the despatch of the *Essay* to Göttingen. He described it as 'though printed ... not published, nor indeed finished'. Wood had, he said, 'caused cast of only a very few copies, to put into the hands of his friends, in order to have their animadversions'.[6] This copy, which Michaelis must have received in late December or early January, is now in the library of the University of Göttingen. The author's name has been written in under the title: 'Mr. Wood, Under-Secretary of State', and below that: 'Donum auctoris. Michaelis.' Michaelis, before reading the book himself, passed it on to his colleague, the classical scholar C. G. Heyne, who reviewed it at length in his *Göttinger Anzeigen von Gelehrten Sachen*, XXXII, on 15 March 1770. Wood's thesis thus became known in scholarly and literary circles and there was a demand for the book itself to be made available in translation. Michaelis must have made such a proposal to Wood almost at once, for Wood writes thanking him on 10 April 1770 – asking, however, that he should await a revised and corrected version before proceeding. He will, he hopes, find time to work on it during the parliamentary recess. In his next letter, on 27 April, Wood, having heard of Heyne's review, is more anxious and more insistent that the copy in Michaelis' possession should *not* be translated, should not, even, be allowed to get into strange hands:

...the Specimen which you have was only intended to be shown to particular freinds & only Six Copies were printed in that hasty & cheap manner, least I should lose the thread of the subject during my attendance upon duties of another kind, which make it absolutely impossible for me to look into my Journal or papers relative to my travells.[7]

As a mark of friendship, and in fair exchange for scholarly gifts already received, Wood sent Michaelis copies of his *Palmyra* and *Balbec*, as well as of the first volume of the *Ionian Antiquities*, together with a work by the abbé Barthélemy, who was to be his translator in France Certainly he was keen to have his book translated into German, but in its finished form. He wrote again in August, his last letter to Michaelis, saying that he hoped to have ready before the end of the year 'a correct copy', which he would then be glad to see put into German – indeed, he would willingly pay for the work to be done. However, no such 'correct copy' came to Göttingen before Wood's death; the job of bringing the revised material to press devolved on Jacob Bryant, who took his time over it, being very busy with his own affairs and, moreover, not at all in sympathy with Wood's arguments.[8] It does not seem likely that Bryant allowed his own opinions to interfere in his editing of his friend's text; he claims that he found the *Comparative View* incomplete, and finished it himself, but this will not have amounted to very much. If John Nichols is right when he says that, instructed by Bowyer, he entered in the printer's copy 'every addition and variation made afterwards by Mr Wood', then it is easy to see, comparing those manuscript insertions with the published version of 1775, that Bryant, in editing the *Essay* at least, did not deviate at all from the author's own words.

In Göttingen, Michaelis did not wait for Bryant to complete his editor's work. Deciding that Wood's death released him from the obligation, he went ahead and made the *Essay on the Original Genius of Homer* known in German, using his own text, that 'Specimen', for the translation and his own son, Christian Friedrich, as translator. Thus was published in 1773, in Frankfurt am Main, *Robert Woods Versuch über das Originalgenie des Homers*. Heyne's review was reprinted in the volume as a preface. The book had a wide circulation in Germany and contributed to literary debate two years before Bryant's full edition came out in England. The ideas were put about as Wood had formulated them, concisely and vigorously, in his provisional version of 1769.[9]

The translation was reviewed as soon as it appeared, in the *Frankfurter gelehrte Anzeigen* of 23 April 1773 – a knowledgeable and enthusiastic review sometimes ascribed to Goethe but not in fact by him. The only sour remarks were meant for Michaelis: the reviewer wondered how any translator had managed to prise the one copy of Wood's work from Michaelis' grasp – by means of a great deal of money, no doubt. He did not know that Michaelis had successfully kept the business in the family.

The times were exactly right for Wood's book. By review and translation, by being discussed, this 'provisional' work came most opportunely to the attention of German scholars and poets. It will be obvious why he was so well received when we examine his views; but the bare facts of publication almost speak for themselves: a book on

Homer by a man who had traced the Scamander to its source and who had searched the country for vestiges of Troy – what better years for such a book to arrive in Germany than those between 1769 and 1773?

We can begin with the journey itself. Wood's thesis – not peculiar to him but part of a new direction in the eighteenth century – was that we should read Homer better if we knew the localities his epics are sited in: 'he enters most into the spirit of the Copy, who is best acquainted with the Original. If, therefore, we would do the Poet justice, we should approach, as near as possible, to the time and place, when and where, he wrote' (*Essay*, p. ix). We should understand his references more vividly, and also – the chief gain – by holding his poetry up to the real places we should see how true he was to Nature: 'the nearer we approach his country and age, the more we find him accurate in his pictures of nature' (p. vi). It is a new – *unclassical* – notion that a writer's value lies mainly in his truthfulness to local circumstances, and it is an unclassical way of reading a text to look for that connection in truthful mimesis between the poetry and the author's time and place. Our attention is turned not to the general and timeless, but to the particular. Many travellers prior to Wood had gone to test the ancient accounts against the present appearance of the famous places; and a few, like Guys or Lady Montagu or, as a contemporary reviewer of the *Essay* pointed out, the orator Aeschines, had read their Homer on the spot;[10] but no one before Wood, so far as I know, had made his journey serve a precise and important literary–critical end. That is his originality.

The new injunction, which Wood's book greatly supported, is this: know the context – pay attention to the circumstances of a work, the nature of the times, the manners, the landscape, the climate. Good art has its roots in particular time and place. It may soar up to universality, but it is rooted in real life, it has the sap of a particular people in it, it enjoys the sunlight of a particular sky. (This was an encouraging thought for Germans in 1770 in their woeful recurrent search for an identity.)

It helps to know the landscape. Why? Because in essence the famous localities are unchanged. I have already mentioned the persuasive sentimental power of that continuity and shall discuss it further (though more with reference to manners) in the chapter on Guys. It was not Wood's concern however to prove that the spirit of Hellas had survived and was only dormant and might be brought to life again in encouragingly unchanged surroundings. His interest was specifically Homer's art, and the survival of the landscape is made to serve his thesis. We can still see the landscape Homer saw, therefore we can prove and admire his truthfulness:

Not only the permanent and durable objects of his description, such as his rock, hill, dale, promontory, &c. continue in many instances to bear unquestionable testimony of his correctness, and shew, by a strict propriety of his epithets, how faithfully they were copied; but even his more fading and changeable landscape, his shady grove, verdant lawn, and flowery mead, his pasture and tillage, with all his varieties of corn, wine, and oil, agree surprisingly with the present face of those countries. (*Essay*, p. 75)

Likewise in manners. Homeric manners survive, and Wood studied them with interest when he was in the East. Among the Bedouin tribesmen, for example, heroic, patriarchal manners survive. They have the violence characteristic of the *Iliad*, but also the hospitality depicted in the *Odyssey*. They love wiliness, Odysseus' chief quality; they accord their women, as do the Homeric heroes, a less than European respect. As a corollary to this last observation Wood notes, both in Homer and among these latter-day Homeric peoples, the absolute absence of sentimental love; which is interesting when we think of Goethe's attempt to treat the Nausicaa episode. A substantial chapter in Wood's book (pp. 143–80) is given over to the examination of contemporary manners in the Mediterranean and Middle Eastern countries and to a comparison of them with those depicted in the *Iliad* and the *Odyssey*, the point being always to demonstrate Homer's truthfulness.

It was in this truthfulness, Wood argued, that Homer's surpassing excellence lay. He was 'the most constant and faithful copier after Nature' (p. 5). As such he was the greatest poet there has ever been. Obviously that is not the whole of the matter, and we should not nowadays want to make quite that emphasis, I think. But Wood was writing at a time when, particularly in Germany, to be a 'constant and faithful copier after Nature' (even if, for the moment, we take 'copier' in its dullest sense), when truthfulness to real circumstances, will have seemed, to progressive minds, a very great virtue in a writer, perhaps the be-all and end-all of good art. It will have seemed very fresh and salutary indeed to turn in that direction after so long a bondage to the imitation of French classicistic forms. Only once realism in art becomes accepted and established do it and its processes then become problematic. Wood was not a professional literary critic, he was a traveller, a statesman, an amateur of classical literature; but he was himself aware that imitation, mimesis, copying, the translation of Nature in Reality into the Natural in Art, is not a simple matter – at least, not a simple matter to discuss. For nearly always when he praises Homer's 'Mimetic Powers' (pp. viii–ix), when he calls him 'a copier', when he praises him for taking a picture faithfully from life, he couples with that notion of fidelity the notion, apparently paradoxical, of originality. The essay is on the *original* genius of Homer: 'in the great province of Imitation he is the most original of all Poets' (p. 5) – 'his natural and unaffected manner carries with it those obvious marks of original invention, which discover . . . that the picture has been faithfully taken from life' (p. ix).

Wood does not untangle the paradox. He lets it stand, sensing that both its sides are true: fidelity to Nature *and* originality. We can look elsewhere to see the matter pursued, by those professionally interested in pursuing it: in Winckelmann's *Gedancken über die Nachahmung* (which Wood may well have read, in Fusseli's translation of 1765), and in the endlessly fascinating *Kunstgespräch* in Büchner's *Lenz* (a discussion that owes a good deal to Winckelmann), where realism is shown to be not at all a straightforward business. *Nachschaffen* is Büchner's word, 'creative reproduction'; and in the word 'creative' all manner of possibilities are contained. It would be out of place to expand on the topic here. But one last point: Wood remarks of Virgil that 'he copied Nature through Homer' (*Essay*, p. 235) – just as Winckelmann advised contemporary artists to get to Nature through Praxiteles and Phidias. Homer was favoured (Wood actually says he was 'original from necessity, as well as by genius' p. 35), the Greek sculptors of the fifth century were favoured, in that beautiful Nature was more evident then. We are disadvantaged, and the mediation of those happier artists will be necessary.

The best thing in Wood is his study of Homer's language. That was what really went home, causing an excitement far beyond the confines of Homeric scholarship. Time and again we hear him saying things of central importance in German *Sturm und Drang* (and in the European Romanticism of which that movement was a part). For he examines Homer's epics as primitive song, as oral poetry; in a most pragmatic and perceptive way he examines the nature and conditions of such poetry, drawing on his own observations in those countries where it still survives. He discerns and celebrates its particular merits. Those exciting new notions – soon commonplaces, but still exciting – in the latter half of the eighteenth century concerning the primacy of poetry over prose, that poetry is the natural first language of Man, that prose is a fall from Nature – those are the criteria he brings to his study of Homer. He is engaged, perhaps without knowing it, in the polemics against sophistication, over-civilization, politeness, artificiality, when he praises 'that noble simplicity of language' (p. 246), that 'simplicity, without meanness' (p. 291) by which Homer is graced. Unobtrusively – but how the Germans must have seized on this – he is anti-French, for in the chapter on Manners he remarks: 'Our polite neighbours the French seem to be most offended at certain pictures of primitive simplicity, so unlike those refined modes of modern life, in which they have taken the lead' (p. 144). Homer has 'that genuine cast of natural simplicity' (p. 145) which the Bible has. And his language exactly suits his own simplicity and that of his times. It is a language concrete and unambiguous; easily intelligible when listened to; sonorous, dignified and expressive. In short, a language supreme

... in the province of Poetry, where the most finished efforts of artificial language are but cold and languid circumlocution, compared with that passionate expression of Nature, which, incapable of misrepresentation, appeals directly to our feelings and finds the shortest road to the heart.[11] (*Essay*, p. 284)

His remarks on the authorship and composition of the epics struck scholars in his own and the next generation with revelation. For noting, as others before him had done, that there is only one reference in Homer, and that very mysterious, to the art of writing (*Iliad*, VI.168), he took seriously and examined as perfectly possible the idea that the poems were composed orally, and only collected and written down at a later date. The Muses, he reminds us, were born of Mnemosyne, goddess of Memory. He points to many things in Homeric verse that have a mnemonic function; to the power of memory among illiterate people, adducing evidence picked up on his travels and contrasting a primitive education with our own: 'In a rude and unlettered state of society the memory is loaded with nothing that is either useless or unintelligible; whereas modern education employs us chiefly in getting by heart, when we are young, what we forget before we are old' (p. 260). It is a marvellous chapter, this on language, both enthusiastic and exact, giving strength to some of the century's most potent myths, and beginning a line in Homeric studies which, proceeding through Wolf (his *Prolegomena* of 1795), has proved valid to the present day.

One obvious application of Wood's remarks on Homeric composition was to Ossian. He was not the first to connect the two poets by any means; but he was, it seems, the first to suggest similarities in the preservation and transmission of their works. It was generally supposed that Homer's poems were brought from Ionia into Greece by Lycurgus, the ruler of Sparta, and collected together in written form. Wood concludes:

> If therefore the Spartan Lawgiver, and other personages committed to writing, and introduced into Greece, what had been before only sung by the Rhapsodists of Ionia, just as some curious fragments of ancient poetry have been lately collected in the northern parts of this island, their reduction to order in Greece was a work of taste and judgment: and those great names which we have mentioned might claim the same merit in regard to Homer, that the ingenious Editor of Fingal is entitled to from Ossian. (*Essay*, p. 279)

That will perhaps be sufficient summary and quotation to indicate in a general way how in tune Wood was with the literary enthusiasms of his age, especially as they were expressed in Germany. The review already mentioned in the *Frankfurter gelehrte Anzeigen*, wholly favourable, accepts the principles of his book without reservation:

> Wenn man das *Originelle* des Homer bewundern will, so muß man sich lebhaft überzeugen, wie er sich und der Mutter Natur alles zu danken gehabt habe. Ohne die genaueste Kenntniß aber der Zeiten und des Orts, wo er gesungen, wird dieß nie möglich sein. Die Zeiten muß man, da uns außerdem keine Denkmale davon übriggeblieben, aus ihm selbst, und den Ort durch Reisen kennen lernen.[12]

> (We shall not appreciate the originality of Homer unless we clearly understand that he owed nothing to anybody but himself and Mother Nature. And without precise knowledge of the times and the place in which he sang we never shall understand this. We must take our knowledge of the times from Homer himself, since no other memorials remain; and our knowledge of the place from travel.)

In *Dichtung und Wahrheit* Goethe acknowledged what he and his generation owed to Wood:

> Glücklich ist immer die Epoche einer Literatur, wenn große Werke der Vergangenheit wieder einmal auftauchen und an die Tagesordnung kommen, weil sie alsdann eine vollkommen frische Wirkung hervorbringen. Auch das homerische Licht ging uns neu wieder auf, und zwar recht im Sinne der Zeit, die ein solches Erscheinen höchst begünstigte: denn das beständige Hinweisen auf Natur bewirkte zuletzt, daß man auch die Werke der Alten von dieser Seite betrachten lernte. Was mehrere Reisende zu Aufklärung der Heiligen Schriften getan, leisteten andere für den Homer. Durch Guys ward man eingeleitet, Wood gab der Sache den Schwung. Eine Göttinger Rezension des anfangs sehr seltenen Originals machte uns mit der Absicht bekannnt, und belehrte uns, wie weit sie ausgeführt worden. Wir sahen nun nicht mehr in jenen Gedichten ein angespanntes und aufgedunsenes Heldenwesen, sondern die abgespiegelte Wahrheit einer uralten Gegenwart, und suchten uns dieselbe möglichst heranzuziehen. (*Werke* (Hamburg ed.), IX, 537–8.)

(It is a fortunate thing for any period of literature when great works of the past surface again and become current, since their effect is then completely new. And thus Homer dawned on us once more, and in a manner suiting our times, which were highly favourable to such a reappearance: for the continual emphasis on Nature finally taught us to consider the works of the Ancients in that light too. What several travellers had already done for the illumination of the Scriptures, others did for Homer. Guys gave us a beginning, Wood added momentum. His book – of which at first there were very few copies – was reviewed in Göttingen and we learned what his thesis was and how far he had gone in expounding it. We stopped seeing in Homer's poems a strained and inflated world of fabulous heroes and saw instead the true reflection of a primitive reality, and did our best to familiarize ourselves with it.)

The emphasis in this appreciation falls on the new understanding of Homer, to which Wood materially contributed, as the product of a particular time and place. When Herder, writing on the songs of Ossian, points to their provenance 'aus den Nordischen, Schottischen Gebürgen, wo alles im Gesange auch Ort, Zeit, Geschichte, Wahrheit ist...' ('among the Northern, the Scottish highlands, where everything in the poetry is also time and place and history and truth...'), then he is close to Wood on Homer. And if the literary work is the product and faithful mirror of particular historical and local circumstances we shall appreciate it better, as the Frankfurt reviewer suggested, by entering into those circumstances as fully as we, in a later age, are able to. The Germans, not in fact great travellers, became enthusiastic exponents of the belief that one must see the place itself. Thus Herder, for the better appreciation of Ossian, was carried away to Scotland, in imagination at least:

Zu den Schotten! zu Macferson! Da will ich die Gesänge eines lebenden Volks lebendig hören, sie in alle der Würkung sehen, die sie machen, die Örter sehen, die allenthalben in den Gedichten leben, die Reste dieser alten Welt in ihren Sitten studiren! eine Zeitlang ein alter Kaledonier werden...

(To the Scots! to Macpherson! There let me hear the songs of a living people *live*, see all the effect they have, see the places which everywhere live in their poems, study in their manners the vestiges of the old world! to be an old Caledonian for a time...)

In fact to read Ossian as Wood had read Homer:

Wood mit seinem Homer auf den Trummern Troja's, und die Argonauten, Odysseen und Lusiaden unter wehendem Segel, unter rasselndem Steuer: Die Geschichte Uthals und Ninathoma im Anblick der Insel, da sie geschahe; wenigstens für mich sinnlichen Menschen haben solche sinnliche Situationen so viel Würkung. Und das Gefühl der Nacht ist noch in mir, da ich auf scheiterndem Schiffe, das kein Sturm und keine Fluth mehr bewegte, mit Meer bespült, und mit Mitternachtwind umschauert, Fingal las und Morgen hofte.[13]

(Wood with his Homer in the ruins of Troy, and the *Argonautica*, the *Odyssey* and the *Lusiads* under a blowing sail, by a rattling tiller. The story of Uthal and Ninathoma in sight of the island where it took place. For me at least – man of the senses that I am – such physical situations are powerful in their effect. And the feeling of that night is still in me when, on a ship run aground that neither wind nor tide would shift, drenched by the sea and howled around by fearful midnight gales, I read Fingal and hoped for morning.)

There is some poetic licence in this. Herder's voyage in 1769 from Riga to Nantes took him nowhere near Ossian's fabulous coasts; still less did the return journey from Antwerp to Amsterdam. But the sentiments are exactly right.

Goethe, a *sinnlicher Mensch* if ever there was one, always responded intensely to particular locality. In Sicily he was excited by landscape in a way that is very close to the spirit of Wood's *Essay*; for the region was thought to be that in which Odysseus had suffered many of his adventures. The public gardens in Palermo so reminded Goethe of the luxuriantly fruitful island of Phaeacia, where the shipwrecked Odysseus was hospitably received, first by the princess Nausicaa then by her father Alcinous, that he rushed off at once to buy a copy of Homer's work:

Aber der Eindruck jenes Wundergartens war mir zu tief geblieben; die schwärzlichen Wellen am nördlichen Horizonte, ihr Anstreben an die Buchtkrümmungen, selbst der eigene Geruch des dünstenden Meeres, das alles rief mir die Insel der seligen Phäaken in die Sinne sowie ins Gedächtnis. Ich eilte sogleich, einen Homer zu kaufen, jenen Gesang mit großer Erbauung zu lesen und eine Übersetzung aus dem Stegreif Kniepen vorzutragen. (*Werke*, XI, 241)

(But that magic garden had made too deep an impression on me. The waves along the northern horizon that were so dark as to be almost black, their persistent advance upon the indented coastline, the peculiar smell of the sea in its haze — all this brought back the island of the blessed Phaeacians to my senses and to my memory. I hurried at once to buy a copy of Homer, read the book in question with great edification, and translated aloud and impromptu for Kniep.)

Thereafter, 'überzeugt, daß es für mich keinen besseren Kommentar zur *Odyssee* geben könne als eben gerade diese lebendige Umgebung' ('persuaded that I could have no better commentary on the *Odyssey* than these the living localities themselves') (XI, 299), throughout his tour of Sicily, Goethe read Homer. In so doing he was following Lady Montagu, Pierre Augustin Guys and Robert Wood, but the experience, of course, was all his own. The truth and beauty of the *Odyssey* were revealed to him with new intensity in the places in which, so he believed, the poem was set.

Was den Homer betrifft, ist mir wie eine Decke von den Augen gefallen. Die Beschreibungen, die Gleichnisse etc. kommen uns poetisch vor und sind doch unsäglich natürlich, aber freilich mit einer Reinheit und Innigkeit gezeichnet, vor der man erschrickt. Selbst die sonderbarsten erlogenen Begebenheiten haben eine Natürlichkeit, die ich nie so gefühlt habe als in der Nähe der beschriebenen Gegenstände.

Nun ich alle diese Küsten und Vorgebirge, Golfe und Buchten, Inseln und Erdzungen, Felsen und Sandstreifen, buschige Hügel, sanfte Weiden, fruchtbare Felder, geschmückte Gärten, gepflegte Bäume, hängende Reben, Wolkenberge und immer heitere Ebnen, Klippen und Bänke und das alles umgebende Meer mit so vielen Abwechselungen und Mannigfaltigkeiten im Geiste gegenwärtig habe, nun ist mir erst die Odyssee ein lebendiges Wort. (*Werke*, XI, 323)

(As for Homer – the scales have fallen from my eyes. His descriptions, his similes etc. seem to us poetic and are in fact unspeakably natural – drawn, it is true, with *frightening* purity and intensity. Even the strangest fictitious incidents have a naturalness that I was never so aware of as now in the proximity of the things described.

Now that I have here present in my mind these coasts and headlands, gulfs and bays, islands and spits of land, rocks and beaches, bushy hills, gentle pastures, fertile fields, splendid gardens, well-cared-for trees, trailing vines, cloudy peaks and always-smiling plains, cliffs and banks and the all-surrounding sea – now that I have all this, in such variation and variety, only now has the *Odyssey* become for me a living word.)

And more than ten years later, preparing to attempt the *Achilleis*, he said this to Schiller:

Uns Bewohner des Mittellandes entzückt zwar die Odyssee, es ist aber nur der sittliche Theil des Gedichts, der eigentlich auf uns wirkt, dem ganzen beschreibenden Theile hilft unsere Imagination nur unvollkommen und kümmerlich nach. In welchem Glanze aber dieses Gedicht vor mir erschien, als ich Gesänge desselben in Neapel und Sicilien las! Es war als wenn man ein eingeschlagnes Bild mit Firnis überzieht, wodurch das Werk zugleich deutlich und in Harmonie erscheint. Ich gestehe, daß es mir aufhörte ein Gedicht zu seyn, es schien die Natur selbst. (*Briefe*, II, 331)

(We inland-dwellers are, of course, delighted by the *Odyssey*, but we are only really affected by its ethical component, we have to help out the descriptive component with our imaginations as best we can, and never very successfully. But in what brilliant light the poem appeared to me when I read it in Naples and Sicily! It was like varnishing a picture, when the colours appear at once in their proper clarity and harmony. Indeed, I ceased to think of the *Odyssey* as a poem – it seemed Nature herself.)

Of that insight and excitement, there on the spot in Sicily, came a response which Wood, a traveller, scholar and statesman, could not give, but which Goethe, a poet, could. Goethe's response to Homer's 'creative imitation' of Nature, there for all to see in the *Odyssey*, was the wish to create, to imitate Homer: 'mir auf und aus diesem Lokal eine Komposition zu bilden' ('to compose a work in and out of this locality') (*Werke*, XI, 298). In that blessed place he had before him Nature herself, the unspoilt original, and Homer's faithful copy. No poem ever sprang from clearer sources than *Nausikaa*. It was the real Sicilian landscape that drove him to read Homer, and out of Homer's lines – almost literally: the pencil marks are still there to be seen in the margins of his copy – out of Homer's own words, Goethe began to draw his *Nausikaa*. Those two elements – Greek landscape and Greek poem – are the ground itself.

But Goethe wrote only 156 lines of his intended five-act tragedy, and of those many are incomplete and disconnected. In details, turns of phrase, imagery and tone there is a great deal of very close allusion to the Homeric original. Odysseus' soliloquy, when he wakes hearing Nausicaa's maids, is a compendium, in 38 lines, of 'Odyssian' details. For the remainder, the best by far are those sketches towards an evocation of the landscape. The *Odyssey* has a greater variety of place than does the *Iliad* and the books Goethe read and reread 'mit unglaublichem Anteil' ('with enormous sympathy') (XI, 299) for his projected play have perhaps a keener sense of place than any others in Homer: where the girls bring the washing, for example, at the river-mouth; or the grove of Athene outside the town, where Odysseus hides to allow Nausicaa to precede him; and, best of all, the garden of Alcinous. This last, a most beautiful and famous evocation, Goethe recreates:

> Dort dringen neben Früchten wieder Blüten,
> Und Frucht auf Früchte wechseln durch das Jahr.
> Die Pomeranze, die Zitrone steht
> Im dunklen Laube, und die Feige folgt
> Der Feige... beschützt ist rings umher
> Mit Aloe und Stachelfeigen...,
> Daß die verwegne Ziege nicht genäschig...
>
> (*Werke*, V, 71)

> (Blossoms come on again with the fruits
> And fruits come in succession throughout the year.
> Lemons, oranges among the dark leaves;
> Figs never-ending... there is a palisade
> Of aloe and prickly-pear...,
> Or the goats, intruders after sweet things...)

Further on, unconnected, there are two lines of his own immediate observation:

> Ein weißer Glanz ruht über Land und Meer,
> Und duftend schwebt der Äther ohne Wolken.

(A white radiance over land and sea;
Scented, cloudless, shimmering pure sky.)

That is to say: what is best realized in the *Nausikaa* fragment are Homer and Nature – in the lines on Alcinous' garden, the two together.

Goethe dwelled on (or in) his project throughout his tour of Sicily, and it died away to nothing when he left the island. The account of his 'excited reverie' contained in *Die Italienische Reise* was written some thirty years later.

Goethe was reading Robert Wood again in the late 1790s. He was then much concerned with epic form and was projecting nothing less than a continuation of the *Iliad* from where Homer left off. His *Achilleis* resembles *Nausikaa* in two respects: first, in that it remained unfinished, but secondly in that its main inspiration and focal point were a particular locality, this time the Troad.

Goethe, Herder and numerous lesser writers can be shown to have read Wood's *Essay* in German translation and to have been influenced by its central idea. Or more properly, perhaps, we should say that they found what he wrote sympathetic; it entered the ethos of their current thinking and was very welcome there. Indeed, the *general* timeliness of the book is very obvious. Its subject is Homer and that alone, in those years, would have got it a hearing; but what is more striking, and characteristic of the age, is the wider applicability of those comments made on the particular subject. It says something for the wholeness of the enthusiasms then that what is said so illuminatingly on Homer could be transferred and applied elsewhere, without loss of power – to the Bible, to Ossian, the folksong, the ballad, even to Shakespeare – and that these remarks of an amateur literary critic have their place in the great discussions and trends of the times: the raising of naturalness as a supreme virtue, the extension of taste to comprehend areas previously despised. Herder on the origins and nature of language, on primitive song, on Shakespeare, on Gothic architecture, is recognizably at one with Wood. Not that he owes his ideas to him, not at all; but that they are contributors together to an innovating and liberating movement.

Robert Wood, alone among the great travellers of the eighteenth century, put his journeys to a literary–critical use. He travelled with Homer in mind; what he experienced he brought to his reading of the texts. His distinction is the belief that literature matters in and derives from real life: that its practitioners and its subjects live and breathe in particular time and place. He had the English practical sense of real connection, which the Germans in his day admired.

4

HEYNE AND WINCKELMANN

Christian Gottlob Heyne, to whom Michaelis passed on Wood's book early in 1770, had been Professor of Eloquence at the University of Göttingen since 1765. He was born at Chemnitz in 1729, and his early life, until the call to Göttingen rescued him, was, like Winckelmann's (until *he* got away to Rome), exemplary in its frustration and servitude. His childhood was one of wretched poverty; his father was a weaver, a class ruthlessly exploited; by no thrift and labour could the family be properly fed. His wish, in these circumstances, to become a scholar must have seemed bizarre. By the age of ten he was giving lessons, to pay for his own. He met with some charity and much heavy patronage and condescension. There is something at once admirable and a little horrifying in his single-minded pursuit of scholarship in circumstances so utterly hostile to it; he was set apart from his fellows, from his class, his whole personality warped to one end, to be learned, to get out. The life of Winckelmann reads the same. In hagiography their wretchedly poor beginnings are set against the great achievements later, like darkness against the light, to point up the triumph. Winckelmann, at least, never forgot the cost.

Heyne at Leipzig University was urged by his professor to follow the example of Scaliger and read all the ancient authors in chronological order. He did what he could. For six months he slept only two nights a week, and naturally enough fell ill of a fever. Instances of manic hard work may be cited from the biographies of several eighteenth- and early nineteenth-century scholars who made it into the light. (Of those who crippled themselves similarly, and without success, nothing, of course, is known.) F. A. Wolf, author of the *Prolegomena*, towards the end of his schooldays 'would sit up the whole night in a room without a stove, his feet in a pan of cold water and one of his eyes bound up' (apparently to rest it – by overtaxing the other). At university 'to save time, he spent only three minutes dressing, and cut off every form of recreation. At the end of the first year he had nearly killed himself.'[1]

Once schooled and learned, to what did that learning give these heroes access? To years of servitude, cataloguing the libraries and doing the academic donkey-work for the idle amateur rich. Waiting to take up such a post (as copyist in the library of Count Brühl, on a pittance) Heyne was given floor-space by a licentiate in divinity and slept with folios for his pillow; often his only meal in the day was peapods, boiled. In the first winter of his employment he and his colleagues in the Count's library were much importuned by a young man visiting them from nearby Nöthenitz with frequent demands for obscure books. This was Winckelmann, then preparing himself to escape from *his* tyrant, Bünau, to Italy, via a change of faith.

In Brühl's library, worked nearly blind, Heyne yet found time and energy to edit Tibullus and Epictetus, his salvation as it turned out. Shortly afterwards the Seven Years War began, Frederick advanced on Dresden, destroyed the palaces and library of Brühl and put Heyne out of a job. In the bombardment of Dresden (July 1760) he lost all his possessions. Nevertheless, in the following year he married, which increased his need of an income. In Göttingen, Gesner died and a successor was needed. Nobody sprang to mind. Rhunken was approached, in Leyden, but he declined; and asked why they were looking abroad when they had someone at home who was more than qualified. This someone, in Rhunken's view, on the evidence of the editions of Tibullus and Epictetus, was Heyne, of whom no one in Germany had heard and whose very whereabouts were quite unknown. To Heyne, destitute and having, by his own admission, wholly got out of the habit of classical scholarship, the call to the chair in Göttingen must have seemed like the direct intervention of an idiosyncratically benevolent deity into his miserable affairs. He came to Göttingen in 1763 and remained there, achieving some eminence and resisting attractive offers to move elsewhere, until his death in 1812.

During his time in Göttingen, as editor of the *Gelehrte Anzeigen*, Heyne wrote between 7000 and 8000 reviews; what he wrote on Robert Wood's *Essay* was one of his most important pieces. His biographer Heeren (his son-in-law) commented: 'Ich zweifele, ob irgendetwas sonst eine ähnliche Revolution in Heyne's Ansicht und Studium des griechischen Alterthums gemacht hat' ('I doubt whether anything else brought about such a revolution in Heyne's view of and work on Classical Antiquity'). As we shall see, Heyne later qualified his enthusiasm, and shifted his allegiance from Wood to Lechevalier, but his first response, when Michaelis gave him the book (that provisional copy, one of only half a dozen printed in 1769) was of wholehearted approval and excitement. Heeren calls his review 'fast begeistert' ('almost enraptured'). 'Wunderbar fühlte sich Heyne davon ergriffen' ('its effect on Heyne was wonderfully strong)'[2] he says; and Heyne himself, looking back, remarked rather ruefully: 'Ich war damals jugendlicher Begeisterung noch fähig' ('in those days I was still capable of youthful enthusiasm').[3] Heyne's importance is of a dated and limited extent no doubt, but to see why Wood came as so enlightening and congenial a spirit to him is to understand those intellectually exciting times a little better. Heyne was not a figure on the stage of German *Sturm und Drang*. He was a man of great learning, of some flair, and of some enthusiasm for Greece and Rome, whom scholarly slavery, years at the treadmill, had physically, mentally and spiritually impaired. The encounter with Wood must have been a dramatic moment; at our remove it has a certain pathos. For there, on the subject of Homer, scholar and traveller meet: not quite as equals, it is true, for, as Heyne presents it in his very full, informative and influential review, his own unaided deductions from the text were simply *confirmed* by Wood's observations from the life. For example: 'So stellten wir uns zwar immer auch die Sache vor; aber Herr Wood bringt physische und geographische Gründe...bey...' ('of course, that has always been our own view of the matter; but Mr Wood has adduced arguments of a physical and geographical kind...').[4] The primacy of scholarship is preserved, but life backs it up nicely on occasion.

Whether Wood actually enlightened Heyne or only corroborated the opinions he already held does not matter very much. Heyne saw that current research in geography and anthropology might be applied to the text of Homer; that the real locality mattered; that Homer, blind or not, knew a real world. The discussion or quarrel over the authenticity and value of Ossian could be brought very directly to bear, since there also local evidence was being adduced. Wood was an agent of this method. If we may believe Heeren, the way Homer was taught to students at the University of Göttingen was quite markedly affected by Heyne's reading of Wood's book. Such an alteration would be a small but characteristic victory of the new spirit of that age.

Ironically, this application of the traveller in the lecture room may best be seen in the foreword Heyne wrote to Lechevalier's book *Beschreibung der Ebene von Troja* in 1792, when Wood himself had fallen out of favour. Lechevalier, with Choiseul-Gouffier in the Troad in 1785–6, announced the conclusions of their joint researches, without ever mentioning his partner's name, in a paper delivered in French to the Royal Society in Edinburgh in the spring of 1791. When the account came out in German the following year, Heyne, whom Lechevalier had visited and charmed, gave it a long preface dispraising Wood the better to elevate the new luminary. The bone of contention was the situation of Homer's Troy, a question not resolved until Schliemann began digging at Hissarlik in 1870; and thus it was the appendage to Wood's *Essay*, the *Comparative View of the Troad* (made known in Germany in the translation of 1773) that came in for most criticism. But Wood's whole work, so enthusiastically reviewed in 1771, is damned with faint praise twenty years later. Where it was sound, says Heyne now, it did no more than encourage him in the way his own deductions had long been leading him; where it was unsound, in the matter of the situation and topography of Troy, it had caused much confusion, and a Lechevalier was needed to put things right. In fact Wood and Lechevalier were equally wrong. Wood and his companion Dawkins, climbing the Scamander, went too far upstream, and sited the crucial confluence with the Simois impossibly far inland. Wood's map was nevertheless an improvement on Pope's (which had the misfortune to be published back to front and was in any case largely fantastic) and on it, Heyne says, in rather aggrieved tones, he, Heyne, had based a course of lectures 'On the Battles in the *Iliad*', wishing to elucidate Homer's text by reference to the topography Wood had suggested. Getting into a terrible mess, he blamed Wood (dead by then). Lechevalier, doing even more violence to the real locality than Wood, sited Troy at Bunarbaschi, and by this hypothesis Heyne was wholly convinced. Printed with Lechevalier's account in German is Heyne's own essay *Über das Local in der Iliade* in which the reliance he placed on his authorities (the travellers) is clear:

Durch das Ansehen von Pope und Wood hatte ich mich verleiten lassen, meine eigne Einsichten zu verläugnen, und das, was ich aus dem Homer gefaßt hatte, nach ihren Vorstellungen umzubilden.[5]

(I had been swayed by the prestige of Pope and Wood into betraying my own insights, and into altering what I had deduced from Homer himself to suit their views.)

Misled by them, he returned to his own divinations – to find these then, in their turn, happily confirmed by Lechevalier. Nobody was right; but what matters here is the new idea that one's reading of Homer would be enhanced by a knowledge of the real landscape in which his heroic poem was sited.

One small indication of the power such contemporary topographical information had on Heyne's understanding of the text is in the matter of Hector's decisive combat with Achilles. Homer has Achilles chase Hector three times round the walls of Troy. At least, that is how the lines are normally understood; περί (*peri*) is normally taken to mean 'around'. But, since at Bunarbaschi, where Lechevalier located Troy, this would have been quite impossible, Heyne is forced, in a long note on Lechevalier's text, to agree with his author and bend the word περί into meaning 'to and fro', a usage for which there is no convincing precedent.[6] Thus, in Heyne's view, Achilles chased Hector to and fro (in a long circle) under the walls of Troy. The ancient commentators, not knowing the topography of Homer's Troy, naturally assumed that περί meant 'around'; but Heyne, thanks to Lechevalier, now knew better. The text, he says, must be understood in the light of the traveller's firsthand experience: 'so muß der Hauptbeweis vom Local hergenommen werden.' In fact Troy *VII*a, unearthed by Schliemann on the hill of Hissarlik and usually identified with Priam's city, was only 550 yards (503 metres) in circumference, and to circle it three times at a run, though strenuous, would not have been impossible for Homeric heroes; whereas the terrain around Bunarbaschi was far too sprawling and precipitous to make the episode even remotely feasible.

Altogether the topography of Troy is a very teasing matter, and scholars wishing to locate the fig-tree and the Scaean Gate, the hot and cold springs where the Trojan women did their washing in times of peace, the site of Achilles' battle with the angry river or Odysseus' and Diomedes' ambushing of Dolon, were avid for whatever facts or speculations the travellers could offer.

The most glamorous sites of all were the barrows of the heroes killed before Troy, supreme among them Achilles and his friend Patroclus. On the subject of their burial Homer is unusually expansive and exact. Knowing that before long he will be dead himself, Achilles raises over the ashes of Patroclus only a relatively modest mound, to be increased, he orders, once the ashes of both of them are mingled there together. In Hades then the ghost of Agamemnon reports to the ghost of Achilles that this was duly done:

> Burning like a forge when the flames had consumed you
> At dawn we collected your white bones, Achilles,
> And laid them in pure wine and oil. Your mother gave us
> A golden urn, the gift, she said, of the god Dionysus,
> The work of great Hephaestus. Therein we placed your bones,

Famous Achilles, together with those of Patroclus,
Son of Menoetius, who died before you. The bones of Antilochus,
Whom you loved above all others when Patroclus was dead,
We placed close by and over all we soldiers raised
A colossal mound on a high headland above
The Hellespont where the waters widen so that in our
Generation and in all generations to come
Men at sea will mark it from a great distance.[7]

In his fragment *Achilleis*, Goethe expands this passage and odd lines in the *Iliad* in a marvellously imaginative and detailed way. His Achilles stands in the barrow of Patroclus as the Myrmidons raise it around him. Athene, taking on the form of Antilochus, visits him there, and he gives precise instructions for the finishing of the monument after his own death. He and the goddess walk on the rim of the open mound together and, with the Hellespont and the open sea below them, she consoles him for his early death with the certainty that his fame will be eternal and that his monument, the tomb, will serve sailors far and wide as a landmark in all ages to come. It is a fine composition, full of the inspiration of place.

In ancient times the Achilleium was confidently identified by sailors approaching the Sigean headland. It was the source of many legends (appearances of Achilles' ghost, for example), and Alexander the Great, who regarded Homer's hero as his ancestor and tutelar spirit, adorned the tomb with flowers, anointed its stone with perfumes and danced around it naked, as he passed through the Troad eastwards on his campaigns. His favourite, Hephaestion, sacrificed particularly to Patroclus, in order to indicate that he was to Alexander what Patroclus had been to Achilles. (When Hephaestion died, Alexander and his men cut off locks of their hair as Achilles and his Myrmidons had done at the funeral of Patroclus.)[8]

The tomb was thus one of the holy places of the cult of heroic friendship – such a friendship as Winckelmann wanted first with Lamprecht, then with Berg – [9] and for that reason Hyperion and Alabanda are drawn there:

Da ich die Wälder des Ida mit ihm durchstreifte, und wir herunterkamen in's Thal, um da die schweigenden Grabhügel nach ihren Todten zu fragen, und ich zu Alabanda sagte, daß unter den Grabhügeln einer vieleicht dem Geist Achills und seines Geliebten angehöre, und Alabanda mir vertraute, wie er oft ein Kind sey und sich denke, daß wir einst in Einem Schlachtthal fallen und zusammen ruhen werden unter Einem Baum... (III, 36)

(When I wandered through the woods of Ida with him and we came down into the valley to ask the silent burial mounds after their dead, and I said to Alabanda that among the mounds perhaps one belonged to the ghosts of Achilles and his beloved friend, and Alabanda confessed that it was often his childish thought that we might some day fall on one field of battle and rest together under one tree . . .)

Modern sentimental travellers found the desire to identify the barrow, and that of Ajax on the northern shore, quite irresistible. The by no means 'enthusiastic' Chandler states simply and categorically:

After walking eight minutes we came between two barrows standing each in a vineyard or inclosure. One was that of Achilles and Patroclus; the other, which was on our right hand, that of Antilochus, son of Nestor . . . We had likewise in view the barrow of Ajax Telamon.[10]

Lechevalier, no less definite, is more expansive:

This curious mass of earth, raised by the hands of the Greeks, still exists. It is not now surrounded with elms, as it once was; the place of these is now occupied with tall poplars, and mournful cypresses, still more gloomy, and better adapted to the nature of sepulchres.[11]

Lechevalier, through bribery, was able to open one of the numerous tombs in the vicinity. Barrows were very much in vogue at the time. William Borlase, whom Lechevalier and his editors frequently cite, was opening the burial mounds of Cornwall and the Isles of Scilly, and comparing what he saw with Homer's description of the tomb of Achilles.[12] When Lechevalier dug away the earth from the tomb at Dios-Tape he discovered two broad stones leaning together and beneath them a statuette of Athene and a metal urn containing cremated human bones.[13] Goethe must have had this in mind when he has his Achilles give these instructions to Antilochus (alias Athene):

> dir sei empfohlen
> In der Mitte das Dach, den Schirm der Urne, zu bauen.
> Hier! zwei Platten sondert ich aus, beim Graben gefundne
> Ungeheure; gewiß der Erderschüttrer Poseidon
> Riß vom hohen Gebirge sie los und schleuderte hierher
> Sie, an des Meeres Rand, mit Kies und Erde sie deckend.
> Diese bereiteten, stelle sie auf, aneinander sie lehnend
> Baue das feste Gezelt! Darunter möge die Urne
> Stehen, heimlich verwahrt, fern bis ans Ende der Tage.[14]

> (Do as I ask then:
> At the tomb's mid-point roof over the urn securely –
> And see, I have set two slabs aside, unearthed whilst digging,
> Massive things; surely Poseidon, shaker of *terra firma*,

Ripped them loose from high on a mountain and flung them here
To the sea's edge, under gravel and earth. Use these
That I set aside and raise them and stand them together
For a solid tent. And place the urn beneath
In secret safekeeping, to the distant end of time.)

That Athene stands in the grave with Achilles – one of the poem's finest details – was, I am sure, suggested to Goethe by Lechevalier's discovery of the statuette. Lechevalier does not *quite* dare to assert that he has in his hands the urn containing the ashes of 'man-slaying Achilles who would not live long', but he is sorely tempted to:

When therefore I behold the Urn of metal adorned with vine-branches, I own I find it very difficult to prevent myself from thinking of that famous Urn, the gift of *Bacchus*, and the workmanship of *Vulcan*, which *Thetis* gave to her son, and in which the Greeks deposited the ashes of their hero.[15]

Dalzel, Lechevalier's Scottish translator and editor, adds a sceptical footnote here: 'A classical imagination naturally indulges itself in these pleasing fancies.' Schliemann was just the same: Helen's jewellery, Nestor's cup, Agamemnon's death-mask, he beheld and handled them all. Many centuries of sentimental preoccupation with the Homeric localities culminate in such discoveries. It is like the Invention of the True Cross; certainly of that order of excitement. Van Krienen's discovery of Homer's tomb (with Homer sitting upright in it) was another such momentous occasion (to be discussed later).

Goethe and Hölderlin, in poetic freedom, took what they liked from the travellers and the factual accuracy or inaccuracy of their sources was of absolutely no importance; Heyne, since his line was academic lectures and not imaginative literature, had to be more circumspect. Still, he was anxious to bring his subject, especially Homer, to life, and what topographical and archaeological information he could in all conscience accept, he made use of. The excitement of the poet and of the academic must have been rather similar.

From 1767 onwards Heyne gave lectures on classical archaeology, by which is meant the study of classical art through its remains. His students were young men of the kind likely to be sent abroad for a year or so, for their further education and amusement, on a tour of Europe's art galleries and collections; and it was Heyne's aim to prepare them beforehand for what they might see. Himself, he kept abreast of the new discoveries, especially through Winckelmann, who sent to him and the Minister Münchhausen accounts of what had lately been found in and around Rome, and these accounts Heyne published in the *Gelehrte Anzeigen*. He saw to it also that the University Library bought all the important new publications in classical art and archaeology, among them, naturally, Winckelmann's *Geschichte der Kunst* and *Monumenti antichi inediti*. The latter half of the eighteenth century was rich in publications that would be useful as teaching-aids: the series publishing the excavations at Pompeii and Herculaneum, for example; D'Hancarville's edition of Sir William Hamilton's vases; the *Ionian Antiquities*, Stuart's and Revett's *Antiquities of Athens* and Choiseul-Gouffier's *Voyage pittoresque de la Grèce*. These are all works consisting largely of lavish engravings, more or less learnedly explicated. (Prints pirated from them were the means by which *gusto greco* was popularized.) Works such as these Heyne bought or, in scholarly exchange, was given for the University Library and used in his courses on ancient art. He used also, like most teachers in his day, collections of coins and gems; especially, of the latter, Lippert's famous and serviceable paste imitations. Coins and gems, bearing exact and often very beautiful depictions of famous men and mythological figures, were an excellent introduction into ancient history. Glyptography was an eighteenth-century mania among the rich. Winckelmann's first substantial work after his arrival in Italy was the cataloguing of Baron von Stosch's vast and valuable collection. The catalogue was to serve, after the gems themselves were dispersed, as a fascinating, encyclopaedic hand-book, since the description of each piece was to entail an exhaustive explanation, through copious reference to ancient authors, of the figures or scene depicted on it. Engravings, gems and coins were what those who never left Germany most easily and profitably studied of classical culture. There were in addition plaster-casts, often of poor quality, of those famous statues, themselves mostly copies, to be seen in the galleries and private collections of Rome. Heyne's library, where he gave his lectures on classical art (beginning at eight in the morning in the summer term), was well supplied with casts. There stood the Apollo Belvedere, the Laocoön and the rest, those works ecstatically described by Winckelmann, which Heyne's young men, when they got to Rome, would have no option but to go and see. Heyne himself, it seems, could scarcely see them, not even in his own University Library, in plaster-cast. Acquiring that scholarship for which he was finally and miraculously called to Göttingen had so ruined his eyes that to see all of a large statue at once was more than he could manage. Even the extremely respectful

Heeren concedes: 'Den vollen Genuß eines Apollo, eines Laocoön konnte Heyne schwerlich haben' ('it is unlikely that Heyne could enjoy the Apollo or the Laocoön *in full*');[16] and adds that a journey to Italy would hardly have benefited him. Of real statues he had seen enough in Dresden, and thereafter plaster-casts, peered at myopically, sufficed.

Carlyle, in his essay on Heyne, though he calls him 'encrusted and encased', yet concludes by numbering him among those 'old illustrious men, who, though covered with academic dust and harsh with polyglot vocables, were true men of endeavour, and fought like giants, with such weapons as they had, for the good cause'.[17]

Relations between Heyne and Winckelmann were never entirely cordial; in a sense the two men were rivals in the business of escaping from horrible conditions. Winckelmann might be thought, and perhaps by Heyne himself, to have been the more successful. From Rome in March 1765, having that winter been, at Heyne's suggestion, elected to the Göttingen Gesellschaft der Wissenschaften, he concluded a long and erudite letter to him as follows:

Von Ihnen möchte ich wissen, ob man an einem Orte, wie Göttingen ist, vergnügt leben könne, und wie man es angebe, es zu seyn. Denn ich kann mir nicht vorstellen, wie dieser und ein jeder Ort, wo Academien in Deutschland sind, Leipzig ausgenommen, und die Ernsthaftigkeit, die ein Professor annehmen muß, hierzu Gelegenheit gebe. Mich deucht, man müsse in dieser Lebensart alt werden, und vor der Zeit, man mag wollen oder nicht. Es würde aber noch schwerer werden für jemand, der einen gütigen Himmel, und ein schönes Land, wo die ganze Natur lacht, lange Zeit genossen hat. (*Briefe*, III, 91)

(I should like to know from you whether it is possible to enjoy life in a place like Göttingen, and how one would go about it. For I cannot imagine that, being in Göttingen or any other German academic town (except Leipzig) and adopting the High Moral Seriousness necessary in a professor, one would have much opportunity for enjoyment. It seems to me that a man would grow old before his time in such a life, whether he liked it or not. But it would be harder still on anyone who had lived for a long time under a kindly sky in a beautiful country where all of Nature smiles.)

Was life possible in Göttingen, life as Winckelmann in Rome had come to know and enjoy it? He writes elsewhere that were he ever to come north again he would need, from any patron taking him on, a very generous allowance for wine – since life without a very great deal of wine north of the Alps would be unliveable. There is often in his letters to Heyne a facetiousness, an obviously unserious belittling of himself before the 'greater' scholarship of his correspondent. Winckelmann's contempt for German academics (though he wanted their approbation) was deep and comprehensive, and Heyne must have felt it. Inevitably,

6 Portrait of Winckelmann

unfairly perhaps, the two men separate as types; one feels they dealt with one another as types. The free spirit, the imaginative, poetic and passionate discoverer and celebrator of beauty versus the pedant, the bookman, the mind full of dead facts – that from Winckelmann's point of view. And from Heyne's: thoroughness, self-discipline and rectitude versus enthusiasm, fantasy and unsoundness in scholarship and morals. Those are the opposites they tend towards, true or not.

Again and again Winckelmann pleads for a learning which will not be just dead facts, which will be more than only the remembered sum total of what other minds have thought before:

Das Leben ... ist viel zu kurz als daß wir es über einem Buche vom Alterthum ... veliehren sollten: und die gantze Wißenschaft des Alterthums ist dieses nicht werth, weil wir wenn wir sehr gelehrt werden, nichts wißen, als was andere gethan oder gedacht haben. (*Briefe*, IV, 7)

(Life is much too short to be wasted over a book about Antiquity: not even to acquire all the classical learning there is, because all our great learning will be nothing but what others have done or thought.)

... daß es eine strafbare Eitelkeit sei, die Vernunft, die uns zu weit edlerem Gebrauche veliehen ist, bis ins Alter fast bloß mit Dingen zu beschäftigen, die nur das Gedächtnis in Bewegung halten. (C. Justi, *Winckelmann*, I, 99)

(... it is a criminal vanity to occupy our minds, which were given us for far nobler purposes, almost solely, into old age, with things that only engage the memory.)

Winckelmann was nearly thirty-eight when he got to Rome. He dated his real life from then, and looked in relief and bitterness on the forfeited years of his youth and early manhood: 'mia gioventù indegnamente perduta' ('my shamefully wasted youth') (*Briefe*, II, 302); 'mein Leben, welches ich in Deutschland unedel verlohren habe' ('my life, ignobly wasted in Germany') (III, 195); 'die erste schönste Hälfte meines Lebens [ist] in Kummer und Arbeit vergangen' ('the first and best half of my life was lost in misery and labour') (I, 180–1). He had outdone even Heyne in manic dedication to learning:

Nur vier Stunden der Nacht widmete er dem Schlafe, und um ja nicht länger zu schlafen, ging er oft gar nicht zu Bette, sondern blieb in seinem Lehnstuhle vor seinen Büchern sitzen, um gleich bei seinem Erwachen wieder bei seinen Arbeiten zu seyn. Ein ganzes Jahr brachte er einmahl so zu, ohne in's Bette zu kommen. (*Briefe*, IV, 199)

(He gave over only four hours of every night to sleep, and in order not to sleep any longer he often did not go to bed at all but sat in his armchair in front of his books so as to begin work again immediately as soon as he woke. He once spent a whole year in this fashion, without ever going to bed.)

Once free, in Rome, marked and marred by academic slavery as he was, he determined that any book he wrote would transcend mere scholarship. 'Gelehrt' and 'Gelehrsamkeit' are words he invariably uses disparagingly. His *Geschichte der Kunst* was, he said, 'eine Arbeit, nicht für Gelehrte, sondern für Leute welche Empfindung haben und denken' ('not a work for the learned but for people of sensibility who think') (I, 416); 'gewiße nicht Universitäts-Kenntnißen' ('a certain non-university knowledge') (III, 72) was what his books were offering.

Denn man muß erstlich bedenken, daß ich in Rom und nicht in Göttingen schreibe, von Dingen die zur Erleuchtung unserer Nation und zum guten Geschmack beytragen, und nicht Sachen, die bloß Gelehrsamkeit betreffen oder für die Canzel oder der Erbauung dienen. (*Briefe*, III, 62–3)

(For you must bear uppermost in mind that I am writing in Rome and not in Göttingen of things that will contribute to the enlightenment of our nation and the growth of good taste and not of things that only concern the learned or that might do for the pulpit or an edifying tract.)

Still his books, if we read them now, might be thought to bear a certain deadweight of superseded scholarship – more than his prose style and his evident love was able to leaven – and in that sense his escape from 'philology' was less than total. But those monumental works, though they occupied him much of the day every day, are not all the man's life nor are they the only witness to his peculiar value. It is when we remember his renown in his own times, the effect he had on men like Herder and Goethe, that the opposition, as types, between him and Heyne clarifies. Only a creative, a passionate and a dedicated person could have worked upon his contemporaries thus.

Heyne, when Winckelmann was dead, criticized him with increasing sharpness and condescension for inaccuracy, scholarly unsoundness, even scholarly dishonesty; ridiculed his ecstasies and his imaginative apprehensions and suggested something morally dubious in his love of beauty. (His turning away from Winckelmann is, like his deserting Wood, a mark of ageing: 'Ich war damals jugendlicher Begeisterung noch fähig.') Yet in 1778, in the same year as the essay on Pliny in which his harshest comments are made, he wrote for the Gesellschaft der Alterthümer in Kassel a eulogy of Winckelmann that won the first prize (being preferred over Herder's, the only other entry). In that public piece he strikes the proper tone, with enough of a semblance of sincerity to convince the judges at least. Still there are qualifications and criticisms of a kind reinforcing the opposition of himself and Winck-

elmann as types. He doubts whether, academically speaking, Winckelmann's death was untimely; he would hardly, in Heyne's view, have
produced much more of value. His life in Italy was not conducive to
good scholarship; he had no time to read; besides, the best editions were
not to be found there. Heyne's criticism of Italy as a place detrimental
to scholarship is the best illustration one could wish for of the difference
between the two men. Rome, said Winckelmann again and again, was
the only place he could live. Italy was quite simply 'das Land der
Menschlichkeit' ('the humane land'), 'das Land der Menschenliebe'
('the land of human love') (*Briefe*, ii, 305, 306); Rome 'der einzige Ort
in der Welt...wo man vergnügt leben können' ('the only place in the
world where one can enjoy life') (iii, 225).

Ich würde sagen: ich habe bis in das achte Jahr gelebet; dieses ist die Zeit meines
Aufenthalts in Rom und in anderen Städten von Italien. Hier habe ich meine Jugend,
die ich theils in der Wildheit, theils in Arbeit und Kummer verlohren, zurück zu rufen
gesuchet, und ich sterbe wenigstens zufriedener. (*Briefe*, ii, 275)

(I think of myself as being in the eighth year of my life – the time of my residence in
Rome and other Italian cities. Here I have tried to retrieve my youth, which I wasted
partly in riotousness and partly in labour and misery, and I shall die happier at least.)

His scholarship, far from being inhibited in Rome, could thrive only
there. He needed around him for his work not only what the eighteenth
century thought most excellent among the remains of classical sculpture, but also the classical city itself, its buildings and people, the
campagna and the climate. By that love of a present place Winckelmann
is redeemed (out of that deepest of all pits, dated learning); and failing
to realize this, his rival's peculiar quality, Heyne rather damns himself.
In fact, repeatedly we hear him dispraising Winckelmann for the very
qualities by which he is remembered and lacking which Heyne himself
is forgotten.

There can be no doubt that Winckelmann's scholarship ran in the
mainstream of his life; there is no division; wholeness and connectedness
are everywhere apparent. We can be sure of this even if – because of
the academic conventions of the day and because of the harm already
done him by his scholarly apprenticeship – not all of that whole pleasure
of life enters or survives in his published works. His letters are proof
that Winckelmann was one in whom the aesthetic sense ran through
all the five senses and through that sixth: the excited mind. The beauty
of certain works of art obsessed him – the damaged head of a young
faun, for example, discovered in 1763: 'von so hoher himmlischer

Schönheit, daß er alles übertrifft was ich gesehen, und was seyn kann. Beständig denke ich an denselben und die Nacht träume ich davon' ('of such high and divine beauty that it excels everything I have seen, everything possible. I think of it constantly and dream of it at nights') (*Briefe*, II, 309–10). Later he acquired the faun's head for himself; it was in his room, as one of his few possessions, until he died. 'Es ist mein Ganymedes, den ich ohne Aergerniß nel cospetto di tutti i Santi küßen kann' ('he is my Ganymede whom I can kiss without offence in the presence of all the saints') (III, 128). Winckelmann's homosexuality, whatever inconvenience and suffering it may have caused him in his personal life, lent his aesthetics erotic passion. The fusion seems to me admirable. One of his privileges was a room in Albani's country villa to which he could occasionally withdraw, to write:

...hier pflege ich allein im August zu wohnèn, und dieses Jahr gedenke ich es in einer schönen Gesellschaft eines *individui* zu thun, weil ich von der Schönheit schreiben will nach einer lebendigen Schönheit. (*Briefe*, III, 170)

(I generally live here alone in August, but this year I intend having the company of a certain beautiful person since I wish to write about beauty after a model of living beauty.)

Friendship, in the Greek manner, was the expression, or one expression we should more properly say, of the love of beauty got from study. What he read of the works of Apelles and Praxiteles, what fragments he saw of copies of copies of their painting and sculpture, filled his imagination with ideals of beauty; and to quite a large extent, so it seems, he was able to find some equivalent or realization of those ideals in what could still be experienced of real human beauty in Italy. He looked for beauty in people – and discovered it:

...wie viel schöner die Natur der Menschen-Kinder in Italien ist, und wie es sich an den Griechinnen, die hier sind, findet. Hier siehet man, daß die Natur in ihrer schönsten Bildung so wenig als möglich von der geraden Linie der Stirn und Nase abgegangen, und ich habe das Vergnügen, diese Betrachtung alle Tage an einem jungen Römer und einem der schönsten Menschen zu machen. An keinem Ort habe ich das Griechische Profil so häufig als in Tivoli gefunden. (*Briefe*, I, 315)

(How much more beautiful Nature in human beings is in Italy, as may be seen in the Greek women here. One observes that Nature, in her best creations, has departed as little as possible from the straight line formed by the forehead and the nose. I have the pleasure of making this observation daily in the features of an extraordinarily beautiful Roman youth. Nowhere have I come across the Greek profile more often than in Tivoli.)

His letters are full of such delighted observations; he urged his friends, as they travelled Italy and Sicily, to be similarly attentive. In 1755, still in darkest Germany, he had written of the great physical beauty of the ancient Greeks, of the freedom with which that beauty was displayed, and of the unique advantage their artists thus enjoyed. It was a constant joy for him, south of the Alps, to see how much Greek beauty had survived; and he worked as he thought the ancient artists themselves worked, perpetually substantiating and enhancing the ideal through the observation of Nature. His aesthetics had the life-blood of real experience. What Heyne must overlook in him or condemn with insinuations was in fact one of his saving graces, an erotic aesthetic sense; and Italy, 'Land der Menschlichkeit', allowed him his own predilections, as Germany could not.

Goethe was freer in his praise; heathen himself, he knew a fellow-spirit when he met one. His essay *Winckelmann und sein Jahrhundert*, published in 1805, exalts above all his subject's wholeness of life: Winckelmann was able to discover in the real world 'antwortende Gegenbilder' ('corresponding images') of his imagination's ideals. Given the passionate and demanding nature of that imagination, even its occasional and temporary satisfaction was a fine achievement, one making human existence worthwhile. The young men with whom Winckelmann fell in love realized for him his life's two highest ideals: that of friendship in the Greek manner, and that of beauty.

A large part in these relationships was the wish to teach. The young men were in Rome, with the freedom of aristocrats, for their edification, and Winckelmann, the cobbler's son, who had got his learning by hard labour, wished them to see as he saw and to share his enthusiasm. That is a connection between scholarship and practical life (one not to be denied to Heyne either) and there can be no doubt that in Rome Winckelmann taught people to see. The addressing of pamphlets on the appreciation of beauty to men, like Berg and Riedesel, whom he loved is a characteristic act. That some of the recipients turned out faithless or unworthy is neither here nor there. And if his friendships are occasionally painful and he appears ridiculous, that too is unimportant; discrepancy is very likely. At least he is never morbid, he is no Aschenbach.

Winckelmann's own dictum, most often pernicious in its application, that 'der einzige Weg für uns, groß, ja, wenn es möglich ist, unnachahmlich zu werden, ist die Nachahmung der Alten' ('the only way for us to become great – indeed, if possible, to become inimitable – is to imitate the Ancients'),[18] did in his own case work creatively. The spirit of what he understood as Greece was deeply congenial to him. He was, in Goethe's phrase, 'eine antike Natur', a pagan; he had the Greeks' sufficiency and straightforwardness, he was of this world and at home in it. That is why there is no divorce in him. His scholarly works express his character:

Wenn bei sehr vielen Menschen, besonders aber bei Gelehrten, dasjenige, was sie leisten, als die Hauptsache erscheint, und der Charakter sich dabei wenig äußert, so tritt im Gegenteil bei Winckelmann der Fall ein, daß alles dasjenige, was er hervorbringt, hauptsächlich deswegen merkwürdig und schätzenswert ist, weil sein Charakter sich immer dabei offenbart. (*Werke*, XII, 123)

(If the chief thing about very many people, and especially scholars, is their achievement, and their characters are not much expressed in this, the opposite is true of Winckelmann – that is, everything he achieves is remarkable and valuable chiefly because his character is always revealed in it.)

The idea of Greece was rooted in him, his 'Nachahmung der Alten' was the flowering of his own personality; the facts acquired by study were the material, on which his imagination worked.

Winckelmann was an archaeologist; as Papal Antiquary he was responsible for the supervision of works coming to light in Rome, and he was well informed about discoveries elsewhere, in Greece too. There was in his day a great expansion of available facts; faced with profusion some minds fragment and others would be exhaustive. But it is only through the imagination, through what Coleridge called (by false derivation from the word *Einbildung*) the 'esemplastic power', that the greater and greater abundance of 'fixities and definites' could be fused into a compelling idea.

Precisely how the ancients were to be imitated worried the more creative of eighteenth-century minds. They knew that nothing vital would come of the steady accumulation (through travellers and archaeologists) of more and more facts. Humboldt, quoted by Goethe in the essay on Winckelmann, actually regretted such discoveries: 'es kann höchstens ein Gewinn für die Gelehrsamkeit auf Kosten der Phantasie sein' ('it can at best be a gain for scholarship at the cost of the imagination') (XII, 109). And there is an equivalent of that to my mind exaggeratedly pejorative view in Hölderlin's *Hyperion*. With

Diotima and his friends the elegiac hero is contemplating the ruins of Athens. He thinks of the travellers, the amateurs, the archaeologists:

... sie haben die Säulen und Statuen weggeschleift und an einander verkauft, haben die edlen Gestalten nicht wenig geschätzt, der Seltenheit wegen, wie man Papagayen und Affen schäzt. (III, 85)

(...they have carried off the columns and the statues and sold them to one another, and have thought highly of those noble forms, for their rarity, as one might value a parrot or a monkey.)

In fact, two of their company, 'zwei brittische Gelehrte, die unter den Altertümern...ihre Erndte hielten' ('two British scholars reaping their harvest among the antique remains') (III, 86), offend his sight next day below the Acropolis. But though they disgust him he is soon consoled since he believes as emphatically as does Diotima that the spirit of ancient Athens is not to be recovered in archaeological remains. 'Wer jenen Geist hat... dem stehet Athen noch, wie ein blühender Fruchtbaum. Der Künstler ergänzt den Torso sich leicht' ('Whoever is in possession of that spirit... for him Athens still stands, like a fruit tree in blossom. The artist, for himself at least, easily makes the torso whole again') (III, 85). Hyperion does have that spirit (that Idea, that Ideal), he *is* an artist, and from that advantage despises the antiquarians.

Hölderlin began but unfortunately never finished an essay on precisely this topic (which is not a dated one) 'Der Gesichtspunct aus dem wir das Altertum anzusehen haben' ('How should we see the Ancient World?'). The question is crucial: how shall a nearly overwhelmingly excellent past be connected creatively with our poor present? He writes, rather desperately:

Es scheint wirklich fast keine andere Wahl offen zu seyn, erdrükt zu werden von Angenommenem, und Positivem, oder, mit gewaltsamer Anmaßung, sich gegen alles erlernte, gegebene, positive, als lebendige Kraft entgegenzusezen. (IV, 221)

(We seem really to have almost no other option: either to be crushed beneath the weight of the received and the positive, or, with a violent presumption, to pit one's self as a living force against everything learned, given and positive.)

There is in this surely the fear that all learning will tend to deaden the mind; the peculiar danger of learning about the Greeks is that we may be induced to think that having the facts about their excellence is the same as its recreation. Hölderlin easily thought of the corpus of learning as a corpse; the accumulation of facts was the way of death. 'Positives Beleben des Todten' ('positive animation of the dead') (IV, 222) was the way of the antiquarians rummaging in the ruins of Athens, and by extension it is the illusion, under many forms, that a living work can be made by assembling enough material. Hölderlin had a horror of 'alles Positive'; his poetry serves the cause of perpetual revolution, against dead forms. That is the obligation of all poetry, to excite resurgence and prove its undying possibility, but scholarship is not necessarily doomed to do the opposite. Cannot a scholarship be imagined which, rooted in one's life and dealing with others, filled every letter to the full with spirit? It was Goethe's final word of praise for Winckelmann that his works with all their great learning were written 'als ein Lebendiges für die Lebendigen, nicht für die im Buchstaben Toten' ('as something living for the living, and not for those entombed in the dead letter') (*Werke*, XII, 118).

5

WINCKELMANN AND GREECE

Nobody did more for the Idea and the Ideal of Greece than Johann Joachim Winckelmann. Through him, who never went there, the idea of the classical achievement clarified and became for much eighteenth-century artistic endeavour a polestar of nearly blinding brilliance. What he said on Greek art, having seen very little of it, went ineradicably into the European consciousness. However we qualify and contradict it now, still it excites and sometimes persuades the imagination. Many lines of thinking on Greece converge in him, in his peculiarly intense vision. Thus what he says on climate – that it favoured the development and appreciation of beauty – or on democracy – that it is a pre-condition of artistic achievement – may be found elsewhere, before and after him, but, bringing into focus the many previous and current lines of perception, he made of Greece a coherent, steady and luminous image. Passionately believed, it excites at the very least assent in others, in us still, as all truly poetic fictions do. He was one of those learned men, one of the very few, with an imagination passionate enough to fuse 'the fixities and definites' of scholarship into a convincing vision. As such, though he refused opportunities to travel to Greece, he is perhaps the pivot of this book.

The tract he published in 1755 – the *Gedancken über die Nachahmung der Griechischen Wercke in der Mahlerey und Bildhauer-Kunst* ('Thoughts upon the Imitation of Greek Works in Painting and Sculpture') – in which he first and with an immediate sureness outlined much of his life's work, was written on so very little that he might serve as proof of the imagination's power to generate ideas by far exceeding their material. The statues in the collection of August der Starke had been vilely restored in the style of the times before they left Rome to come to Dresden. They were moreover, during the time of Winckelmann's residence in nearby Nöthenitz, never properly displayed. He describes them (years later, it is true) as being packed together like sardines, in sheds, and able to be seen but certainly not studied. Nor, so it seems, did he actually trouble to go and look at them more than once, and then late on in his stay, shortly before he left for Rome. For the writing of the *Gedancken* he found it more convenient to study the statues in plaster-casts: that is, then, plaster-casts of restored Roman copies of, on the whole, Hellenistic originals. We need constantly to remind ourselves how little work of the best periods was to be seen in Western Europe in the eighteenth century. In Germany, almost nothing. In England and France, thanks to the travellers and their wealthy patrons, not much but rather more (which is not to say that amateurs and scholars could always distinguish it). The great bronzes in the National Museum in Athens, which now more than any other works constitute or confirm our idea of classical excellence in sculpture, are the happy discoveries of the last half century. Winckelmann and his contemporaries were in that respect by no means so well off. Still, what he had to go on in Dresden – the circumstances if not the works themselves – seems remarkably unpropitious. Yet Dresden was Athens for him. His tract opens with fulsome praise of August der Starke for bringing firstrate works of Greek art to Saxony:

Die reinsten Quellen der Kunst sind geöffnet: glücklich ist, wer sie findet und schmecket. Diese Quellen suchen, heißt nach Athen reisen; und Dreßden wird nunmehro Athen für Künstler.[1]

(The purest springs of art have been broached: happy the man who finds and drinks at them. In search of those springs we must journey to Athens, and Dresden henceforth will be the artist's Athens.)

Goethe said much the same about London, once Lord Elgin had brought the Parthenon marbles there. Earlier Winckelmann had called Potsdam Athens (and Sparta to boot), but whether by that he meant chiefly the classical sculpture there – 'die erstaunenden Wercke, die ich dort gesehen habe' ('the astonishing works of art I saw there') – or Attic pleasures with his friend Lamprecht – 'ich habe Wollüste genoßen, die ich nicht wieder genießen werde' ('I have had pleasure such as I shall never have again') (*Briefe*, I, 111) – is not clear. Both, I should say. Being with Lamprecht would naturally enhance his pleasure in the statues, and vice versa.

Since what we are discussing here is the ability of the imagination to conceive of or sustain an ideal in the real presence of very little, it might be worth citing Schiller's response to the collection of plaster-casts that he visited in Mannheim in 1784. He was no traveller, even Switzerland was too far for him; when he needed local colour for *Wilhelm Tell* he turned to Goethe, who had been there. In the Gypssaal in Mannheim he could imagine himself in Greece:

Mein ganzes Herz ist davon erweitert. Ich fühle mich edler und besser...

Empfangen von dem allmächtigen Wehen des griechischen Genius trittst du in diesen Tempel der Kunst. Schon deine erste Ueberraschung hat etwas ehrwürdiges, heiliges. Eine unsichtbare Hand scheint die Hülle der Vergangenheit vor deinem Aug wegzustreifen, zwei Jahrtausende versinken vor deinem Fußtritt, du stehst auf einmal mitten im schönen lachenden Griechenland, wandelst unter Helden und Grazien, und betest an, wie sie, vor romantischen Göttern.[2]

(My whole being is enlarged. I feel myself to be a nobler and a better man.

Entering this temple of art you are received into the almighty inspiration of Ancient Greece. Even in your initial astonishment there is something dignified and holy. It is as though an invisible hand gently removed the veils of the past from before your eyes, two thousand years fall away as you approach and you are suddenly standing amidst the beauty and radiance of Greece and walking among the heroes and the Graces and worshipping romantic deities as they do.)

Another instance, rather more in the manner of Winckelmann's visit to Potsdam, is Hölderlin's visiting the Museum Fridericianum in Kassel in the summer of 1796 accompanied by Susette Gontard, her beautiful friend Marie Rätzer and the writer Wilhelm Heinse, author of *Ardinghello und die glückseligen Inseln*, a book notorious then for its sensuality. Hölderlin, the house-tutor, and Susette, wife of a banker, were by that time illicitly in love. When the French marched against Frankfurt, in July, Gontard sent his wife and the children and sundry hangers-on away to safety in Westphalia. (He remained behind to safeguard his business, his motto being: 'Les affaires avant tout.') In the museum in Kassel Hölderlin saw his first few pieces of classical sculpture, among them an Athene.[3] He saw these in the company of the woman he loved – whom he called 'eine Griechin', 'Athenäe', 'die Athenerin', who became the Diotima of his novel and of numerous poems – under the benevolent eye of 'Vater Heinse', a passionate lover of Greece and champion of a pagan sensuality. The fusion of the aesthetic and the erotic into their proper wholeness is easily imagined. She must indeed have seemed to Hölderlin the confirmation of his idea:

Ich hab' es Einmal gesehn, das Einzige, das meine Seele suchte, und die Vollendung, die wir über die Sterne hinauf entfernen, die wir hinausschieben bis an's Ende der Zeit, die hab' ich gegenwärtig gefühlt. Es war da, das Höchste, in diesem Kreise der Menschennatur und der Dinge war es da! (III, 52)

(Once at least I have seen it, the one and only, the object of my soul's longing, and perfection, which we remove to a place beyond the stars, which we postpone to the end of time, I have felt here present. The best we ever aspire to was once here, here in the circle of our human nature and of earthly things.)

A beautiful, a talented woman among barbarians (as he put it), there are busts of her in the style of the age that lend the idea great persuasive power. She was perhaps a little in love with him before he ever came into her household, since she had read fragments of his Greek novel already published in Schiller's *Thalia*. When Hölderlin next saw any classical sculpture – Napoleon's trophies in Paris – in the early summer of 1802, his mind was already close to collapse, and a few weeks later Susette Gontard died. They are relevant here, and may be remembered throughout, as persons in whom the classical ideal, established in the previous generation, lived.

The Hellenic Ideal, if not quite all things to all men, did answer a variety of needs, that for sexual freedom being one of them. Winckelmann and Heinse, though their tastes differed, may be thought of together as writers to whom Greece meant joy and freedom in the sexual life. Heinse's novel continually opposes the rigid and unnatural, indeed barbaric morality of Christian northern Europe with the healthy and innocent will to pleasure among the pagan Greeks. His story ends, perhaps rather absurdly, with the establishment of a new Hellas, in which free love replaces marriage, on the 'glückselige Inseln' of Naxos and Paros. In his aesthetics he allowed, as Winckelmann did, the sexual sense to play a large and even dominant part. His response to pictures or statuary is often a matter, frankly admitted, of their more or less successful erotic appeal; and the same strain, with his own bias, is evident in Winckelmann's rhapsodic descriptions of the Apollo Belvedere, the Antinous and the Belvedere torso. Art for both of them belonged in the sensual mainstream of life, as it had done, so they believed, among the Greeks before Christ. Heinse thought excellence in art could only be achieved if life itself were being lived with passion and pleasure. 'Zu der Zeit, wo die Menschen am mehrsten lebten und genossen, war die Kunst am größten' ('in times when men lived most and enjoyed life most, art was at its greatest').[4] He thought it impossible that art should flourish in a repressed society. In such a society men and women made aware, by love, of the rich possibilities of life and art would inevitably find themselves isolated and embattled. And that is how the young Hölderlin and Susette Gontard must have seemed to Heinse when he served them as guide in the museum at Kassel.

Soon after publishing the *Gedancken*, by means of a conversion to Catholicism, Winckelmann moved to Rome. Rome 'valait bien une messe'. The contrast with Germany (especially with the Germany *he* had known) was so great that, in a sense, one can well understand his feeling, for the rest of his life, that he was living in the midst of a superabundant good fortune and need not travel further to add to it. The reasons for his not going to Greece are complex and interesting and will be discussed; but it is as well to emphasize at the outset how very well off he felt himself to be in Rome. One can almost say that what he imagined in Germany he realized in Rome. When the comparison is made, in no respect is Germany the better place. There he was enslaved, in Rome he is free, academically and in his sexual life. Like Goethe thirty years later (whose German circumstances were however infinitely more favourable) he uses again and again the metaphor of rebirth to describe his move to Rome. Heinrich Heine said: 'Ask a fish how it feels in water and it will reply: "like Harry Heine in Paris."' Winckelmann was similarly in his element in Rome. To him, as to most of his contemporaries who thought about such matters, Italy, and not Greece, was the classical land. There are reasons for this – the historical fact of the shift westwards of culture, and easy access – that I have already indicated. Winckelmann's immense physical well-being in Rome combining with the conviction that there was nowhere better for the study of classical art, inclined him very strongly to stay put; particularly when he thought of the slavery, the gloom, the pedantry, the bigotry etc. from which he had escaped. He kept to the end of his life the endearing characteristic of not being able to believe his own good luck: 'Dieses ist das Leben und die Wunder Johann Winckelmanns, zu Stendal in der Altmark, zu Anfang des 1718. Jahrs gebohren!' ('the life and miracles of Johann Winckelmann, born in Stendal in the Altmark at the start of the year of our Lord 1718' (*Briefe*, II, 276).

Coming from Dresden – the *Elbflorenz*, the Athens of Germany – with its few bits and pieces packed up higgledy-piggledy in garden sheds, he found the libraries and galleries of Rome at his disposal – a wealth of the very greatest classical works, as he believed, quite unexplored and unexpounded. After years of study, and knowing his own passion, he believed himself, quite rightly, uniquely able to exploit the vast treasure-house of Rome for the enhancement and dissemination of a great idea. His frequent protestations, which may sound like excuses, that he has too much to do, have to be taken seriously. He comes suddenly into great riches; and having had no cause, prior to that, to think himself a lucky man, he busies himself with what he has and is cautious of asking for or even of accepting any more.

He says many times that no one can write on classical art without having been in Rome; indeed, without living in Rome and having access to the collections daily for a long period. He is sceptical of Lessing's qualifications since *he* had not been in Rome.[5] But Winckelmann never once says that for the classical scholar a trip to Greece was necessary. At times he rather doubts whether he would get much out of such a journey at all. Again we must emphasize that he was not odd in such a view. It was exceptional in his day, and until long after his day, to think a journey to Greece essential for a Hellenist. There was *in fact* more to be seen in Rome – that is, there was more to be seen of what, conventionally, was felt to be typical and best in classical art; and more easily to be seen, since sites in Greece were for the most part chaotic and private collections almost non-existent. It only appears odd of Winckelmann to refuse the journey because it was offered him so often and in such relative comfort; and also because he was, for his age, until the great poets of the next generation succeeded him, the exponent to Western Europe of the Ideal of Greece.

Winckelmann, favoured by cardinals, had access to the best in Rome. As Papal Antiquary, after 1763, it was his job personally to keep check on the new discoveries (and to prevent their illicit export). To those of his correspondents whom it would interest he nearly always in his letters gave news of more finds, in Rome and on the country estates. To his protector Bianconi, until their rift, he sent detailed reports of what had come to light, praising the beauty of the new things and assessing their importance in the history of classical art. The finds seem very numerous; those were exciting times for collectors and archaeologists.

Constant discovery, the continual addition to the already extensive corpus of works – this kept Winckelmann's scholarship alive. His classifications were continually tested. Of course, not everything that came to light was good (not by our more discriminating standards); and on one notorious occasion he was sent into raptures by a forgery, done by his friend Mengs, for which he never forgave him. Still, the 'objective' value of the discovered work and the rightness or wrongness of the discoverer's assessment of it matters less than the quality of the enthusiasm that the discovery generates. The excitement one feels still living in Winckelmann's accounts is due very largely to the immediacy of his contact with the works he is describing. As they came to light he was on the spot to see them. Occasionally – the faun's head, for example – he possessed them. To describe the Apollo Belvedere he visited the gallery many times; he saw the real thing, which was quite unlike his procedure in Dresden. For his *Geschichte der Kunst* he drew on works never described before, and on many being unearthed literally whilst the book was being written. The *Monumenti Inediti* are just that – works which he himself, after his classification of classical art, put into circulation among scholars and amateurs in England, France and Germany. The Idea of classical beauty was continually confirmed and substantiated by new finds. In one memorable instance – the Pallas head – it was actually exceeded by the new reality come to light:

Es ist vor wenig Tagen ein Kopf einer Pallas zum Vorschein gekommen, welcher alles an Schönheit übertrifft, was das menschliche Auge sehen können, und was in eines Menschen Herz und Gedanken gekommen. Ich blieb wie von Stein, da ich ihn sahe. (*Briefe*, III, 50)

(A few days ago a head of Athene came to light that exceeds in beauty anything a human being can ever have seen or felt or thought. I stood as if turned to stone when I saw it.)

It was, he said, 'so schön, daß ich mich glücklich preise, durch dieses Werk meinen Begriff noch erhöhen zu können' ('so lovely, that I count myself blessed in being able, through this work, to enhance my conception of beauty still further') (III, 49). He would, with luck, have made or seen such discoveries in Greece too; but in the richness, in the increasing richness of Rome, the pull of Greece was resistible. Ironically Winckelmann, surrounded, indeed nearly overwhelmed, by 'classical art' was not able to distinguish a pure Greek style through the plethora of Roman copies. He is rather a proof of the enormous pre-eminence of Rome before the shift in taste, encouraged notably by Stuart and Revett, was really under way. Winckelmann saw only their first volume, in 1762, in which there is little depiction of sculpture (only the friezes of the Tower of the Winds and the Choragic Monument of Lysicrates), and thought it rather slight.

From Rome Winckelmann went four times to Naples, and from there visited the excavations at the buried cities of Pompeii and Herculaneum. He was not well received. In fact, on his fourth visit he went in fear of a beating or worse, because of the harsh criticisms he had published of the Italian scholars in charge of the sites. In the museum they watched him like hawks, for fear not that he would steal the exhibits but that he would make notes and publish what they regarded as theirs. The excavations, begun at Herculaneum in 1738 and at Pompeii in 1748, continued throughout the century and were a great attraction. Goethe, visiting the sites in March 1787, commented: 'Es ist viel Unheil in der Welt geschehen, aber wenig, das den Nachkommen so viele Freude gemacht hätte' ('There have been many catastrophes in the world, but few that have given succeeding generations so much pleasure'). The findings were published first in sumptuous folios; and then in cheap pirated prints were disseminated widely and started a fashion in dress and furnishings. Visitors to Sir William Hamilton's home in Naples, though after Winckelmann's time, were entertained of an evening by the beautiful Emma Hart, Sir William's mistress, who became his wife and the mistress of Lord Nelson. She would dress *à la grecque*, in costumes designed after those of the dancers of Herculaneum and Pompeii, and would strike what were known as *poses plastiques*: 'stehend, kniend, sitzend, liegend, ernst, traurig, neckisch, ausschweifend, bußfertig, lockend, drohend, ängstlich etc.' ('standing, kneeling, sitting, lying, serious, sad, teasing, extravagant, penitent, tempting, threatening, timid etc.') (*Werke*, XI, 209), Goethe says. In a hidey-hole, where Hamilton kept such of his antiquarian acquisitions as he dared not display, Goethe came upon a large black upright box, open at the front and framed in gold. Against or in this Emma had been wont to stand, imitating as exactly as possible certain of the poses found in the wall-paintings at Pompeii. But unfortunately these performances had been discontinued, and the box consigned to the Milord's lumber-room.

The wall-paintings were what interested Winckelmann most. Since nothing survived by the great Apelles and Zeuxis, on whom he had already written authoritatively in the *Gedancken*, these works of much later date were like teasing after-images of the lost originals. It was Winckelmann's enthusiastic response to these pictures that made him an easy dupe to Mengs and Casanova when, in 1760, they 'discovered' for his delectation, a mural of Zeus and Ganymede – a subject in the contemplation of which, as they well knew, Winckelmann could scarcely be expected to keep a balanced mind. He wrote: 'Ganymedes schmachtet vor Wollust und sein ganzes Leben scheinet nur ein Kuß zu seyn' ('Ganymede looks faint with desire and his whole existence seems no more than a kiss') (*Briefe*, II, 111).

It was only towards the end of his life, in October 1766 through the Prinz von Mecklenburg, that Winckelmann got to know Hamilton, who was the English Ambassador at the Court of Naples. In letters he refers to him as both friend and patron; even allowing for the boastfulness usual in Winckelmann's letters to Germany it is certain that the two men were on the friendliest terms. In Naples, in the autumn of 1767, he frequented the Hamilton household, along with Riedesel, D'Hancarville and the numerous other more or less famous personages who were *de passage*. When Sir William and Lady Hamilton came to Rome the following February Winckelmann in his capacity as cicerone (but only to the discriminating) gave up two days a week to show them round. Rare among English aristocrats (his friend Lord Stormont was another exception) he won the difficult Winckelmann's wholehearted approval: 'dieser große Liebhaber und Kenner der Alterthümer' ('this great lover and connoisseur of antiquities'), he calls him (III, 343). 'Ich freue mich auf Herrn Hamiltons Ankunft in Rom, um jemand zu haben, mit dem man vernünftig über das Alterthum sprechen könne' ('I look forward to Sir William's arrival in Rome since he is someone with whom a rational discussion of classical matters is possible') (III, 289). He was a great collector, and ahead of his time in that his particular passion was the Greek vases of southern Italy, then still called Etruscan. The publication of his first collection (sold to the British Museum in 1772) had been undertaken by the adventurer D'Hancarville; Winckelmann – so Hamilton hoped – would provide a description, an explanation of the scenes from history and mythology with which the vases were decorated, such as he had done of Stosch's collection of gems. Winckelmann agreed – at first reluctantly, fearing years of work, but then enthusiastically; and he speaks of the project as definite in several letters throughout 1767. When he came to Naples in the autumn he saw the vases themselves and discussed them in detail with D'Hancarville (in whose house he lived). The first, very fine, engravings were sent to him in Rome, and he saw the first published volume. But for his death he would surely have gone on with the work: 'die Erklärung dieser Stücke bleibt mir vorbehalten' ('I have reserved for myself the commentary on these pieces'), he wrote as late as February 1768 (III, 366). In the *Monumenti Inediti* and in the last edition (published posthumously) of the *Geschichte der Kunst* there are the beginnings of a proper assessment of these important and truly Greek works. In looking at these vases, generally thought to be of local origin and only hesitantly beginning to be ascribed to Greek artists, Winckelmann was getting closer to the real thing than he knew. So much of his time was spent studying and describing the cardinals' collections of, for the most part, not first-rate sculpture. In Rome, almost too rich in works of art, he perhaps could not see the wood for the trees. The vases, for which his enthusiasm was awakened too late in life, and some of the gems – these were the best things he saw. In time, had he had time, his instinct would have led him nearer and nearer to Greece – figuratively speaking at least. One plan that did look like coming off was to cross to Sicily with a hired artist to publish the vases of Prince Biscari in Catania.

Another approach was to tour Magna Graecia, and this too was one of Winckelmann's recurrent plans. Magna Graecia is *very* Greek, whereas in Rome Greece was all but totally obscured. He conceived the idea of such a tour less than a year after his arrival in Rome. Then in April 1758, from Naples, he went as far as Paestum. That was all he ever saw of the cities of the Western Greeks, but Paestum is superb and he was greatly impressed. The three archaic temples had only recently been rediscovered, by surveyors, it seems, planning a new road for the King of Naples. They saw them through the trees. It is one of the great moments of discovery, like Bocher's first sight of Bassae or Wood's of Palmyra in the desert. Thereafter the tourists went, but still not in any significant number, so that Winckelmann could feel himself to be among the first. His visit to Paestum is the nearest he ever came to that excited exploration of a classical site which his predecessors, contemporaries and successors enjoyed in Greece. The temples are truly Greek, and their situation in Winckelmann's day was exactly of a kind to excite the Hellenist mind with admiration and nostalgia. 'Diese erstaunenden Ueberbleibsel' ('these astonishing remains'), he calls them (*Briefe*, 1, 350), 'das erstaunendste und liebste' ('the most astonishing, my best-loved') (1, 371), 'cosa stupenda!' ('a stupendous thing!') (1, 356), 'mir das ehrwürdigste aus dem gantzen Alterthum' ('to my mind the noblest relic of all Antiquity') (1, 404). There is frequent and enthusiastic mention of the visit in his letters that year. This to Berendis on 15 May:

Es ist eine wüste verlaßene Gegend, wo man so weit das Auge gehet nur etliche Hirten-Häuser siehet: denn es ist eine ungesunde Luft daselbst: Es ist an 70 Ital. weit von Neapel. Mitten in diesem wüsten Lande stehen 3 erstaunende Dorische fast gantz und gar erhaltene Tempel in den alten Ring-Mauren, welche ein Viereck machen und 4 Thore haben. Die Mauren sind an 40 Römische Palmen dick: welches unglaublich scheinet. Man findet daselbst den Bach vom saltzigen Waßer von welchem Strabo redet und viel andere Dinge bey den Alten. (*Briefe*, 1, 366)

(It is a wild and desolate area, only a few shepherds' dwellings as far as the eye can see, for the air is unhealthy. It lies about 70 Italian miles from Naples. And in the middle of this desolation stand 3 astonishing Doric temples almost completely preserved within the old precinct walls which form a square and have 4 entrances. The walls are about 40 Roman palms thick, which seems incredible. The stream of salty water is there that Strabo speaks of, as well as many other things mentioned in the works of the ancient writers.)

His mention of Strabo is almost poignant: so his fellow-Hellenists found their way more or less surely around the wilder sites of Greece. With all his reading, Winckelmann would have been well equipped to identify monuments and give back the ancient names to forgotten places.

There is an account of the temples at Paestum in Winckelmann's *Anmerkungen über die Baukunst* of 1762. It might seem perfectly to be expected that he should like and appreciate the site; but in fact he was exceptional in doing so, so immediately and discerningly. His appreciation of Paestum, like his appreciation of Hamilton's vases, is proof, if any were needed, that his instinct about the Greeks was sound and that, given time and the courage to seize every opportunity, he would have made his way more and more surely through the Roman confusion and copies to the 'true style' – or to real, visible instances of that style which in the imagination he had already perceived. When James Adam visited the temples in 1761 he found them 'inelegant'. Goethe's response, in March 1787, is instructive and, though familiar, is worth quoting here in full:

Von einem Landmanne ließ ich mich indessen in den Gebäuden herumführen; der erste Eindruck konnte nur Erstaunen erregen. Ich befand mich in einer völlig fremden Welt. Denn wie die Jahrhunderte sich aus dem Ernsten in das Gefällige bilden, so bilden sie den Menschen mit, ja sie erzeugen ihn so. Nun sind unsere Augen und durch sie unser ganzes inneres Wesen an schlankere Baukunst hinangetrieben und entschieden bestimmt, so daß uns diese stumpfen, kegelförmigen, enggedrängten Säulenmassen lästig, ja furchtbar erscheinen. Doch nahm ich mich bald zusammen, erinnerte mich der Kunstgeschichte, gedachte der Zeit, deren Geist solche Bauart gemäß fand, vergegenwärtigte mir den strengen Stil der Plastik, und in weniger als einer Stunde fühlte ich mich befreundet, ja ich pries den Genius, daß er mich diese so wohl erhaltenen Reste mit Augen sehen ließ, da sich von ihnen durch Abbildung kein Begriff geben läßt. Denn im architektonischen Aufriß erscheinen sie eleganter, in perspektivischer Darstellung plumper, als sie sind, nur wenn man sich um sie her, durch sie durch bewegt, teilt man ihnen das eigentliche Leben mit; man fühlt es wieder aus ihnen heraus, welches der Baumeister beabsichtigte, ja hineinschuf. Und so verbrachte ich den ganzen Tag. (*Werke*, XI, 219–20)

(A peasant had begun showing me round; my first response was simply astonishment. I found myself in an utterly foreign world. For as the centuries pass in their development from what is grave and weighty to what is light and agreeable so they change human beings too, create them, indeed, after the changing taste. Now our vision, and through it our inner selves, have advanced to and been decisively determined by a lighter architecture, so that these blunt, squat, cramped and massive columns seem to us oppressive or even horrible. But I soon took myself in hand, remembered the history of art, thought of the times to whose spirit such a manner of building was congenial, recollected the austere style in statuary, and in less than an hour I was in sympathy with the place. Indeed, I praised my good fortune in being allowed to see these extremely well preserved remains with my own eyes, since pictures of them can give no real idea. For an architectural drawing will show them more elegant than they are and in any perspective reproduction they will appear more ponderous. Only by walking around and among them can one impart to them their proper life; one absorbs out of them, by sympathy, what the architect intended and built in. I spent the whole day thus.)

It is the shock of the real thing. One can actually see an adjustment in taste occurring. It is a shock such as artists in London experienced when they first saw the sculptures from the Parthenon frieze. The eye, accustomed to the smoothness of the Apollo Belvedere, had to get used to the emphatic musculature of Phidias' classical figures.

Goethe went back to the site in May and discovered then 'die letzte und, fast möcht' ich sagen, herrlichste Idee, die ich nun nordwärts vollständig mitnehme' ('the final and, I am tempted to say, most splendid idea – which I take back with me now to the north, complete') (XI, 323).

Winckelmann was at Paestum in the company of two courtiers from Cologne and the Hamburg author, J. J. Volkmann. (He wondered whether his party were not the first Germans at Paestum, though he ought to have known that his friend Graf Firmian, Ambassador in Naples, had been there three years before.) It was Volkmann who, just off Paestum, in the Bay of Salerno, recited passages from Geßner's *Idylls*, to Winckelmann's delight. It is clear from the letters in which Winckelmann recounts this that both he and Volkmann thought the combination of Geßner and Paestum a happy one. That Winckelmann loved and appreciated the archaic temples at first sight and yet thought Geßner – 'der delphische Geßner', as he calls him, absurdly – in place there, is a curious detail in our examination of taste and changes in taste. But his close friend Riedesel provides another instance of the same. He found the Greek islands not at all to his liking: too hot, too barren, too windy. 'Quiconque aime l'ombrage des arbres, le ramage des oiseaus, le dous murmure des eaus, ne peut se plaire dans ces contrées' ('Lovers of shady trees, warbling birds and the gentle murmur of waters will not be happy in these parts'). And he then quotes Gresset, to show what he had hoped it would be like:

> Ces ondes tendres & plaintives,
> Ce sont des Nymphes fugitives,
> Qui cherchent à se dégager
> De Jupiter pour un Bergér :
> Ces fougéres sont animées,
> Ces fleurs, qui les parent toujours,
> Ce sont des Belles transformées;
> Ces papillons sont des amours.[6]

> (These gentle and plaintive waves
> Are nymphs in flight
> Seeking to escape
> Jupiter in favour of a shepherd:
> These heaths have living souls,
> The flowers, their constant ornament,
> Are girls metamorphosed;
> These butterflies are cupids.)

Physically Winckelmann got no nearer to Greece than Paestum, 50 miles (80 km) south of Naples. I propose now to examine the opportunities he had of travelling to Greece, and to discuss his reasons for refusing or being unable to take them. Relying chiefly on the letters, one is of course faced with the difficulty of assessing how realistic or honest Winckelmann is being when he speaks of his projects to his friends, especially those in Germany. He liked to present his liberty and opportunities as limitless, which by comparison with his circumstances in Germany they were. So his letters are full of projects, mostly of travel; to a succession of correspondents he repeats his latest plan, often in identical words, reiterating it until, with a casual mention, it dies, to be replaced by another. The disproportion between what was projected (and much advertised) and what was done, particularly in the matter of journeys, is very striking indeed. Winckelmann was not a bold traveller – journeys even to Naples cost him a great deal of worry – but he seems to have felt that he ought to be bold, and he compensates or torments himself with projects. It throws his final abortive journey north into a peculiarly tragic light: that he finally plucked up the courage for a wrong and fatal trek.

Being in Rome Winckelmann was almost permanently under the temptation or incitement (like the prick of conscience) to go to Greece. The journey was in the air, at times like a fever: 'Es ist eine Gährung in der Welt diese Reise zu machen' ('the world is in ferment, everyone seems under a compulsion to make this journey') (III, 304). Quite simply, being in Rome and occupying a prominent position there, Winckelmann came into contact with many people who were projecting journeys to Greece and several who did in fact go or had already been. Rome was the natural meeting-place for travellers to Greece and Winckelmann, staying put, inevitably met them or heard of them as they came and went. And it was to Rome that works of art discovered in Greece came for restoration before following their new owners home to England or France. Especially once he had become Papal Antiquary it was Winckelmann's concern to know of such imports. But even prior to that he notes in a dispatch to Bianconi on 30 April 1763 (II, 316) the arrival of a statue and two bas-reliefs from Greece. An English friend has an agent in Smyrna, a doctor with the Turkey Company, who stands in such good credit with the Porte that he can buy what he likes and ship crate-loads of finds to England via Rome. Describing the temples at Paestum, Winckelmann could adduce as evidence in support of his theory that architecture among the Greeks developed later than sculpture a drawing by Stuart of the Parthenon frieze, which, he said, he had seen in Rome.[7] Winckelmann moved freely in a world of travellers, amateurs, dealers, restorers, forgers; he corresponded with men, like Stosch and Montagu, who had spent time in Greece and Turkey. Through all such contacts he was in nearly permanent touch with the land itself, whose artistic products, mostly in debased form, he had in superabundance around him in Rome.

There is another element in Winckelmann's being drawn towards (and yet resisting) Greece. As his reputation grew, it began to be hoped and expected of him that for the sake of European scholarship he would go. Hagedorn urged him as early as 1759: 'Reisen Sie erst nach Griechenland, sehen sich um so viel besser um, da Sie auf Spons Schultern stehen können, und arbeiten für Welsch- und Deutschland' ('but go to Greece, you will have a much better view of things since you can stand on the shoulders of Spon, and labour for Italy and Germany') (IV, 81). His friends among themselves said the same. Brandes to Heyne, in August 1767: if he went to Greece 'was würde man für die Gelehrsamkeit und Kunst sich davon nicht versprechen können' ('what benefit there would be in it for scholarship and the arts') (III, 299). That he had missed the journey was one element in the general regret after his death. And Winckelmann himself certainly thought there was nobody fitter in his generation for the enterprise: 'ich könnte mir auch schmeicheln, daß nicht leicht jemand dieselbe mit mehrerer Erleuchtung und Erfahrung thun wird' ('and I flatter myself that not many men will undertake it with more vision and experience at their disposal') (III, 301). Though he read earlier and contemporary travellers avidly, excerpted them at length and cited them as authorities in his books,[8] he was nevertheless quite often scathing about their achievement. They do not have eyes to see, each sees only what his predecessors saw: 'véritablement tous les Voyageurs répètent ce que d'autres ont dit' ('truly, all the travellers repeat what others have said') (III, 187). The sense that he would himself be the best possible traveller to Greece lends the discussion of his projects almost a public importance; and his excuses assume at times an indignant tone: why should he put himself out for an ungrateful world? 'Der Undank der Welt verdienet nicht, daß man sein Leben tausend Gefährlichkeiten aussetzet.' ('why should one, to reap the world's ingratitude, expose one's life to a thousand perils?') (II, 130). (And *were* he to go, he says in the same letter, he would burn his findings before he died. But that is unusually bitter. Normally his wish for recognition is stronger than his conviction that the world is unworthy of him.)

Winckelmann first mentions the possibility of a trip to Greece in a letter of 1 June 1756 to his university friend Genzmer. It is a remark very much in the tone of those to come:

Mein Hauptwerk...ist eine Abhandlung von dem Geschmack der Griechischen Künstler. Ich werde diesen Sommer vermuthlich in Neapel zubringen, und nachher nach Florenz gehen, um alles zu untersuchen. Meine Absichten erfordern wenigstens einen Aufenthalt von drey Jahren in Italien, und vielleicht habe ich noch das Glück nach Griechenland zu gehen. Nach Syracus werde ich von Neapel reisen. (*Briefe*, 1, 223)

(My chief work ... is a treatise on taste in Greek art. I shall probably spend the summer in Naples, and go to Florence afterwards, to have a look at everything. My purposes require a stay of at least three years in Italy, and perhaps I shall even be fortunate enough to go to Greece. I shall go to Syracuse from Naples.)

He had been in Rome only six months. He wishes to impress an old friend. The next mention, as it happens, exactly characterizes the opposite tone: the resigned or the timorous. It is in a letter to Caspar Füssli, 27 July 1758, and the topic is the same, his *Geschichte der Kunst*. He hopes to begin printing before the winter. In the meantime he is making last-minute additions to his material. He plans another visit to Naples, possibly he will cross to Sicily; he must go to Tuscany. Then he adds: 'Ich wünschte die Ruinen von Athen gesehen zu haben, allein man muß seinen Wünschen ein Ziel setzen' ('I should like to have seen the ruins of Athens, but one must set some limit to one's wishes') (1, 399). 'It would have been nice to have gone, the book might have benefitted...' A bit wistful, not very insistent. That note recurs often during the next ten years, until his death.

In September of that same year (1758) – he was then in Florence cataloguing Stosch's gems – there was for the first time serious talk of a definite project. Bianconi was himself planning a journey to Greece, with his brother, and Winckelmann was to go as the party's antiquary. A painter was going too. Winckelmann was ecstatic at the prospect, and effusively grateful. In letters until January 1759 to friends in Germany and Switzerland he speaks of the project as definite: 'Meine Reise nach Griechenland ist festgesetzt' ('my journey to Greece is settled') (1, 435). 'Unterdessen ist die Reise nach Athen fest beschlossen' ('meanwhile the journey to Athens is quite decided upon') (1, 440). With laughably exaggerated understatement he mentions, to Hagedorn on 13 January 1759, 'eine kleine Reise, die ich vielleicht nach Griechenland zu thun gedenke' ('a little trip to Greece I perhaps have in mind to take') (1, 445). But by that time it is already 'perhaps' and by June, again to Hagedorn, he admits that the journey is off. Everything was planned, he says; money was waiting in Athens. Writing to Berendis at the end of the year he adds that he had letters of introduction to all the English consuls. His reasons for not going were not simply that Bianconi had called the whole thing off, since there was talk in letters *before* Bianconi made the proposal and again after it had fallen through of his undertaking the journey himself in the company of one Colin Morison, a Jacobite refugee. The reason he gives Hagedorn is one he reverts to thereafter whenever such a project comes to nothing: he needs peace and quiet, he is well off in Rome, he wants to get on with his work:

Nunmehro ist es Zeit an ein System des Lebens zu gedenken, welches mir die Reise nach Griechenland verleiden wird...Ich will die Ruhe suchen und in der Ruhe, die ich genieße und in dem Ueberfluß von Materien zu schreiben, das Beste und Nützlichste zu wählen suchen. (*Briefe*, 11, 9–10)

(The time has come to put my life in order, and the journey to Greece would get in the way of that...I want peace and quiet and I want to use what peace and quiet I already have to choose from among the plethora of things to write the best and most useful.)

Essentially he has no need to go to Greece: 'Ich habe alles, was man in der Antiquität und in der Kunst wünschen kann, bey der Hand' ('everything one might want for the study of antiquity and art I have here to hand'). In a letter to Francke (his colleague in wretched circumstances in Nöthenitz) he speaks of 'dieses wilde unstätige Leben' ('this wild unstable life') (1, 422) – and that with reference to a trip to Sicily. Goethe was scarcely more bold thirty years later. He was in Naples, and after much dithering and fussing had made up his mind to cross to Messina:

Der Fürst von Waldeck beunruhigte mich noch beim Abschied, denn er sprach von nichts weniger, als daß ich bei meiner Rückkehr mich einrichten sollte, mit ihm nach Griechenland und Dalmatien zu gehen. Wenn man sich einmal in die Welt macht und sich mit der Welt einläßt, so mag man sich ja hüten, daß man nicht entrückt oder wohl gar verrückt wird. Zu keiner Silbe weiter bin ich fähig. (*Werke*, XI, 223)

(Prince Waldeck unsettled me still further just as we were leaving, for he proposed nothing less than that on my return I should make ready to accompany him to Greece and Dalmatia. Once in the world, once having taken up with the world, you run the risk of being carried away, or of going clean off your head. I am quite dumbfounded.)

Winckelmann wrote to Berendis in December 1759: 'Ich gehe noch immer mit einer Reise nach Griechenland schwanger' ('I am still full of the idea of a trip to Greece') (II, 59). He wants a congenial travelling companion, that is all. Then Stosch wrote from Florence saying that a genteel acquaintance of his, Lady Orford, was off to Greece and would be glad to have Winckelmann with her as an antiquary (as *direttore*, Winckelmann says). Winckelmann wrote back, again ecstatic: 'Dieses ist das Ziel aller meiner Wünsche, und ich wüßte nicht was ich vor Freuden thun würde' ('there is nothing I want more, and I should be beside myself with delight') (II, 68). She would not be disappointed in him, he promises; and the published account of their journey would be to her, not to his, greater glory. This 'donna matta e stravagante' ('crazy and extravagant lady'), as he calls her behind her back (II, 82), intended hiring a ship, as Dawkins did for his expedition with Wood and Bouverie. In subsequent letters Winckelmann pestered his friend for more details: 'Ich wünschte in allen Ihren Briefen ein paar Worte von dem *dessein* der Mylady zu lesen' ('say something in all your letters about Mylady's project'); 'Ich baue auf derselben itzo meine Luftschlösser. Der Himmel gebe daß der Grund nicht sinke' ('I'm building my castles in the air on it. Pray heaven the ground won't sink') (II, 68 and 69). In protestation of his earnestness he produced what must be the *locus classicus* of longing for Hellas:

Nichts in der Welt habe ich so sehnlich als dieses gewünschet; ich ließe mir gerne einen Finger abhauen, ja die Klöße wegschneiden, um in solcher Gelegenheit diese Länder zu sehen. (*Briefe*, II, 69)

Winckelmann and Greece

(I have never wanted anything so passionately as this. I wouldn't mind losing a finger, in fact I wouldn't mind losing my balls for such a chance of getting to see those countries.)

Lady Orford's project was never realized and it is doubtful whether Winckelmann's offer could have altered that. Neither she nor Bianconi actually went to Greece; nor did the Jacobite Morison: 'ce compagnon', Winckelmann says, 's'est laissé épouvanter par la difficulté de l'entreprise. Pour moi je n'y ai encore renoncé' ('my companion has let himself be put off by the difficulty. Myself, I still haven't given up the idea') (II, 99). For Winckelmann, not a rich man, the undertaking would indeed have been a difficult one. He might have got there at his own expense, but to do any useful work on the spot he would have needed considerable sums with which to bribe Turkish officials and to hire labour. This sort of expense could only really be met by the aristocratic or at least very wealthy amateur like Nointel or Dawkins, or by some royal or public body: the French Kings who sent Tournefort and Fourmont, or the Society of Dilettanti who aided Stuart and Revett and totally financed Chandler's expedition. Certainly Winckelmann's best hope was to be taken on as antiquary or learned travelling-companion by a wealthy patron. Several such offers, more or less promising, do seem to have come his way. He might, he says, have gone with the English architect Robert Adam; or with Lord Henry Grenville (and Stosch); or with the reprobate Edward Montagu; or with the frequently mentioned but still mysterious Lord Hope; or with the Duc de la Rochefoucauld, at the French Court's expense. Winckelmann writes of Adam:

Es stehet derselbe im Begriff, auf seine Kosten eine Reise nach Griechenland, durch die ganze Levante und durch Aegypten zu thun. Ich könnte sein Gefährte seyn, wenn ich wollte. (*Briefe*, II, 238)

(He is about to undertake a journey, at his own expense, to Greece, throughout the Levant and through Egypt. I could go with him if I liked.)

But Adam did not in fact go. Stosch and Grenville sailed to Constantinople in February 1762, and in their company Winckelmann would surely have been well off. Stosch was his close friend, and Grenville, according to Boswell at least, was 'a man of merit', 'stately but affable'.[9] Had he gone with Montagu he would have had an exciting time; what serious work he would have done is another matter. It is not possible to identify Hope exactly, nor to say whether he was by

121

rights or courtesy or his own deceit a lord; but he was certainly very rich, and there is evidence that he did indeed make the journey to Greece. His offer must surely have been especially tempting since by then Stosch was already in Constantinople and Winckelmann would have been able to join him there. He talks of advertising the journey publicly, as a tribute to their friendship. And yet he adds: 'In Rom muß ich befürchten alles zu verliehren, wenn ich reise' ('I run the risk of losing everything in Rome if I go') (III, 34). In the end the terms of Hope's offer did not suit him. It is impossible to say whether his refusal was reasonable or not. The conditions were not what he called 'advantageous' (even to see Greece and his good friend?), and the matter was allowed to drop, Hope travelling without him. There is unmistakably a note of relief in his reporting this to Stosch: he would have had to interrupt his work on the *Monumenti Inediti* (then being prepared for the press), he would have forfeited his advantages in Rome.

We cannot say for certain exactly how many offers of a journey to Greece were made to Winckelmann, nor how serious they all were. He is given to boasting of his opportunities. But we can say for certain that some offers were made, some apparently serious and advantageous, and that he accepted none of them. The characteristic tone whenever an opportunity approaches too near is one of extreme caution, indeed of anxiety; and when opportunities come to nothing what we hear in his letters is relief rather than disappointment. In fact despite his frequent and extreme protestations of longing to go to Greece he could also admit to feeling quite indifferent:

Im übrigen ist mir die Lust, nach Griechenland zu gehen, ganz vergangen. Ich werde alt und etwas bequem, und will suchen, meine übrigen Tage in Ruhe zu genießen. (*Briefe*, II, 243)

(Besides, I have quite lost my desire to go to Greece. I'm getting old and somewhat lazy and what I want is to enjoy the days that are left to me in peace.)

His desire could be excited by proposals made to him by friends and acquaintances, but in himself, we must conclude, he had no sustained and determined wish to go to Greece. 'Der Wille des Menschen machet alles möglich' ('through human willpower anything might happen'), he wrote towards the end of his life (III, 331), 'man darf nur wollen und nicht ablaßen, wie ich aus eigener Erfahrung weiß' ('only want a thing enough and don't let up, as I know from my own experience'). That determination got him out of Germany to Rome, but was there not applied to getting him to Greece. That is what one misses in all his reports and discussions of opportunities and proposals: the will to go.

In the last twelve months of his life Winckelmann, far from achieving the peace and quiet he was so anxious to have, suffered agonies of indecision, and in the end chose tragically wrongly. The last great issue of his life was the journey to Greece. He was earnestly prompted by two friends, Pierre Augustin Guys and Johann Hermann von Riedesel, and especially by the latter; and since Riedesel's journey to Greece and his urging Winckelmann to accompany him are well documented I can conclude my survey of Winckelmann's lost opportunities with the last and clearest case.

Winckelmann first met Riedesel in October 1762 in Rome. Their correspondence began in March 1763, when Riedesel began his leisurely journey home, via Florence and Venice. The suggestion that they should visit Greece together, Winckelmann serving his younger and wealthier friend as cicerone (through places neither had ever seen), seems first to have been made, by Riedesel, in January 1764. The journey would be at his expense. He was by that time back in Germany, but planning and being ardently urged by Winckelmann to return south as soon as possible. In fact it was three years before they met again. During that time Riedesel was in southern Germany – on state business – then in Switzerland (from March to October of 1765), and reached Bologna early the following year. He and Winckelmann must then have spent nearly a year together in Rome, though perhaps they were not able to be so much in one another's company as they had hoped and expected. Riedesel went on to Naples in January 1767. From there, between March and May, he undertook a tour of Sicily that was, for himself and for Winckelmann, a sort of prologue to the journey to Greece in the following year. On numerous previous occasions Winckelmann had planned to go to Sicily and had spoken of the project as certain. Now he was urged to accompany his friend, but did not. Instead he gave him a commission for Sicily – to search for a fragment of Doric capital among the ruins of the Temple of Zeus at Agrigento – advised him on what to read in preparation, and referred him to a scholar in Palermo who would be of assistance. When Riedesel returned and wrote up his account Winckelmann read it, edited it and saw to its publication through Swiss friends. In a word, he toured Sicily vicariously, in the person of his friend. Riedesel, for his part, saw the sites to a very large extent through his mentor's eyes. On the Temple of Zeus, for example,

Winckelmann had already written a scholarly piece – which, he suggested, Riedesel might like to compare with his own observations on the spot. The published book – *Reise durch Sicilien und Großgriechenland* – is in the form of two letters (*Sendschreiben*) addressed to Winckelmann in Rome.

Back from Sicily Riedesel was determined to go to Greece. For the next months, until the game was lost, he subjected his friend to persistent persuasion. This was the culmination of all offers and opportunities, quite the most favourable and tempting. Furthermore, to compound his trouble, Winckelmann's plans to visit Germany had by now become definite, so that the decision posed itself as a choice between Germany and Greece: 'ich bin getheilt zwischen Ihnen [Riedesel] und dem entfernten Freunde [Stosch], zwischen Griechenland und dem väterlichen Himmel' ('I am divided between you [Riedesel] and my more distant friend [Stosch – who was back in Germany], between Greece and my native land') (III, 274). That is how he formulates it, repeatedly. His indecisiveness is painful: 'Der Böse Feind reitet mich itzo mit Gedanken einer Reise nach Griechenland, und noch mächtiger als der leidige Teufel ist Riedesel, welcher mir keine Ruhe läßt' ('the foul fiend is riding me at present with thoughts of a journey to Greece, and worse than the Devil himself is Riedesel, who gives me no peace') (III, 301). He seems on the verge of giving in to forces beyond his control or to an unholy temptation:

... weil mich vielleicht mein Geschick, dem ich nicht werde widerstehen können ... nach Griechenland treiben wird. Ich stelle mir von dieser Reise mehr die schlimme als gute Seite vor; aber der böse Feind leget allezeit in der schlimmen Wagschale ein Übergewicht. (*Briefe*, III, 301–2)

(... since perhaps my fate, which I shall not be able to resist, will drive me to Greece. I see the worse and not the better side of the enterprise, but the Devil weighs down the scale of the worse with all his arguments.)

He knows it will be his last chance. His reasons for hesitating are: that he is too busy (III, 302); to do the job properly would require at least two years – 'denn man müßte keine Insel unbesuchet laßen' ('for no island could be left unvisited') (III, 308); on the other hand he is not convinced that he would make any worthwhile discoveries (III, 307). And a new excuse enters or becomes dominant: he is too old. What folly, he writes to Berendis, to contemplate such a thing at his age: 'da ich mehrentheils 50 Jahre auf dem Nacken habe' ('with nearly 50 years on my back') (III, 281). He concludes: 'Große Dinge würde ich machen, wenn ich nur 10 Jahre weniger hätte' ('I should do great things if I were 10 years younger'). By then (July 1767) he had been thinking about going to Greece for rather more than ten years. To Riedesel, the devil riding him with this idea, he offers, in lieu of the thing itself, a characteristically literary evocation: he imagines them strolling together along the banks of the rivers of Greece: 'Ueber alles was groß in der Welt geachtet wird, werde ich mich mit dem Freunde erheben, und im Geiste längst denen Ufern des Ilissus und des Eurotas hingehen' ('I shall rise with my friend above everything the world holds great and stroll with him in the spirit along the Ilissus and the Eurotas') (III, 275). In the end he chose Germany. Greece was the lesser attraction, he says; he must conserve his energies – 'ich bin in den Jahren, wo mit dem Leben nicht zu scherzen ist' ('I am too old to be frivolous with my life') – he must translate into French and oversee the publication in Germany of his revised *Geschichte der Kunst* (III, 336–7). That was his choice, to go north, leaving Riedesel to travel through Greece alone; and by the most bizarre of fates his choosing the 'safer' course led to his brutal and pointless murder.

His death in Trieste lends the decision a tragic seriousness. He is for ever now the man who, offered Greece or Germany, chose wrongly and was punished for it; as though, afraid of Greece, he took the emotionally easier course, and forfeited not only Greece but his life. When Riedesel first made the proposal Winckelmann could still think, quite rationally, of doing both – of going to Germany, then to Greece. There were indeed quite pressing reasons why he should return home: the advancement of his reputation primarily, the wish to shine in his fame in the country of his obscure and laborious beginnings. After that triumph he might still go to Greece. But increasingly he must have felt confronted by a stark either–or. That must have been his feeling – that he had chosen the wrong but binding alternative – when on the journey north he lost his nerve and fled. But by then the Fates had blocked his way with the murderer Arcangeli. Perhaps throughout, but especially in this last year, Winckelmann's life is as Keats says of Shakespeare's, one 'like the Scriptures, figurative'. The biographical facts, equivocal and inconclusive as all such details are, seem unable to resist the pull of the myth, and order themselves according to the terrible idea: a man punished for choosing wrong. Fleeing south, Winckelmann reached Trieste, and there he was stabbed to death in his hotel bedroom. Riedesel then was among the Greek islands.

Was it as a salve to his conscience that he wrote (to Heyne) that he was coming to Germany, in part at least, to further his pet scheme: the excavation of Olympia (III, 358)? Elis captured his imagination as nowhere else in Greece. In a late interpolation – that is 1767 or 1768 – into the *Geschichte der Kunst* he evokes the stadium with its statues of the Olympian victors. Elis, the site of the games, was for him, as for Hölderlin, one of the supreme places of Greece, where the spirit of that civilization was most apparent. Hyperion visits its ruins with his mentor Adamas. In his poetry Hölderlin frequently looks to that locality: 'Gehöret hab' ich/Von Elis und Olympia…' ('And I have heard / Of Elis and Olympia…'). He wishes his own fragmented country had some such unifying point: 'Wo ist dein Delos, wo dein Olympia?' ('where is your Delos, where your Olympia?'). The athletes' competition in excellence – 'müßigernst' ('leisurely–serious'), Hölderlin calls it – was for the eighteenth century a hallmark of the Greek achievement, and Olympia was perhaps its best setting. Winckelmann's idea was to get permission from the Porte, hire a hundred workers and excavate the stadium. In Germany, so he told Heyne, he hoped to raise contributions towards the cost of the enterprise. He concludes:

Was jemand ernstlich will, kann alles möglich werden, und diese Sache liegt mir nicht weniger am Herzen, als meine Geschichte der Kunst, und wird nicht leicht in einer andern Person gleiche Triebfedern finden. (*Briefe*, III, 359)

(Anything is possible if a man wants it enough, and this business is as near to my heart as is my *History of Art*. I can't think it will ever be undertaken by anyone else with a like enthusiasm.)

The combination is significant: his *Geschichte der Kunst* and the excavation of Olympia. His own attempt to wrest out of obscurity and chaos a clear image of Greek art was, he said, as strenuous an exercise as that of the athletes.

Winckelmann thought himself the first German at Paestum, and was not. He imagined he would be the first modern traveller at Elis – Fourmont in 1728 had been called back, before reaching the site, by his royal patron – and in this too he was wrong. Chandler's party had reached Elis in the summer of 1766. It is true they did not find very much (no full excavation was begun until 1875) and Hölderlin, drawing on Chandler, had to take details from elsewhere (the Troad) when he wished to evoke the place for his hero, Hyperion. It is characteristic of Winckelmann that he should be dreaming of doing something that somebody else, more pragmatic, had already done. Things found at Olympia since – the Apollo especially – would have confirmed Winckelmann in his vision. The stadium is laid bare. Inspired by Pindar he would have peopled it, as Hölderlin did, with 'die müßigernsten Kinder' ('the leisurely-serious children')

> Beim Kampfspiel an des Alpheus Bäumen
> Wo beschattet die glühenden Wagen des Mittags
> Und die Sieger glänzten und lächelnd die Augen des Richters.
>
> (II, 693)
>
> (At the games by the Alpheus, under
> That river's trees where the burning chariots of mid-day
> And the victors shone, and the eyes of the judges smiling.)

6

WINCKELMANN AND RIEDESEL

Riedesel's account of his journey to Greece, written in French, though not outstanding for fullness, novelty or style, deserves attention since it is the first by a German; more, perhaps, since it is a work ghosted by Winckelmann. It is very unlikely that Riedesel would have gone to Greece had it not been for Winckelmann, who chose not to accompany him, with fatal consequences. Riedesel toured Greece, as he had toured Sicily, with his mentor's teaching in mind.

Johann Hermann von Riedesel, Freiherr zu Eisenbach, to give him his full title, set off on his Grand Tour in December 1761 and, travelling through France and Northern Italy, reached Rome in October 1762, and there met Winckelmann. He was nearly twenty-two and had behind him legal studies at the University of Erlangen and the beginnings of a diplomatic career in the service of the House of Württemberg. What made him attractive to Winckelmann was not his physical appearance. He is described as 'ein kleiner buckliger Mann' ('a small hump-backed man').[1] What Winckelmann discerned and admired in him was the quality he rated almost above all others: aesthetic sense – 'die Fähigkeit der Empfindung des Schönen', as he called it in the tract addressed to another of his friends, Friedrich Reinhold von Berg. Given that sense, Riedesel was able and willing to develop it, under Winckelmann's tuition. Their relationship was from the start, and remained, very much that of pupil and teacher. Riedesel was one of those few whom Winckelmann thought worthy of being favoured with his time.

Thirty-nine of Winckelmann's letters to Riedesel survived and were published by Daßdorf in 1777, doubtless with some interference. (The originals are lost, as are Riedesel's replies.) Even allowing for the tone of the age they are often effusively affectionate.[2] Riedesel soon became, so Winckelmann told him, one of the very few real friends he had. Absence made him fonder, he longed for their reunion in Rome. In the letters he praises him repeatedly for his extraordinary receptivity to beauty: 'da Sie unter vielen Tausenden der einzige sind, der das Schöne

gleichsam von Natur kennet, und diese Kenntniß richtig gemacht hat'
('since you alone among many thousands know beauty, so to speak,
naturally and have made that knowledge sound') (*Briefe*, II, 348).
Writing to him as he passes through Switzerland, he calls him the
sighted man in the country of the blind. Naturally, Winckelmann
reports to Riedesel on the new discoveries being made in Rome, and
it is to him that he makes some of his warmest and most perceptive
observations on art and the aesthetic sense – on the faun's head, for
example, and the head of Pallas. He charged him when travelling to look
out for beauty in the local inhabitants: 'Schreiben Sie mir, ob Sie
Schönheiten unter dem Weiblichen Geschlechte entdecken' ('write and
tell me of any beauties you discover among the female sex') (III, 234).
On his Sicilian tour Riedesel did as he was bid, and discovered in the
women of Erycia a beauty to justify among them the ancient cult of
Aphrodite.[3] Riedesel could be trusted wherever he went in Sicily to see
with his master's eyes. Winckelmann's letters to him rest on the
assumption of sympathy and common interest.

There is another element in their relationship: the plebeian's envious
affection for the aristocrat. When they met, Winckelmann was more than
twice his pupil's age; but he had lived, as he said himself, only seven
years, only since he came to Rome. He had behind him, before that, years
of bitter slavery; he was self-taught, self-made, nothing had been easy,
he had warped his whole life and gone against his conscience to get the
freedom he had in Rome. And the young men coming to him, Riedesel
their epitome, had enjoyed since birth as an unquestioned right a surer
liberty than he would ever achieve (dependent as he was on cardinals
and kings). Had he had their freedom how much further he would have
advanced along the road of scholarship. The accident of birth put a man
half a lifetime ahead. He applied to himself the Greek term ὀψιμαθής –
spätklug – but not that he thought himself what we should call 'a late
developer', rather that he was born into a class intended to be kept
ignorant, and that by dint of a heroic and crippling exertion, at the cost
of years of his life, he got himself out of it, so that he stood at the age
of forty in a freedom at least comparable to that enjoyed by Riedesel
as a birthright. That understandable envy, never personally bitter
towards the advantaged friend, is apparent in his feelings for Riedesel:

Mein Unglück ist, daß ich einer von denen bin, die die Griechen ὀψιμαθεῖς, *sero sapientes*,
nennen... denn ich bin zu spät in die Welt und nach Italien gekommen; es hätte, wenn
ich gemäße Erziehung gehabt hätte, in Ihren Jahren geschehen sollen.[4]

(I am unfortunately one of those the Greeks call ὀψιμαθεῖς, *sero sapientes*... for I came out into the world and to Italy too late. It should have happened when I was your age, had I had the right education for it.)

To instruct young men of wealth, taste and leisure was then, in the years of his fame, something of a compensation, vicariously, for his own youth 'theils in der Wildheit, theils in Arbeit und Kummer verloren'. The leisure that wealth bought seemed to him, who had earned it the hard way, the *sine qua non* for the study and appreciation of beauty. The aesthetic sense might be developed, Winckelmann argued in the tract addressed to Berg, but only in young men of leisure and not in those

... welche nur um ihr notdürftiges Brot lernen, und weiter nicht hinaus denken können... Denn die Betrachtung der Werke der Kunst ist... für müßige Menschen, das ist, die nicht den ganzen Tag ein schweres und unfruchtbares Feld zu bauen verdammt sind.

(... who learn nothing but what they need for their bare existence and can think no further than that... The contemplation of works of art is... something for people of leisure; for those, that is, who are not condemned to spend the whole day tilling a hard and fruitless field.)

Riedesel had 'nebst der Fähigkeit, Mittel, Gelegenheit und Muße' ('not only the ability but also the means, the opportunity and leisure')[5] for the appreciation of works of art, and he used that privilege wisely in learning from Winckelmann.

He toured Sicily and Magna Graecia between 10 March and 8 June 1767. Winckelmann, who had, so to speak, conducted the journey at a distance, from Rome, urged the traveller to write up his account forthwith. That winter he had Riedesel's journal in his possession and began editing it. He actually commends the work to friends in Switzerland as his own (*Briefe*, III, 380). By them it was duly published, in Zurich in 1771, anonymously as Riedesel insisted, but also lacking the foreword Winckelmann had promised. The book was written in German – *Reise durch Sicilien und Großgriechenland* – as Winckelmann had wished, though as a literary language French came more easily to Riedesel. By that time he had toured Greece too. In May 1768 he had looked across the Straits of Otranto at the mountains of Albania, quoted Virgil (*Aeneid*, Book III) and added:

Meine Begierde war nicht klein, von hier nach Griechenland überzuschiffen; und wenn ich mit den nöthigen Briefen und Geld versehen gewesen wäre, so hätte ich diese Reise gewiß von Otranto aus fortgesetzt. (*Reise*, pp. 223–4)

I must own my desire was great, to go over to *Greece*, and had I the necessary recommendations, and a sufficient sum of money with me, I should certainly have continued my voyage from *Otranto* on that side. (Eng. ed., p. 189)

This intention he then carried out, one year later, sailing from Naples on board an English ship. His book of the tour of Greece, written in French, the language of a culture he had gone to Greece to forget, appeared in 1773, in Amsterdam and Stuttgart, as *Remarques d'un voyageur moderne au Levant*.[6] By that time Winckelmann was five years dead and the anonymous author had been appointed Frederick the Great's ambassador in Vienna. His journeys for pleasure and education, which, after Greece, had taken him to Egypt, Spain, Portugal, England and Scotland, were over and he was a successful, well-liked and respected diplomat, between Vienna and Potsdam, until his death in 1785.

Riedesel, though he could quote his authors when the occasion prompted him, was not a classical scholar but an educated young man of some sensibility professing many of the ideas and sentiments current in his day. His very unoriginality makes him an interesting figure in Greece; for he travelled, as most people do, taking his personal and local prejudices with him. These are, on the whole, of a sympathetic nature and his transporting them through Greece has, at our remove, the charm that all very aptly historical details have. He is not a traveller who tells us very much that is new about Greece; but about the eighteenth-century sentimental preoccupation with that land he is, unconsciously, very revealing. And there is, in his case, the added interest of Winckelmann's ghostly presence in his observations. It is *not* Winckelmann, to be sure: we miss his passion and perception. It is rather the commonplaces of his work that Riedesel is able to carry to Greece, the current ideas and sentiments that were his foundation, not his peculiar insights. The interest lies in the meeting of these received ideas with the real localities themselves; and although Riedesel did not have the originality to drive such a confrontation into the production of something new, still the very inadequacy of his correspondences is instructive. He is, like several of the early travellers, a point of orientation in the shifts of taste.

Rather than describe Riedesel's itinerary I shall discuss some of the expectations with which he went to Greece, drawing the evidence from wherever is most convenient. We can begin with his *Avant-Propos*, since it resumes the intention and spirit of his journey:

Ennuié de voir toujours en Chrétienneté les mémes moeurs, les mémes usages, les mémes habillemens du corps & la méme moulure d'ésprit; voïant que Paris habille l'Europe entiére & que les femmes la dominent, je fûs tenté de voir un païs, ou l'habillement, les moeurs & usages, la religion, le sistéme d'Etat, ne fussent autant sujéts, que chés nous, à des variations continuelles; ou les hommes, vivant moins avec les femmes, fussent plus hommes; lequel enfin aïant moins de loix & moins de connaissances, que nous n'en avons, fût plus original & dont les habitans fussent plus prés de la nature. Je jettais les yeus de loin sur la Turquie; le souvenir des anciens Grécs enflamma mes désirs; entre les monumens d'Athénes je crus pouvoir retrouver des traces du Génie & de la grandeur d'ame de ses anciens habitans. Je désirais de connaitre les Grécs modernes, & de me rappeller en comparaison les Anciens, de marcher sur la terre, qui avoit produit Socrate, Aristide, Sophocle & Xénophon. Je partis de Naples pour Smyrne, le 10 mai 1768, à bord d'un vaisseau anglois.

(Tired of for ever seeing in Christendom the same manners, the same customs, the same bodily apparel and the same intellectual moulds; seeing that Paris clothes all Europe and that women govern it, my eyes were drawn to a country in which costume, manners and customs, religion and the system of government were not so subject to continual change as they are with us; where men, living less in the company of women, were more men; a country finally which, having fewer laws and less science than we do, was closer to the source and lived more naturally. I glanced from a distance at Turkey; the memory of the Ancient Greeks excited my longing; I thought that among the monuments of Athens I might discover traces of the genius and the greatness of soul of its former inhabitants. I wanted to get to know the modern Greeks and to remember, by comparison, the Ancients; to tread the ground that had brought forth Socrates, Aristides, Sophocles and Xenophon. I left Naples for Smyrna on 10 May 1768 on board an English ship.)

It is almost certain that in the spring of 1765 Riedesel, like Boswell shortly before him, visited Rousseau at Môtiers near Lausanne. Riedesel was at that time frequenting the household of Prinz Ludwig Eugen of Württemberg on Lake Geneva. This prince, who astounded Winckelmann by his serious interest in the *Geschichte der Kunst* – 'ich hätte nimmermehr geglaubt, daß ein Deutscher Prinz ein systematisches deutsches Buch lese' ('I should not have thought any German prince capable of reading a scholarly book') (*Briefe*, III, 91) – was an enthusiastic disciple of the solitary philosopher; and introduced Riedesel to him as a young man 'd'autant plus intéressant, que la nature semble avoir donné autant de laideur à sa petite figure que de beauté à son caractère' ('all the more interesting in that nature seems to have endowed his meagre features with as much ugliness as she has his character with beauty').[7] Certainly Rousseau was, with Winckelmann, Riedesel's great mentor, and he travelled Greece in search of that natural humanity which, according to Jean-Jacques, civilization had eradicated in the cities of western Europe. On such a quest, of course, he need not have gone to Greece. If we may believe the *Avant-Propos* his interest in going there was not primarily antiquarian or Hellenist, but rather cultural and philosophical. He at first avoided Constantinople, where the search for unspoiled manners would be hopeless, and visited the islands and the small provincial town of Athens (as it was then):

Partant du principe, que toutes les Capitales de l'Univers sont peuplées de l'ambition & de l'intérét, & que ces deus passions doivent guider les caractéres de leurs habitans, j'ai suivi le conseil de *J. J. Rousseau*, qui dit, que pour connaitre les Français il faut aller en Tourraine & non à Paris: & j'ai observé les caractéres des Insulaires & des Habitans d'Athénes, lesquels éloignés du Trône & hors de la carriére de l'ambition, simplement attachés à l'agriculture & à un chétif commerce, doivent étre plus originaus, plus vrais, & moins corrompùs par le Mahometisme. (*Remarques*, pp. 198–9)

(Starting from the premise that all the world's capitals are full of ambition and self-interest and that these two passions must govern the characters of those who live there I have followed the advice of Jean Jacques Rousseau who says that if you would know the French you must go to Tourraine and not to Paris: and I have studied the character of the islanders and the inhabitants of Athens, who, being remote from the Throne, away from the paths of ambition and bound to the simple life of agriculture or humble commerce, must be truer to their original nature and less corrupted by Islam.)

Sick of civilization, *europamüde* and searching for an unspoilt people, it was inevitable that Riedesel should be strongly anti-French; that despite his French education and his greater facility in French than in his native German. France was, to Rousseau and his sympathizers, the politest, that is to say, the most over-sophisticated and unnatural of the European nations. Hellenism very often has a colouring of Francophobia. In Winckelmann's damning formulation: 'Ein Franzose ist unverbeßerlich: das Alterthum und er wiedersprechen einander' ('the French are irredeemable: classical antiquity and the French are at opposite poles') (*Briefe*, 1, 235). Robert Wood makes the same antithesis in his *Essay*: Homer and the French. Riedesel, it should be remembered, was writing his account at the same time as Herder and Goethe were formulating likes and dislikes in the violently nationalistic language of *Sturm und Drang*: Art and Nature, Racine and Shakespeare, the French and the Germans. And from Lessing's *Laokoon* (1766) the same irreconcilable differences can be deduced: on the one hand French classicistic drama, on the other Greek tragedy, poles apart. Already a follower of Rousseau, Riedesel will have had from Winckelmann in Rome the strongest possible corroboration of his bias against the French. Both his travel-books are strewn with sharp asides: on Naxos, for example, when he observes that M. de Nointel's carved initials have been effaced: 'heureusement que la postérité ne perd rien, en ignorant qu'un Ambassadeur de France y a été!' ('fortunately posterity can do without knowing that a French Ambassador passed this way ') (*Remarques*, p. 76).

Riedesel, the aristocrat, was, in his writings at least, a decided opponent of feudalism. He believed what Winckelmann had taught him: that democracy was a pre-condition for the achievement of excellence in a nation. Without individual and civil freedom the arts and sciences could not flourish. Winckelmann, understandably bearing in mind his enslaved youth, was an extremely vociferous champion of such liberty. What he had struggled for and in part won in his own life he imagined as the possession of his beloved Greeks. He extolled the tyrannicides Harmodius and Aristogiton (as did Hölderlin, nineteen when the French Revolution began); and the unruly Wilkes, whom he frequently met in Rome, seemed to him admirable chiefly as a fighter in the cause of freedom, 'dieser zweyte Milton' ('this second Milton'), he called him, inappropriately. Hellenism had revolutionary potential: it deduced from Ancient Greece, especially Periclean Athens, the model of a just society.

Compared with France and Germany, England, because of her parliament, could be thought of as a free country, producing great libertarians, like Wilkes. Riedesel was a confirmed Anglophile; all his passing references to English institutions are complimentary; he was happy in England and disappointed not to get an ambassadorial posting there. J. R. Forster, translating his first book into English in 1773, noted approvingly that 'it breathes a love of liberty, not frequently met with in transmarine publications'. That Riedesel entered the service of the King of Prussia is, I suppose, of no more significance than that, as a Francophobe, he wrote his tour of Greece in French. Perhaps Forster had in mind his high pathos in Malta (pp. 67–8; Eng. ed. pp. 55–6) or on Etna:

Glücklich ist nur derjenige, welcher frey und ungezwungen wenigstens auf der Erde seinen Aufenthalt sich wählen kann, und denselben ohne Kummer geniesset, da so viele Menschen als Sklaven an güldenen Ketten ihre Lebenszeit zubringen! (*Reise*, p. 133)

He alone can be called happy, who can freely choose his place of abode on any spot of this globe, and who can enjoy his life without trouble, whilst thousands pass their lives like slaves in golden chains! (Eng. ed., p. 112)

– though the freedom he means there is, characteristically, as much philosophical as political.

In Greece, of course, Riedesel had enslavement perpetually under his eyes. It disgusted him, as it did all travellers from Western Europe, to see the descendants of Themistocles, Miltiades etc. servilely accepting Turkish rule. The Maniotes, among whom the abortive revolt broke out a year later, were an honourable exception. But for the rest – he comes close to contempt. It should be stressed that this standard view is a sentimental one, deriving not so much from a real assessment of the modern Greeks' predicament as from a nostalgia for the Battle of Marathon. The modern Greeks were always the more despised for having had such ancestors. So Riedesel remembers the willingness with which they first embraced their chains – under the Romans:

En vils esclaves ils baisérent les chaines, qu'ils portaient, & ils subirent le sort de toutes les nations trop libres, de tomber sous un gouvernement déspotique, tels que les Romains, & les Turcs çi devant Scythes libres; le méme sort, qui pensà tomber sur l'Angleterre du tems de Cromwell! (*Remarques*, pp. 131–2)

(In vile slavery they kissed their chains and suffered the fate of all nations enjoying too much freedom, which is to fall under despotism – so it was with the Romans and with the Turks (formerly the free Scythians) and the same fate threatened England at the time of Cromwell!)

And he concludes, having seen the worst all over Greece:

Tels sont les hommes! la méme chaine, qui devrait les faire rougir, les enorgueillit. J'ai peine à croire que tous les hommes sont faits pour la liberté. Il y en a peu, qui en savent user. Le sage seulement en jouit, le vulgaire en abuse. (*Remarques*, pp. 229–30)

(But men are like that – taking a pride in the very chains they ought to be ashamed of. I find it hard to believe that all men are made for freedom. There are few who know how to use it. Only the wise man enjoys his freedom; the common man abuses his.)

That conclusion renders 'the love of liberty' socially harmless; a generous passion becomes simply one more notion that the aristocratic philosopher could comfortably afford to entertain.

The comparison of Greece under the Romans with England under Cromwell is characteristic of Riedesel. His books are full of such more or less unapt analogies. He was interested in the government of nations, in a just and efficient ordering of social affairs; and especially in discovering the form of government proper to each national character. Thus he says of Greece:

Il parait que cette nation avec ce caractére inquiét est destinée à se gouverner par des petites Republiques comme anciennement, ou pour porter le joug du Déspotisme comme aujourd'hui. Jamais on ne ferà de ce païs une Monarchie, tout comme l'Angleterre portera plutôt les fers de l'esclavage, que de reconnaitre un Monarque Souverain. (*Remarques*, p. 207)

(This restless nation seems destined either to govern itself in small republics as formerly or to bear the yoke of despotism as it does today. It will never be possible to make a monarchy of Greece, just as England will suffer slavery rather than recognize an absolute monarch over her.)

Corruption and mismanagement pained Riedesel's enlightened mind; and he saw a great deal of it, of course, in Sicily, Magna Graecia and Greece. It was particularly painful when a government failed to engross upon its country's natural advantages. Here, near Naples:

Die Bevölkerung, der schöne Feldbau, der Ueberfluß an Lebensmitteln, der Anblick glücklicher Menschen, alles zeuget von dem Wohlbefinden dieses Landes: Wie noch viel seliger könnten die Einwohner desselben leben, wenn eine weise Regierung dazu beytragen wollte! (*Reise*, p. 269)

The populousness, the cultivation, the abundance of provisions, the sight of contented people, all are proofs of the happiness of this country; and how much more happily could the people live, if a wise government would contribute to their welfare! (Eng. ed., p. 227)

And in Sicily: 'Wenn eine gute Regierung die Ordnung, Gerechtigkeit und Gleichheit hier herstellte, würde dieses der glücklichste Winkel der Erde seyn' (ibid. 58) ('if a judicious government would re-establish order, justice, and equality, this would be the happiest spot on earth' (Eng. ed., p. 47)). Bad government offends against good sense and natural justice.

Riedesel shared Winckelmann's anti-clericalism too. There were reasons why Winckelmann should detest the clergy. It was through them, against his conscience, that he had got to Rome and on them there that his freedom depended. Essentially, as Goethe observed, he was indifferent to the Christian religion in any of its forms. He sang the old Lutheran hymns in the privacy of his own room but that was a piety having very little to do with any established Church. If he was not outspoken in Rome it was for fear of the Inquisition[8] and because honesty in religious matters was less important than the liberty to continue his work on pagan antiquities. Surrounded by clerics, he valued them more or less according to their ability as classical scholars and their humanity in social intercourse.

Riedesel's objections to the Church, quite frequently and openly expressed in his two books, are those of the rationalist and moderate social reformer. He dislikes superstition wherever he sees it, even among the ancients. He is harsh on Greek Orthodoxy (far less balanced than Spon): 'On sait à quels ridicules éxcés ils poussent le Fanatisme pour l'observation de leur Caréme' ('we know to what ridiculous excesses their fanaticism runs in their observation of Lent') (*Remarques*, pp. 210–11), and damns the dervishes (then housing in the Tower of the Winds) 'Tellement les hommes ont toujours éxtravagués, en voulant adorer Dieu d'une façon particuliére!' ('such are the extravagances into which men have invariably fallen in wishing to worship God in peculiar ways') (*Remarques*, p. 129). He abhors the collusion of clergy and aristocracy that keeps the peasantry of Sicily poor: 'so viele Menschen mangeln Brod, weil die Edelleute und Mönche alle Güter besitzen!' (*Reise*, p. 134) ('many people want bread, whilst the nobility and the monks are in possession of all the lands!' (Eng. ed., p. 113)). In fact monks everywhere disgust him, in Catania, San Nicolo, Otranto, on Naxos, living rich, abusing alms, and generally parasiting on the body politic. Rome is infested with them – he quotes: 'Des Prétres fortunés foulent d'un piéd tranquile / Les tombeaus des Catons & la cendre d'Emile!' ('well-heeled prelates trample without qualms / Over the tombs of the Catos and the ashes of Aemilius') (*Remarques*, p. 113) – and Constantinople is just as bad. In remarks à la Montesquieu that were far too strong for his German translator he compares Christianity unfavourably (in the matter of tolerance) with the Muslim Church: 'au lieu que le Christianisme, le fér & le feu à la main, les Cortéz & les Pizarre avec leurs cruautés ont extirpés & pàs convertìs les peuples d'Amérique' ('but Christianity came with fire and sword and all the cruelties of such men as Cortez and Pizarro, and the peoples of America were not converted but exterminated') (*Remarques*, p. 275).[9] They are sentiments of which Lessing would have approved, but the less progressive Christian Wilhelm Dohm, though he does translate fairly, 'corrects' them in long footnotes and puts the reader on his guard against 'Ausfälle dieser Art' ('outbursts of this kind').

Riedesel's objections to modern religion are not of a very radical kind. He is outraged by obvious abuses and disgusted, as a rational man, by all superstition and excess. There is nothing Hellenist about his anti-clericalism; that is to say, he does not have in his imagination as the contrary pole to Christianity the pagan religion of Greece. Winckelmann did, and that is an essential difference between them. One feels that Riedesel would use the word 'enthusiastic', in religious matters at least, just as pejoratively as the ordained Sir George Wheler did of the Bacchic rites on Mount Parnassus. It was the poets, and the poetic art-historian Winckelmann, and not the travellers, who in the eighteenth and early nineteenth centuries countered the otherworldliness of Christianity with the earthly glory of Greece.

Riedesel's particular *manie* was climate. That climate helped or hindered a people in their pursuit of excellence was an eighteenth-century commonplace, but Riedesel will have had it at firsthand and especially well expressed from Winckelmann. Riedesel brooded obsessively on climate and its effects during both his tours. To his surprise, since he seems to have expected a Greece in the style of Gresset and Watteau, he found the climate, especially of Athens and the islands, disagreeable. This was not just personally but also philosophically inconvenient, because in the simplest view of things Greece was thought to occupy the ideal temperate zone between the frozen north and the torrid south; and all the Greek achievements in the arts and sciences were believed to have been favoured by an ideal climate. On the spot Riedesel made more or less successful adjustments to this simplest line. Rounding Cape Matapan, for example (he did not land), he was easily persuaded that the geographical situation of Ancient Sparta and the climate ensuing from it explained the Spartan character and achievement. The lie of the country exposed its inhabitants to the cold winds of the north and the east, whilst the mountains kept out the soft airs of the west. This happy combination toughened the Spartans up. And their supposed descendants, the Maniotes, enjoying the same situation and being similarly virile and independent, confirmed the equation.

He thought the people of Tenos

...les plus fins & les plus subtils des Grécs Insulaires. Ils sont forts, robustes & vieillissent beaucoup; éffét du climat pur & de l'air subtil de l'isle. (*Remarques*, p. 60).

(...the most astute and subtle of the island Greeks. They are strong and healthy and live to a great age. This is due to the pure climate and the light and delicate air of the island.)

But coming with the same supposition to Athens he was disconcerted:

J'avoue, que je ne puis pas combiner l'imagination de leurs Artistes, leur délicatesse & sensibilité dans le goût, la finesse du sentiment de leurs Poëtes, cette urbanité Attique, qui suppose une douceur dans le caractére & les moeurs, avec un climat si rude, un vent du Nord si impétueus, & de si subits changemens du froid au chaud. Comment cependant nier l'influence du climat sur les peuples, qui les habitent? (*Remarques*, pp. 142–3)

(I confess that I cannot reconcile the imaginativeness of their artists, their delicacy and sensitivity of taste, the sophistication of feeling in their poets, that Attic urbanity which implies a certain gentleness of character and manners, with so rude a climate, such a blustery north wind and such sudden changes in temperature. And yet how can it be denied that climate has an effect upon the inhabitants of a place?)

He came in the end to a sensible compromise: climate explained some things but not others:

L'inconstance, la finesse, la légéreté, la sagacité Grécque tant ancienne que moderne, la valeur méme & le courage ancien s'expliquent fort bien par les influences d'un climàt tempéré, plus froid que chaud, séc, serein & d'un air vif & picquant...Mais l'imagination heureuse & créatrice de leurs anciens Artistes, le génie de Phidias & de Praxitéle, d'Appelle & de Zeuxis, ne s'accorde point avec l'impétueus vent du Nord. Leur gout, leur délicatesse, & sensibilité ne pouvaient convenir avec les subits changemens du froid au chaud du climàt d'Athénes, de tout le Péloponnése & de l'Archipel. (*Remarques*, pp. 285–6)

(The inconstancy, sophistication, liveliness and intelligence of Greeks ancient and modern, as well as the ancient heroism and courage, can perfectly well be explained as the products of a temperate climate, one more cold than hot, dry and clear, and of the sharp and stimulating air...But the happy and creative imagination of the ancient artists, the genius of Phidias and Praxiteles, Apelles and Zeuxis, does not conform at all with the blustery north wind. Their good taste, their delicacy and sensitivity did not belong with the sudden changes in temperature characteristic of the climate of Athens and of all the Peloponnese and the Archipelago.)

Riedesel offers instead the suggestion that great things may be achieved not with the help of the climate, but against it. Thus Greek artists were helped to their achievement by factors in their native culture, namely the spirit of competition and the games that were its public form. This argument is Winckelmann's (in the *Gedancken*) and Riedesel reproduces it less exactly than does the learned merchant Guys; but the slant he gives it is his own. Factors of character and culture, he says, 'concoururent à forcer les obstacles du climat' ('combined to overcome the obstacles of climate') (p. 286). That is a shift from his first belief, according to which character and culture themselves were the products of climate; and it is a shift occasioned by his actually going to Greece. It may be that neither his untried presupposition nor his adjustment on the spot is significant or convincing; but his moments of disconcertment are interesting, I think, when his commonplaces meet a strange reality.

Riedesel had in fact in his earlier book already sketched out a theory that in other writers, in Hölderlin for one, assumed some force and subtlety: namely that, by opposition, a people must compensate, and seek to appropriate from elsewhere what it does not possess locally and naturally. Of the Sicilians Riedesel wrote: 'bey einem erstaunlichen Feuer haben sie kein Phlegma, das zu der Ausführung in den Künsten nöthig ist' ('they have amazing vivacity, but not the least phlegm, which is very necessary in the cultivation of the arts, and in the execution of its works' (Eng. ed., p. 143)); they have 'ein übermäßiges

Feuer' ('their great degree of vivacity') (*Reise*, pp. 169 and 170). Hölderlin said of the Greeks that what was natural to them was 'das heilige Pathos' ('holy pathos') and what they needed to complement it was 'die Junonische Nüchternheit' ('Junonian sobriety') (VI, 426). This quality they appropriated, cultivated and finally excelled in. The predicament of the moderns in the North was, according to Hölderlin, exactly the opposite: cold by nature they needed passion. Riedesel's Sicilians, lacking 'phlegm', are volatile and unruly in their lives and in their art.

Climate cannot supply everything. Its effects may need to be qualified or even contradicted by a nation's conscious institutions. And the good effects of a favourable climate may be quite nullified by other interferences. If this were not the case then, climate altering little over the centuries, we might expect to find throughout Greece a people as like (as worthy of) their ancestors as the Maniotes in Sparta. But in fact the traces of such continuity are few and far between. One intention running throughout Riedesel's books, and most apparent in the seventh chapter of his *Remarques*, is to compare ancient and modern, to seek for connections, to discern survivals. Guys, perhaps better disposed than Riedesel and looking about him with the eye of faith, found abundant evidence of unbroken continuity. But this was Riedesel's view:

Il est vrai, que l'on découvre encore ces traits originaus & caractéristiques, qui donnent la ressemblance déjà à l'esquisse d'un portrait. Mais ce sont des traits obscurcis, éffacés à demi. (*Remarques*, p. 200)

(It is true that something like a sketch of the original may be discerned in certain surviving characteristics. But the features are unclear, half-effaced.)

The reasons for this very partial transmission are not hard to find:

La conformité, que le même climat devrait maintenir dans les génies de la nation, qui habite le même païs, dans leurs moeurs, leurs usages & leurs caractéres, est altérée par les Etrangers établis parmì ces Indigénes, par les revolutions qu'ils ont soufferts, mais sur tout par la forme du gouvernement, qui les opprime. (*Remarques*, pp. 196–7)

(The continuity of spirit, manners, customs and climate that we should expect an unchanged climate to maintain in a people continuing to inhabit the same country is disturbed by foreign immigration and social upheaval, but above all by oppressive government.)

As Homer said, in a line frequently quoted by the travellers, take away a man's liberty and you take away half his worth. No climate, however favourable, can compensate a people who have lost their freedom. It needs more than climate and the survival of physical surroundings (however beautiful and rich in glorious associations) to keep the identity of a people alive.

As the achievement of Ancient Greece ascended ever more brightly over Western Europe the wish to explain it grew naturally into a desire to recover or recreate it; and if purely physical causes such as climate could be believed to be crucial, and if their survival into the present day could be demonstrated, then enthusiasts and optimists at least, seduced by a simple logic, looked for the imminent realization of their ideals. Guys was among these, and the line leading to political action, to the re-establishment of the ideal state in its proper unchanged surroundings, is obvious. Riedesel on the other hand, finding that excellence in Greece was, despite the survival of some congenial circumstances, absent, followed what is essentially the same logic and explained its absence and the improbability of its re-achievement by pointing to other circumstances that, being unfavourable, nullify the favourable ones.

Herder, who never went anywhere near Greece but who was nonetheless an admirer and important transmitter of her culture, enlarged these very deterministic speculations on the character and achievements of nations with his more mystical but also more potent notion of palingenesis. According to this the Spirit of Civilization progresses from place to place and nations flourish and fade with its coming and with its passing: 'Immer verjüngt in seinen Gestalten, blüht der Genius der Humanität auf und ziehet palingenetisch in Völkern, Generationen und Geschlechtern weiter' ('in continually rejuvenated forms the spirit of humanity flowers and passes palingenetically through peoples, generations and dynasties') (xiii, 253). Hölderlin, who followed Herder closely in his poetical–historical thinking, expressed the same belief thus: 'Doch, wie der Frühling, wandelt der Genius / Von land zu Land' ('but the spirit passes like the spring / From country to country') (ii, 4). This 'Gang Gottes über die Nationen' ('God's passage across the nations'), as Herder called it (v, 565), was from east to west – from Asia to Asia Minor, from there to Athens, thence to Rome... Riedesel himself, before Herder, offered a version of these speculations. He concludes his remarks on the once great kingdom of Naples thus:

Kein Schatten dieser alten Grösse ist mehr übrig. Die Macht, der Handel, die Kriegs-und Seewissenschaft, die Verbesserung des menschlichen Verstandes, alles scheinet sich immer mehr nach Norden zu ziehen. Mit der Zeit werden die Europäer in Amerika Schutz, Erziehung, Sitten und Cultur des Verstandes suchen müssen. (*Reise*, p. 270)

Now not even the shadow of their ancient grandeur is left. Power, commerce, naval and military sciences, and the improvement of human understanding, all seem to go northward. In time, the *Europeans* will be obliged to look for protection, education, manners, and the cultivation of the intellectual powers in *America*. (Eng. ed., p. 228)

There are several points of general importance here. The first is the conviction, contrary to that of Guys and most Philhellenists, that excellence has gone from Greece for ever. The genius, the spirit of excellence, has passed, in the normal way of things, elsewhere. Such a belief gives hope to the modern nations. German thinkers in the late eighteenth century were inclined to be persuaded that the Spirit of Civilization, once at home in Athens and thereafter in Rome and Renaissance Italy, was due in Germany. Around 1800, in the midst of the Revolutionary Wars, a sense of Imminent Coming was very strong, especially in Hölderlin's Swabia, rich in the chiliastic hopes of Pietism. He imagined a resurgence of the Greek spirit, on German soil and in a form proper to the German people. For that is the crucial element in Herder's teaching: the spirit is 'immer verjüngt in seinen Gestalten' – that is, each nation will flourish according to its character. This relativizes the Greek achievement: it is the product of particular time and place, of unique circumstances, and as such is unrepeatable. What is immortal in it, the spirit, is released and passes elsewhere, into new forms. Winckelmann's view of Greece, despite his thorough work as an art-historian, his careful differentiation of developing styles, was in fact quite ahistorical; and he presented the artistic achievement of the Greeks to his contemporaries as an absolute, not relativized in any way, really as an abstraction, and urged them to imitate its externally valid forms. This could lead of course to the academic and the classicistic, to the 'positives Beleben des Todten' ('positive animation of the dead'), in Hölderlin's words, though it was not Winckelmann's intention that it should. Herder's is, on the face of it, the more exciting idea, since it makes for a national, or indeed individual, *Auseinandersetzung* with Greece, a struggle for self-discovery and self-expression against the powerful beauty of the past. The ideal may well appear at its clearest in Greek form, and may be admired or even worshipped thus; but in that form it cannot again be realized in the personal or the national life.

My concentration on the philosophical and cultural concerns in Riedesel's travel-books fairly represents, I think, the emphasis of his own interests. He travelled Sicily, Magna Graecia and Greece as a man soon to embark on a diplomatic career. He was at least as interested in the management of the modern states as he was in their classical past. There is much in his accounts that concerns in a quite precise way the economy and government of the regions through which he passed. Weary of Europe though he was, he knew full well that he was going back there, to serve its potentates. His nostalgia for the simple virtues was doubtless genuine, but he must have known that his career would be at Courts and in capital cities. Perhaps a large proportion of what I have related of his observations in Greece is not specifically Hellenist at all; rather they are the observations of a young man, a reader of Rousseau and Montesquieu, preparing himself for a political career. By the time he reached Greece he was already well travelled, and in his account he draws frequent comparisons and analogies between places widely separated in Europe. But what Winckelmann loved in him was not these qualities of the enlightened young statesman, but his sensibility and love of beauty. In print, however, he appears far less interested in aesthetics and less sensitive to beauty around him than the merchant Guys. It must be said that he was not a traveller who notably expanded Hellenism. He added – from Greece at least – no new, accurate information of an archaeological kind, nor did he extend or intensify the sentiment. He confirmed some of the commonplaces; and some, it is true, he tried to adjust.

Perhaps his enthusiasm rather deserted him in Greece. He was unwell in Athens, and by then no doubt he had heard of Winckelmann's murder. For one reason or another he did not have the heart to make the usual trips to Marathon, Eleusis, Megara and into the Peloponnese, but took a ship to Constantinople instead. There is more Hellenist sentiment and archaeologically useful information in his book on Sicily than in his book on Greece. Goethe had the *Reise* with him on his journey and always spoke of Riedesel with the greatest gratitude and respect. In such a passage, for example, describing a relief at Agrigento, he writes in a manner not unworthy of his mentor Winckelmann:

Alles, was das Alterthum von schönen Formen und Ideen bis zu unseren Zeiten erhalten, ist an [der Hauptfigur] zu finden; man siehet einen der schönsten Menschen, aber nicht einen gemeinen, sondern von der Natur zu besondern Unternehmungen bestimmten Sterblichen; er ist über die anderen Figuren erhaben, grösser als dieselben, schöner, vollkommener, kurz ein Meisterstück der Natur, und ihrer Nachahmerin, der Kunst. (*Reise*, p. 33)

... all that gracefulness of form, and beauty of ideas, which is handed down to us by the ancients, is to be met with in this figure; you see the form of one of the most beautiful men, visibly singled out by nature for peculiar exploits, preferably to the rest of mortals: he is raised above the other figures, more tall, more beautiful, more perfect than they; in a word, the master-piece of nature and of art. (Eng. ed., pp. 26–7)

A female profile in the same relief is, he says, 'so vollkommen und harmonisch, als ein Sterblicher solches sich vorstellen kann' ('as perfect and harmonious, as a mortal can imagine'); the garments 'so schön, edel und ungezwungen, als solche zu erdenken sind' ('a model of the greatest beauty: the drapery is elegant, noble, and easy' (Eng. ed., p. 27)). He is full and informative on Prince Biscari's collection in Catania (the vases of which Winckelmann had intended to catalogue) and admirably thorough and exact at the Temple of Zeus in Agrigento (which Winckelmann had commended with especial earnestness to his attention). But his published response to things in Greece is disappointing. He saw nothing of archaeological interest not already seen and fully described by his predecessors, and to them – to Spon, Wheler, Tournefort and Stuart – he very readily refers, partly out of deference to their greater knowledge, but partly also, one suspects, out of ignorance and weariness. He seems not to have tried to respond to the great sites with feelings and in language of his own. It really amounts to very little that he admires the Parthenon – 'le plus beau monument que j'aie vu, tant à Rome que par-tout ailleurs'('the finest monument I have seen, in Rome or anywhere else') (*Remarques*, p. 123) – or that he notes with a proper regret the barbarous abuse of ancient remains. There is nothing in his account of Delos to match that of Tournefort, Stuart or Wheler. Perhaps his Hellenism, as an enthusiasm, was undermined by that modern, sceptical, rationalistic bent that was, I think, his characteristic habit of mind. He says of Delos: 'Apollon y avoit un temple superbe, & le fanatisme & la superstition y avoit assemblés d'immenses richesses' ('Apollo had a magnificent temple there: fanaticism and superstition had heaped the place with riches') (p. 63). That is language very like Wheler's on the same subject: his was prompted by seventeenth-century Anglican piety, Riedesel's by the rationalism of Voltaire. I have already mentioned his quoting Gresset among the islands. That is a peculiarly telling, not to say damning, detail. Likewise his preference for 'paysages champetres', rare in Greece. He discovered one such, along the Gulf of Smyrna, and described it thus: 'une belle verdure, des arbres d'haute & basse futaïe, des tapis de gazon, quelques maisons rustiques éparses d'un coté & d'autres' ('beautiful greenery, trees of all sizes, lawns, and a few rustic dwellings scattered here and there'). He was reminded, he says, of 'l'innocence de l'age d'or & les belles vües de la Suisse champétre' ('the innocence of the Golden Age and the beautiful prospects of rural Switzerland') (p. 25).

In Riedesel's Sicilian book the presence of Winckelmann is closely felt. The letters are addressed to him in a quite personal way. The pupil defers to his absent teacher: 'Hier zu entscheiden, würde von mir apocryphischen Antiquario eine grosse Verwegenheit seyn; welches ich also dem Patriarchen der Alterthümer überlassen will' (*Reise*, p. 154) ('to decide here would be great presumption in an apocryphal antiquary like myself; I therefore leave it to the great patriarch of antiquities' (Eng. ed., pp. 130–1)). There are several close correlations between Winckelmann's published writings and Riedesel's observations – on Eryx and Agrigento, for example. In praise of works of art Riedesel uses phrases that are Winckelmann's own – 'die Schönheit der edlen Einfalt mit wenigen Zierrathen' (p. 40) ('the beauty of that architecture, where a noble simplicity and few ornaments are employed' (Eng. ed., p. 32)), 'der gute Geschmack und die edle Einfalt ... der alten Griechen' (p. 114) ('the excellent taste, and the noble simplicity of the ancient *Greeks*' (Eng. ed. p. 96)). His sentiments on friendship are exactly Winckelmann's, and when Winckelmann read the journal he recognized them as such.

Riedesel's 'Zweytes Sendschreiben' has this conclusion:

Ich möchte wünschen, daß ich Ihnen in allen Dingen, welche Sie zu wissen verlangen, genuggethan hätte. Sie glauben, mein Freund, wie groß mein Vergnügen dabey seyn würde ...
... Entschuldigen Sie indessen durch Ihr Verlangen diese unvollständige Nachrichten, welche für mich, und, nach Ihrem Willen, für Sie gemacht sind.

I wish I could have satisfied your curiosity in every point; you will easily conceive how great my pleasure would be in that case ...
... incline you to excuse my imperfect accounts the more readily, as you expressly desired to see them. (Eng. ed., pp. 229–30 – more exactly: 'these imperfect accounts, which were composed for myself and, since you wished it, for you too')

This first book was very much a work of collaboration between two friends, the scholar and the traveller, the teacher and his pupil. In Greece Riedesel was far more remote from Winckelmann, and not only geographically. The real country would have been a shock to Winckelmann too, but his confrontation with it would have been more fruitful than Riedesel's. The Hellenist Riedesel was a creature almost wholly of Winckelmann's making; and he failed in Greece, and became there instead what perhaps he essentially always was, an economist, a *philosophe*, an administrator. There is no mention of Winckelmann throughout the *Remarques*. Some phrases still seem his – 'les nobles & vraies beautés de la male simplicité' ('the true and noble beauty of manly simplicity') (*Remarques*, pp. 124–5) – but in the main he is absent and – by us now – much missed. Riedesel, the only German of any consequence whatsoever to visit Greece before Jakob Bartholdy in 1803 was unfortunately, as a Hellenist, at a loss without the company of the man who had inspired him to go.

7

PIERRE AUGUSTIN GUYS

Pierre Augustin Guys was born in 1720 in Marseilles. A combination of commerce and scholarship was traditional in his family. His father had explored and published antiquities in Provence. Guys was a successful merchant and became very wealthy. He distinguished himself and honoured his profession 'par sa probité et la simplicité de ses moeurs' ('by his honesty and the simplicity of his manners').[1] He made his name as an antiquarian and literary man with the *Voyage littéraire de la Grèce*, first published in two duodecimo volumes in 1771 and going through two further, grander editions before he died.

Guys travelled young, being first established in business in Smyrna and Constantinople. He went to and fro among the islands several times; visited Bulgaria and Syria, as well as Italy, Denmark and Holland. It is impossible to say what all his itineraries were. His earliest published account is of a journey from Constantinople to Sofia in 1744. The letters that compose the 1771 edition of the *Voyage littéraire* go back as far as 10 January 1750; but the third edition of 1783 contains one of 3 February 1748, written on Melos, during a voyage from Marseilles to Smyrna. Though his affairs shifted to Marseilles in the latter part of his life, he still travelled and, indeed, died far away from home, on the island of Zante in 1799.

Since one point of discussion in this chapter will be Guys' close knowledge of the works of Winckelmann it might be useful to include here, as a preface, what little is known of their personal dealings.

Winckelmann first mentions Guys in a letter of 7 March 1767. He is writing to Stosch, back in Germany after his second stay in Constantinople, about the placing of orders for the *Monumenti antichi inediti*:

So gar ein Negotiant aus Marseille hat zwey von mir selbst verlanget. Sie werden diesen vermuthlich kennen; er heißt Guys, und ist in Constantinopel gewesen, wo er sich mehr mit Büchern als mit Rechnungen abgegeben. (*Briefe*, III, 240)[2]

(I have even had a request from a Marseilles merchant, for two copies. You will probably know him – his name is Guys and he has spent some time in Constantinople where he had more to do with books than with bills.)

The book was expensive – 8 *zecchini*, 4 guineas in England (III, 223) – but Guys took two copies and with them copies of the *Description des pierres gravées*, one of each for himself, we may assume. Winckelmann wrote to Wilkes that he was sure Guys – 'Negotiant connu de Marseille et mon ami' ('a well-known merchant from Marseilles and a friend of mine') (III, 290) – would be happy to transmit copies of the *Monumenti inediti* to Paris (where Wilkes was).

And it was Guys who, with Riedesel, urged Winckelmann in the last year of his life to make the journey to Greece:

Ein reicher junger Negotiant zu Marseille, welcher einige Jahre zu Constantinopel, nebst einem guten Vorrath von Büchern, gewesen ist, und Griechenland durch gewandert, erbiethet sich zu solcher Reise alles, was er kann, beyzutragen. Er höret nicht auf mir von den hohen Schönheiten zu schreiben, und wünschet, daß ich dieselbe sehen und beschreiben möchte. (*Briefe*, III, 268)

(A wealthy young merchant in Marseilles, who was some years in Constantinople together with a good supply of books and who has toured Greece, offers to make whatever contribution he can to such a journey. He writes to me continually of the great beauties of Greece and would like me to see them for myself and describe them.)

Guys was forty-seven, not really so young. Winckelmann, who had for ten years felt himself to be too old for the journey to Greece, was only a couple of years his senior. But Guys had sailed more than once through the Archipelago before Winckelmann had got even out of Prussia into Saxony, and continued his travels long after Winckelmann was dead.

There is no evidence that the two men ever met. It is certainly very possible that Guys passed through Rome during Winckelmann's residence there, or perhaps they coincided in Naples; on the other hand their acquaintanceship, friendship even, might well have been established entirely through letters (none of which have survived). What is certain is that Guys knew Winckelmann's books: the *Description des pierres gravées*, the *Geschichte der Kunst* (in the French translation) and the *Monumenti inediti*. Furthermore there is the closest correspondence between his own reflections on the production of beauty (*Voyage littéraire*, chapters 31–4) and those of Winckelmann in the *Gedancken*.

Guys lived for years and travelled extensively in the Greek regions. His book is the bodying-forth, with material culled from that long experience, of one simple and attractive idea. In both these respects – the intimate knowledge of the places, and the singleness of the idea – he resembles Robert Wood. Their journeys in part coincided in time, and their ideas too are in essence, if not in emphasis and application, the same. Goethe thought of the two men together as formative influences upon him in his youth. Wood looked in Greece for evidence of Homer's truthfulness to Nature; that is, for survivals, in topography and manners, of the world Homer depicted; and Guys believed more generally (but with frequent and especial reference to Homer) that a great deal had survived (and manners were his particular concern) out of the ancient times into the modern. The notion that one did well to read Homer (and the other ancient writers) on the spot is common to them both:

Homere a peint fidelement les moeurs & les usages des hommes de son tems. C'est à Troye, sur le Cap Sygée, à Tenedos & à Smyrne, qu'il faut lire ce Poëte.[3]

Homer has justly described the manners and customs of men in his time. It is at Troy, on Cape Sygeum, at Tenedos and at Smyrna, that this poet... should be read. (Eng. ed., 1, 3)

Wood first published his work, it will be remembered, in 1769, but only in half a dozen copies; and it is nearly impossible that Guys should have seen one of these. His own *Voyage littéraire* came out in 1771, before either the German translation or Bryant's full edition of the *Essay*. Thus there is no question of literary influence either way. Characteristically though (he was an avid reader of anything on or near his topic) when Wood's book became generally available in 1775 (a French translation appeared in 1777) Guys acknowledged it, with generous praise, in the third edition of his *Voyage* (II, 242, 339).

The full title of Guys' book is *Voyage littéraire de la Grèce ou Lettres sur les Grecs anciens et modernes, Avec un Parallele de leurs Moeurs*. No educated traveller could travel Greece without bearing the ancients in mind. Those early travellers primarily interested in archaeological remains used the ancient authors, especially Strabo and Pausanias, to elucidate the sites and the buildings. But it is rather a different process, in fact almost a reversal, when a traveller – Lady Montagu being one of the first – applies what is there to be seen, particularly in climate, topography and manners, to the ancient texts, to Homer and Theocritus, to elucidate them and enjoy them all the more. She wrote to Pope, for example, that being in the East she no longer looked upon Theocritus

as 'a Romantic Writer': he had, she said, 'only given a plain image of
the Way of Life amongst the Peasants of his Country'; and she added,
flatteringly and exactly in the manner of her successors Wood and Guys,
'I read over your Homer with an infinite Pleasure, and find several little
passages explain'd that I did not before entirely comprehend the beauty
of, many of the customs and much of the dress then in fashion being
yet retain'd.' She had seen great ladies working at their looms who
reminded her of Helen and Andromache; old men with reverend beards
sitting basking in the sun, like Priam and his counsellors; girls dancing,
like Artemis and her nymphs as Homer describes them in the *Odyssey*;
belts such as that worn by Menelaus and veils like Helen's. Pope replied
that she might indeed, by her letters from the East, provide 'great
Eclaircissements upon many passages in Homer'. Heyne sought the
same in Wood, then in Lechevalier. Pope writes: 'you may see his
Images rising more boldly about you, in the very Scenes of his story
and action; you may lay the immortal work on some broken column
of a Hero's Sepulcher, and read the Fall of Troy in the shade of a Trojan
Ruin'. His translation would be very much the worse, he said, from
not having been done in Asia.[4]

Wood's *Essay* is the fullest product of that wish to site the classical
text in its country of origin. Guys' is another emphasis, not uniquely
his (we see it in Riedesel too), but pursued by no one more thoroughly
and systematically. He is not so much concerned to elucidate the past
by means of the present, or the present by means of the past, but rather
to insist on continuity. So far we have met with such insistence chiefly,
almost solely, in the matter of landscape. Most travellers observed the
survival of physical features there since Homer's day, of localities
famous in poetry, and the more sentimentally minded derived some
consolation from this. But in the matter of manners and character, in the
question of their continuity, the most generally received view, especially
among Europeans at home, was that the modern Greeks had fallen away
utterly from the ancient and that all connection and continuity were lost.
This made for a powerful discrepancy between the surviving beauty of
the landscape and the irredeemably altered condition of its inhabitants.
A curious, presumably fictitious incident exactly illustrating the
derogatory view, is described by Guillet in his *Athènes ancienne et nouvelle*.
The author, or hero, and his companions, when regaling themselves
over the pitiable ignorance of their Greek hosts, are suddenly ashamed
to realize that the ignorance is feigned. The Greeks are deliberately

fulfilling the foreigners' low expectations, for their own private amusement. 'Il ne vient pas un seul Franc à Athènes', says a Greek monk in the party, 'qui voyant l'estat du pays si different de ce qu'il estoit, ne déplore notre condition' ('There is not a stranger comes to *Athens*, but observing the present condition of the Country, he deplores our misfortunes, with great expressions of sorrow').[5] That was in 1675. A century later Edward Gibbon, who had no more been to Greece than Guillet had, produced the classic statement of Western disdain: 'It would not be easy in the country of Plato and Demosthenes, to find a reader, or a copy, of their works. The Athenians walk with supine indifference among the glorious ruins of Antiquity; and such is the debasement of their character that they are incapable of admiring the genius of their predecessors.'[6] Such was the general view, and the uprising of 1770 (which gave Guys' book great topicality) only tended to confirm Western Europe in their poor opinion of the Greeks and was the occasion for much sentimental indignation in the newspapers of London and Paris. The modern Greeks have always had a hard time of it satisfying the largely inappropriate hopes of Western enthusiasts, particularly those from English public schools. If the view is that the modern Greeks are vile, then how else should one expect them to behave but vilely? Yet when they do – like Hyperion's men at Mistra – their detractors feel a terrible rage and disappointment.

Guys denied that they were wholly vile. He discerned much good in them. In fact his book, through three enlarging editions, performed something of an act of rehabilitation. By the Greeks themselves it was recognized as such and Guys was given the freedom of the city of Athens in thanks.[7] But by insisting on continuity, on the survival of much that was good in ancient times, Guys helped raise the expectations of the liberal West. It is a powerful incitement to revolution that the land itself survives (from a time when the idea of democracy was born); even more persuasive is the notion that the people too are alive – only dormant, only 'obscurcis par l'oppression' in Riedesel's phrase (*Remarques*, p. 201). Guys' book is thus a small contribution to the half-century-long recovery and preparation for the successful revolution of 1821 – a revolution that, though successful in that it drove out the Turks, still disappointed those Philhellenes who wanted Periclean Athens back again.

The thesis that there is more continuity in manners and character than has hitherto been supposed soon begins to mean that there is more good in the modern Greeks than has been supposed; since the past was universally thought to be excellent, proof of its survival into the present could not but raise the reputation of the modern Greeks. This needs some qualification: the Greeks always were untruthful, untrustworthy and quarrelsome, and are shown to be so still; but even here the fact of continuity – even the continuity of flaws – is itself encouraging and strengthens the whole thesis whose *Tendenz* is positive.

Guys states his intention at the outset: 'Je vous exposerai les traits de ressemblance que j'ai trouvés entre les anciens Grecs & les modernes' (1, 4) ('I will lay before you those strokes of resemblance I have found between the ancient and modern Greeks' (Eng. ed., 1, 4)). This intention distinguishes his book from those of previous travellers, whose attention was given wholly or mainly to the residual monuments of the great past:

M. Spon cherchoit Delphes au milieu de Delphes. Il n'en reste plus en effet, de traces; mais on y retrouve les Grecs, en les examinant de près. (1, 21)

M. Spon sought Delphos in the midst of Delphos itself. Indeed no traces of it are to be found, but the Greeks themselves are to be distinguished upon a slight examination. (Eng. ed., 1, 27; more accurately: 'upon a close examination')

Il est bon que les Voyageurs avides de retrouver... des monumens qui n'existent plus, sachent qu'à leur défaut les habitans des lieux qu'ils embellissoient, méritent encore notre attention. (1, 3)

It cannot but be pleasing to a curious traveller, searching in a country for monuments which no longer exist, to find that notwithstanding this defect, the inhabitants of the places those monuments once served to embellish, are still worthy of his most minute attention. (Eng. ed., 1, 3)

It is Montesquieu who encourages him to believe that the character of a people survives despite the interferences of history.[8] And the Greeks are conservative, they are not touched by the passing fads and fashions of Europe, they have kept themselves more intact than have the sophisticated peoples further west.

Guys had, like Riedesel and Wood, a nostalgia for the simple life. The rediscovery of Greece, to which he contributed, the rediscovery of good surviving in the modern Greeks, was part of sophisticated Europe's preoccupation in the late eighteenth century with childlike cultures from Canada to Tahiti, with the naive in literature, with childhood. Our disparagement of Greece, says Guys, is a factor of our own decline. Declined though they may be from their Golden Age, they are still closer to Nature than we are 'car on s'en éloigne en se civilisant'

Pierre Augustin Guys

(1, 102) ('the more a people become civilized the further they recede from it' (Eng. ed., 1, 119)).

Il faut étudier & suivre la nature pour la copier; il faut vivre avec ce Peuple, qui a conservé la simplicité des moeurs & des anciens usages, pour peindre ce bon vieux tems que nous sommes forcés de regretter, comme le siecle d'or tant vanté par les Poëtes. (1, 39)

He who would copy nature, must study and follow it. If he would paint the times which we look back upon with regret, as the golden age, so much boasted of by the poets, let him live with the Greeks, who have to this day preserved the simplicity of the manners and customs of the earliest periods. (Eng. ed., 1, 46)

They are passionate and honest in the expression of their sentiments: 'Que nous sommes froids en comparaison, parce que nous sommes trop façonnés & contrefaits à force d'art!' (1, 103) ('How cold and superficial our behaviour in comparison with this people's! We are indeed fashioned and new formed by the force of art, but nature has deserted us' (Eng. ed., 1, 120)). And among the Greeks, all as a nation comparatively simple, Guys looks for preference to the peasantry, since among them the old traditions – remnants of the Golden Age – survive clearest. There is, as in Riedesel and somewhat in Wood, a running comparison not only of ancient and modern Greeks, but also of an amalgam of them with ourselves, never to our advantage. On the Nausicaa episode in the *Odyssey* he comments: 'Telles étoient la simplicité & la sagesse des moeurs de l'ancien tems; nous en sommes aujourd'hui bien loin' (1, 54) ('such were the simplicity and good sense of ancient manners; we are far removed from them today' – this sentence is missing from the English translation).

The sense of loss and the longing usual in Hellenist travellers, nostalgia for the ancient Greek past, is of course also strong in Guys. It heightens a general melancholy à la Young in the chapter 'Les Ruines' of which the engraving, in the third edition, serves as illustration. The draughtsman and the writer do all they can to recover and preserve what vestiges remain among the ruins of time. The ancient sites and the modern Greeks themselves are analogous – in both traces remain, and more evidently in the latter, so Guys believed. But, like Riedesel, he used the metaphor of the archaeologist to describe his study of the people:

Regardez-moi comme un antiquaire, qui au lieu de négliger, comme tant d'autres voyageurs, une médaille de cuivre parce qu'elle est brute & mal conservée, prend la peine de la laver, de la nétoyer avec soin, & découvre enfin des caracteres qu'on croyoit

7   Frontispiece from the third edition of Guys' *Voyage littéraire*

entierement effacés, ou une tête, un revers rare & précieux. J'ai toute la satisfaction de cet antiquaire, lorsqu'en observant pas-à-pas le Grec moderne, & le comparant à l'ancien, dont j'ai tous les signalemens, je reconnois celui que je cherche. (1, 338–9)[9]

In every case consider me in the light of an antiquary, who, instead of disregarding a medal of copper, because it is rusty, and in a dirty condition, on the contrary, washes, cleanses it with care, and in the end discovers characters, which were totally concealed; and by the appearance of the head, or a rare and precious reverse, is, to his great satisfaction, enabled to elucidate some obscure passage in the history of ancient times.

The pleasure that results to me from these enquiries is no less transporting and solid. In tracing the modern Greeks, and comparing them with the ancients throughout every department of life I have had the satisfaction always to find a complete resemblance. (Eng. ed., 11, 137 – a very inaccurate version. This would be closer: 'Think of me as an antiquary who, instead of disregarding a copper coin because it is unpolished and in poor condition as many travellers would, takes the trouble to wash it and clean it carefully and finally discovers characters thought entirely effaced or a head or something rare and precious on the reverse. That antiquary's satisfaction is mine when, in my constant study of the modern Greeks and my comparison of them with the ancients (whose particulars are all known to me) I see the resemblance I am looking for.')

The picture thus recovered, though partial or defaced, substantiates an already conceived ideal. The modern Greeks, an approximation at the lost ideal (a fading after-image of it), are themselves, to the sophisticated European, an object of nostalgia and admiration. Past and present tend to merge for Guys, into one admirable condition – that of Nature – from which he himself, as a modern European, has fallen. (That despite his reputation as a man of probity and simple manners.)

At times Guys seems almost to have the Homeric world or the idylls of Theocritus before his eyes. Modern real people continue these ideal ancient forms, and he is separated from them not by an unbridgeable gulf of time but by the gulf, equally unbridgeable, that his culture makes. The ideal is not actually recovered, not for him, since ideals never can be. His way of looking is not unlike Werther's *vis-à-vis* the village girls in their Homeric simplicity. There isn't the intensity, of course, but the sentimental basis is the same.

An *idée fixe* can always be substantiated. Guys has no trouble assembling evidence to prove his point. He enlarged upon the idea through three editions and was preparing a fourth, with yet more material, when he died. He was aware that he might be thought to be nourishing a prejudice: 'Peut-être trop prévenu pour mon plan, vous paroîtrai-je forcer quelque-fois les ressemblances, pour rapprocher le Grec moderne de l'ancien' (1, 338) ('Perhaps, too much attached to my plan, I appear to you, as if some of the resemblances between ancient and modern Greece, were forced, and strained to gratify my own predilections' (Eng. ed., II, 136–7)). But really he had no doubts about the justness, indeed the obviousness of his parallel. Prejudice, he says, prejudice of an adverse kind, had caused previous travellers to overlook the obvious.

There are two areas of comparison, two lines in the proving of continuity: the one is customs and manners; the other, rather more difficult, is character. I shan't exhaust the list of Guys' examples since the point with every new one is the same. Among the customs and manners that he examines are: women at work, at their embroidery; dances; marriages and funerals; commerce and navigation. These were greatly expanded in the later editions, with essays by other hands, notably by Mme Chénier, the poet's mother, on dances and burials.

The method of comparison is first to establish what went on in ancient times, then to describe how things are now; and then to point the strong similarities. What the ancient practice was is established by reference to classical authors: to Terence, Virgil, Theocritus and, especially, Homer: 'Consultons Homere, qui, pour les usages & les moeurs, sera toujours la plus pure source de toute l'Antiquité Grecque' (I, 335) ('In consulting Homer upon the customs of the primitive Greeks, we have the purest source of knowledge on that head, ever before us' (Eng. ed., II, 133)). This will often suffice, and since Guys is himself an eye-witness of how things are now he can conclude: 'Voyez, dans la quatorziéme Idylle de Théocrite, la description d'un repas rustique à la Grecque: c'est un tableau fidéle de ce qu'on voit aujourd'hui' (I, 123) ('Theocritus in his fourteenth Idyll, gives the description of a rural feast, which is the exact representation of a modern repast' (Eng. ed., I, 143)). But other authorities, modern ones, are also frequently cited to establish that past with which the present is to be compared. They are eighteenth-century writers on classical matters, such as le comte de Caylus and, very often, Mme Dacier; but above all Winckelmann. Guys, as an eye-witness of the present, valued strongly visual depictions of the past, such as he found in the ancient poets, and real images, such as Winckelmann collected and commentated in his *Description des pierres gravées* and *Monumenti inediti*. The correlation between (almost the interchangeability of) the literary and the pictorial or plastic arts seemed self-evident to eighteenth-century archaeologists and aestheticians, until Lessing. Homer was the great Painter – Caylus, in the *Tableaux tirés d'Homère* – praised him for precisely that – *ut pictura poesis* went without saying, and the two arts, poetry and painting (or sculpture), were used for the elucidation of the one by the other. Guys is very much in that line:

On sait que la Poésie & la Peinture se sont toujours aidées mutuellement par les images qu'elles se fournissent l'une à l'autre. Homère a dû sur-tout faire de grands Peintres, parce qu'il l'étoit lui-même, & parce qu'il ne voyoit, ne sentoit, ne peignoit que la Nature. (II, 57–8)

We know that poetry and painting have ever been mutual assistants, by the images they have furnished to each other. Homer may indeed be called the father of painting, and claim the honour of having formed the greatest proficients in that art; everything he described, he saw, felt, and painted from nature. (Eng. ed., III, 67)

He deals in vignettes, in tableaux. The images offered on gems, coins or reliefs – published and explained by Winckelmann – suited his purpose peculiarly well. They matched what he could abstract from Theocritus or Homer, and those extracts themselves pleasingly matched the tableaux he discovered in the villages and fields of modern Greece. Thus at a country dance he recalls to mind the Dance of the Hours as depicted on a relief published by Winckelmann in the *Monumenti inediti*; and discovering evidence of continuity in a kind of chair that has not changed its form since ancient times he refers, for proof, to a gem in the Stosch collection (II, 46 and I, 33). We see the books that Guys himself purchased from the author thus being constructively used.

Even better suited to Guys' purpose, and systematically used by him, were the collections issuing from Pompeii and Herculaneum. These magnificent folios, which the wealthy merchant Guys could afford for his personal library, serve throughout chapters 25, 26 and 27 of his first volume as a basis for the parallel and comparison. He recognizes, particularly in the wall-paintings, many details, especially of dress, whose survival he had noted during his travels through Greece. Some of the dresses, being transparent, were for his modesty rather too alarming: ' Je ne m'étendrai pas d'avantage sur un sujet trop dangereux à traiter – N'imitons pas trop les Anciens' (I, 378) ('I shall say no more of this subject: it is of too dangerous a nature to dwell upon. Let us not follow the ancients in their vices' (Eng. ed., II, 180 – then follows a moralistic expansion of Guys' text)). Perhaps Emma Hart wore such a one in her *poses plastiques*.

Finally, there is one authority whom we might be surprised to see among the classical scholars and the archaeologists, and that is Racine.

Guys cites him frequently as an 'imitateur exact & fidèle des coutumes de l'ancienne Grece' (I, 264) ('a faithful and exact imitator of the customs of ancient Greece' (Eng. ed., II, 53)) on all sorts of matters: on Greek jewellery and dress – 'Que ces vains ornements, que ces voiles me pèsent!' ('how this vain finery and how these veils oppress me!') (*Phèdre*, I.iii). On the situation of Greek cemeteries outside the town – 'Aux portes de Trézène, et parmi ces tombeaux' ('at the gates of Troezen, among the tombs') (*Phèdre*, V.i); and, with extensive quotation from *Mithridate*, *Andromaque* and *Iphigénie*, on Greek patriotism and love of home (*Voyage*, I, 62, 264; II, 181–3).

It seems odd to us, but is quite characteristic of the age, that Racine should be used, like an amalgam of honorary ancient and contemporary classicist, as an authority for how things were in classical times.

Chief eye-witness of how things are now in Greece is Guys himself, but being both a modest and a well-read man he continually substantiates his own observations with those of contemporaries and predecessors in Greece. The list of these authorities is long: he was clearly very knowledgeable in the literature. He cites Belon (on the beauty of Greek eyes), Spon, Rycaut, Smith, Tournefort, Lady Montagu, Leroy and, in later editions, Wood. Also Peysonnel, the French Consul in Smyrna, doubtless a personal acquaintance, whom both Chandler and Choiseul-Gouffier refer to with respect. Guys' own experience was wide and sound and these authors are used to corroborate it. This gives both fullness and persuasiveness to the argument. His English translator (1772) lays great emphasis on the book's authenticity (too many, he says, are 'manufactured in the closet, and obtruded for originals upon the world'). It is pleasant then to see among Guys' authorities the ingenious Guillet de Saint-George. But Guys refers to him as one 'qui a voulu faire, ainsi que moi, la comparaison des Grecs modernes avec les Anciens' (II, 79–80) ('I shall not go so far in my comparisons of the ancient with the modern Greeks, as a brother author, who is also my countryman, has done' (Eng. ed., III, 94)).

The continuity of customs and manners is easier to prove than that of national character, since the former may be observed by an eye-witness now, and visual depictions abound in ancient literature and the plastic arts. Still, in the latter also a comparison between ancient and modern is possible. A Greek national character may be deduced from ancient literature, particularly satirical drama and history; and what the Greeks are like nowadays, how they behave, what their temperament is, a traveller through their country will be able to say. To begin with the worst:

... j'ai trouvé les Grecs tels que nous les peignent leurs Historiens, & Thucydide sur-tout, artificieux, vains, souples, inconstans, avides de gain, amateurs de la nouveauté, peu scrupuleux sur les sermens, &c. (I, 20)

I have found them, I confess, such as they are represented by ancient historians, Thucydides in particular; artful, vain, flexible, inconstant, avaritious, lovers of novelty, and not very scrupulous observers of their oaths. (Eng. ed., I, 25)

That might seem rather damning, and not the sort of verdict for which one would be awarded the freedom of the city of Athens. The book as a whole, however, is anything but an indictment of the Greek national character. The author's deference, as an over-sophisticated European, will not allow him to think worse of the Greeks than he does of his own nation:

... ce Peuple, tout léger qu'il est, tout amateur de la nouveauté qu'on le représente avec raison, n'a pourtant jamais dépendu, comme nous, des caprices & de l'inconstance de la mode qui nous subjugue. (I, 116)

... this people, flighty as they are, and lovers of novelty ... have notwithstanding, always resisted the absurd caprice and inconstancy of fashion, which so eminently prevails with us. (Eng. ed., I, 135–6)

They are mendacious – *Graecia mendax* – like their ancestors, (so Terence and Plautus and Racine depict them); and quarrelsome among themselves. Enslavement has degraded them, as it does any man and any nation. But much of what was good in their national character survives: piety in the family; hospitality to strangers; here and there at least, deep in the Peloponnese and on certain of the islands, the old love of liberty and a fierce patriotism. It is the continuation of these latter qualities that most encourages the hope of revolution. Add to them a spontaneity and a simplicity that Europeans have long since forfeited and the modern Greeks easily become, to imaginations excited by Rousseau, one of those model races like the Swiss, the Corsicans, the Tahitians or the Huron Indians. And because of their thoroughly documented glorious past and their still existent beautiful native land the Greeks hold a peculiar and tantalizing power. When the race survives with its language and the famous places, many with their old names, the temptation to evoke and to reimpose the past is well-nigh irresistible. So the Greeks suffered now adulation and now contempt. Too much survives in Greece, the mind is continually lured towards the ideal there, and so continually disappointed. Guys was a writer who increased yet further the persuasive power of Greece, and so her power to disappoint.

In the second volume of his book, for the first four letters, Guys applies his belief in the continuity of Greek customs and character to one particular topic: the arts. He writes with great enthusiasm; in fact his ideas run away with him. Nowhere in the book is Guys' extreme, even slightly foolish but always sympathetic passion for Greece more apparent than in these chapters. He writes as an amateur, but one well read in the literature on the subject. Webb, Caylus, Mariette, Mme Dacier and Winckelmann are the modern authorities he refers to; and Winckelmann is, I think, his nearest. What Guys writes is not new, but it is in any case difficult to ascribe the first authorship of ideas among the numerous writers on aesthetics in the latter half of the eighteenth century. Guys' letters 'Sur les Arts' are interesting and amusing chiefly for their author's personal and idiosyncratic application of current ideas. He reads like a man who has seen the *truth* of certain academic theories with his own eyes. Not one among his authorities had been to Greece. Their speculations in the study and his real experience of the country's landscape, climate, customs and people are an odd but potent mixture. It is as though he realized with his own senses on the spot the correctness of Winckelmann's *Gedancken über die Nachahmung*. And this *is* odd, since Winckelmann and the others were writing about the production of art in ancient times, by Praxiteles, Phidias, Apelles and Zeuxis; but Guys, there in the land itself in the middle of the eighteenth century, has an amusingly intense apprehension of how beauty at least *might* be produced still, here and now.

It will, I think, easily be appreciated why Guys, obsessed with continuity, should be drawn to deal with aesthetics at such enthusiastic length. The writers whom he cites, and Winckelmann the clearest, believed that the Greeks were aided in their production of beauty by peculiarly congenial circumstances. First the climate. Winckelmann writes:

Der gute Geschmack ... hat sich angefangen zuerst unter dem griechischen Himmel zu bilden. Alle Erfindungen fremder Völker kamen gleichsam nur als der erste Same nach Griechenland und nahmen eine andere Natur und Gestalt an in dem Lande, welches Minerva, sagt man, vor allen Ländern, wegen der gemäßigten Jahreszeiten, die sie hier angetroffen, den Griechen zur Wohnung angewiesen, als ein Land, welches kluge Köpfe hervorbringen würde.[10]

To the Greek climate we owe the production of TASTE ... Every invention, communicated by foreigners to that nation, was but the seed of what it became afterwards, changing both its nature and size in a country, chosen, as *Plato* says, by Minerva, to be inhabited by the Greeks, as productive of every kind of genius. (Fusseli's translation (London 1765), pp. 1–2 – omits 'wegen der gemäßigten Jahreszeiten' ('on account of its temperate climate'); and 'size' should be 'form'.)

Climate survives: 'Le même Soleil qui éclaira autrefois la Grèce, y brille toujours sans nuages, tandis qu'il laisse croupir tant d'autres peuples dans les brouillards épais qui les environnent' (II, 18) ('The same sun which formerly enlivened this country, continues to shine with undiminished splendor, while so many other nations are environed with fogs and a clouded atmosphere' (Eng. ed., III, 21)).

It is true that other conducive conditions no longer obtain. The ancient Greeks had no horror of nudity; artists had ample opportunity, at the games, in the gymnasium, in the baths, to see the human body naked:

Die Schule der Künstler war in den Gymnasien, wo die jungen Leute ... ganz nackend ihre Leibesübungen trieben. Der Weise, der Künstler gingen dahin ... Die schönsten jungen Leute tanzten unbekleidet auf dem Theater ... Phryne badete sich bei den Eleusinischen Spielen vor den Augen aller Griechen ... und man weiß, daß die jungen Mädchen in Sparta an einem gewissen Feste ganz nackend vor den Augen der jungen Leute tanzten ...

Also war auch ein jedes Fest bei den Griechen eine Gelegenheit für Künstler, sich mit der schönen Natur aufs genaueste bekannt zu machen.[11]

The Gymnasies, where ... the youths exercised themselves naked, were the schools of art. These the philosopher frequented, as well as the artist ...

The fairest youths danced undressed on the theatre ... *Phryne* went to bathe at the Eleusinian games, exposed to the eyes of all Greece ... During certain solemnities the young Spartan maidens danced naked before the young men ...

Then every solemnity, every festival, afforded the artist opportunity to familiarize himself with all the beauties of Nature. (Fusseli, pp. 9–11)

Guys follows exactly:

Les Artistes Grecs s'étant soumis à une scrupuleuse imitation de la nature & à ne s'en écarter jamais, n'ont pû manquer de dessiner correctement, mais ils ont eu avec cela des secours qui nous manquent. La nudité des bains leur a fourni des idées justes & précises de la beauté du corps, & de cette fleur de jeunesse qu'ils exprimoient si bien. Ils avoient encore des Athlètes & des Luteurs qui les mettoient en état d'étudier tous les mouvemens des nerfs, le jeu des muscles, & l'emmanchement des membres; des objets nobles & agréables étoient sans cesse sous leurs yeux. C'étoit des modèles qu'ils étoient partout à portée d'observer utilement & de surprendre dans les attitudes les plus avantageuses. (II, 25–6)

The Greek artists having laid it down as a rule, to copy nature exactly, without ever deviating from her, could not fail to design correctly in every instance: They had beside other advantages which we have not. The opportunity of seeing men and women go into the baths, at all times, have furnished them with the most precise and just ideas of the beauties of the human body, and of that floridness of youth so well expressed in their works. They had likewise the further advantage of the wrestlers and the *Athletae*, from whom they studied the movements of the nerves, the play of the muscles, and the inflexions of the limbs; the most noble and agreeable objects were perpetually before them. They watched for these models of imitation, in order to surprise and observe them in the most advantageous situations. (Eng. ed., III, 30–1)

Guys notes with cautious regret (cautious because he is after all a decently Christian man) that such freedom no longer exists:

...une Religion sainte, la plus propre à réformer les moeurs, à réprimer les passions, pour mettre, dans un climat dangereux, la chasteté à couvert des occasions & des chûtes, avoit... borné les progrès des Arts, en proscrivant les nudités. (II, 2)

...the catholic religion, (a system, the best adapted to repress the passions, correct the manners, and screen chastity from seduction in such a dangerous climate;) I say, our holy religion had already proscribed the use of naked figures, and of course very much impeded the progress of the arts. (Eng. ed., III, 2)

The Muslim objection to any depiction of the human form, combining with a Christian horror of the body itself, militates massively against the production of an art such as the Greeks formerly achieved.

Men more radical than Guys at this point in the argument expressed their love of Greece by frankly repudiating the 'pale Galilean'. Christ appears as the skeleton at the Greek feast; life thereafter diminishes in colour and gaiety. Schiller laments the crossing of this threshold in his poem 'Die Götter Griechenlands', Goethe in his 'Die Braut von Korinth'. And in the latter poem, as *passim* in Heinse, it is the loss of the old sexual freedom that is chiefly regretted. Goethe, in his 'Roman Elegies', was able to recover triumphantly a pagan ease of body and soul; Heinse for his part produced illustrations, shocking to his public, of those aesthetic-cum-sexual ideals stated defiantly by Winckelmann and repeated rather nervously by Guys. Thus in *Ardinghello* a discussion between the hero and a fellow-artist (a modern Greek) proceeds to the usual vehement regret that the days of public nakedness are over:

Man kann wohl sagen, daß die Werke der alten griechischen Meister eine Frucht ihrer Gymnasien waren, und daß, wo diese nicht sind, sie schwerlich kann eingeerntet werden. Der erfahrne und geübte Sinn des ganzen Volks am Nackenden, dies ist die Hauptsache, die uns fehlt, nebst dem der Arbeiter selbst; das schönste Nackende der Kunst wird endlich nur durch Erinnerung geschaffen und genossen.[12]

(It is fair to assert that the works of the ancient Greek masters were a product of their gymnasia and that where these are lacking such works will scarcely be produced. That sense which was tried and tested on nakedness and shared by the whole people, is what we lack most; as well as the same sense in our craftsmen themselves. Our best work nowadays, in the depiction of nakedness, is done and enjoyed only through memory.)

Then, rather like Guys in the impulse to assert continuity nevertheless but unlike him in being boldly unambiguous, Heinse concludes his 'academic' debate on the conditions of ancient and modern art by having its participants stage with their models – 'echte Römerinnen an Wuchs und Gestalt, mit der erhabnen antiken, noch republikanischen Gesichtsbildung' ('true women of Rome in stature and form, lofty, classical and still republican in their looks') – a bacchanal, at first in antique costume and finally in none at all. The Hellenic Ideal, in this version, becomes a matter of personal energy and morality, and might thus indeed be realized in the here and now. Guys himself, insisting on continuity, is perhaps, like most of the Hellenists, half-hoping he might *realize*, in the present, ideals best imagined in the terms of a distant past. His interest in Greece is not antiquarian, and for that reason he may be included, with Wood, in the company of more obviously creative writers.

Having admitted that his modern Greeks no longer enjoy, in the matter of sexual morality, the pagan open air, Guys has then to admit that they have lost their political liberty too. Thus doubly deprived, what hope have they of ever achieving anything in the arts? Conditions could scarcely be less propitious:

Les Grecs ne peignent plus comme autrefois, parce qu'ils ont perdu leur liberté; & l'esclave du despotisme (le plus doux peut-être) content de jouir de ce qu'on lui laisse posseder, s'accoutume par l'habitude, à ne rien voir au-delà. (II, 9)

(The Greeks no longer paint as they once did, for they have lost their liberty; and the slave under a despotism he seems almost to welcome contents himself with what he is permitted to possess and grows accustomed, by habit, to seeing nothing beyond that.) (This should be English ed., III, 11 but the long paragraph in the French ed. at II, 9–10 is not translated.)

'And yet, and yet...', Guys says. What *can* he say? Certainly not that anything *has* been achieved. He resorts instead to saying that it might be, the potential is still there, the material, only awaiting the artist. He, for one, cannot believe as Winckelmann did (when he wrote the *Gedancken* at least, before he got to Italy) that there is actually less beauty in the world now than there was then. Guys, the merchant, to his eternal credit, was obviously interested in a good deal more than the cloths and currants he shipped. Quite simply the Greek sunshine persuades him, as did the Roman sunshine Goethe and Heinse, that valuable traces of the ancient miracle remain. Climate survives, and in it beautiful women:

En Grèce, un air pur, un climat doux, des jours sereins m'annoncent à chaque instant, que je vais découvrir les Vénus de Praxitèle & d'Apelle, les formes les plus régulières, des yeux noirs, vifs, animés d'un feu naturel, des tailles élégantes & majestueuses, un habillement simple & léger qui laisse voir toute la beauté du corps, & qui ne cache aucun défaut. Telles sont les femmes Grecques. (II, 18)

The pureness of the air, the softness of the climate, the serenity of the day, inspire ideas superior to any thing, but the objects to be met with in this country. Every woman I meet conveys to my imagination a Venus from the chisel of a Praxiteles, or the pencil of an Apelles; a regular form; black sparkling eyes animated with natural fire; a shape, elegant and majestic; a plain dress, with robes of the finest transparent stuff, so contrived to discover the beautiful symmetry of the body and limbs. Such are the women of Greece. (Eng. ed., III, 21–2 – this is pretty free. The latter part of his first sentence is an invention; '& qui ne cache aucun défaut' is omitted – 'and hides no defect': which might mean that the women's physical flaws are all revealed, or that they have none.)

That is the tone of these chapters. What Guys is doing, in his naive and enthusiastic fashion, is to bring together numerous images in his memory. Some are remembered from the world of art: gems, reliefs, engravings of statues and wall-paintings, as well as 'scenes' from Homer, Theocritus and Virgil. And others are the *tableaux vivants* he has come across on his travels. The images in art are from the glorious past, the tableaux exist still in the present thought hopelessly mediocre. That is what he means when he says, repeatedly, that the models, the material, still exist. The works themselves – he says it again and again – have gone from Greece. They are in Rome if anywhere, in museums, in folios such as he himself acquired. But 'on peut du moins reconnoître encore, dans l'ancienne Patrie des Arts, quelques modèles de ces ouvrages inimitables' (II, 3) ('yet it must be acknowledged that in this country, the ancient seat of the arts, there still remain some models of those inimitable works' (Eng. ed., III, 3)). We have, partially at least, scattered and fragmented, the products of the past; but we also have their surviving models, their material:

Je voudrois . . . opposer aux plus beaux tableaux trouvés récemment à Herculanum . . . à ceux même qu'ont décrits Pausanias & Lucien, les tableaux vivans, animés, qui pourroient continuer de servir de modèles aux Peintres, aux Sculpteurs & aux Poëtes de l'ancienne Grèce, s'ils reparoissoient. (II, 3–4)

I would willingly oppose to the finest paintings lately discovered at Herculaneum, and even to those described by Pausanias and Lucian . . . the striking scenes before me. These might serve as models to the painters, sculptors, and poets of ancient Greece, were they to appear again in the world. (Eng. ed., III, 4)

He discerns, with the eye of faith, 'sous le même Ciel, le même génie qui fit autrefois les Peintres & les Poëtes' (II, 4) ('in the same climate the very identical genius which formed the masters so renowned in Greece for the practice of the arts' (Eng. ed., III, 5)). The four chapters are then filled with remembered 'tableaux vivans & modèles animés' seen or imagined on his travels and compared then or since with their images in art. An irreproachably respectable *voyeur*, he follows 'une jeune beauté Grecque' through the stages of her day: her *lever*, her toilette, her siesta, even her bath (twice), her dancing etc. Emma Hart comes to mind again. I wonder if M. Guys ever saw her perform. In all the poses of his young Greek beauty the Hellenist observer recognizes great equivalents or archetypes in the world of classical art.

One entire letter – no. 33 – is given over to the difficult matter of imitation and idealization, of how the artist works when he contemplates Nature. This is a familiar topic, one touched on by Wood: whether the artist simply copied or whether it was necessary in some way to improve upon beautiful Nature. In Winckelmann and Webb – and Guys follows them – the solution is the same: the artist is able, in the state of creative excitement, to imagine something surpassing even the beauties he has before him. By this process of idealization, in Winckelmann's view, the best Greek art was produced:

> Diese häufigen Gelegenheiten zur Beobachtung der Natur veranlaßten die griechischen Künstler noch weiter zu gehen: sie fingen an, sich gewisse allgemeine Begriffe von Schönheiten sowohl einzelner Teile als ganzer Verhältnisse der Körper zu bilden, die sich über die Natur selbst erheben sollten; ihr Urbild war eine bloß im Verstande entworfene geistige Natur.[13]

> These frequent occasions of observing Nature, taught the Greeks to go on still farther. They began to form certain general ideas of beauty, with regard to the proportions of the inferiour parts, as well as of the whole frame: these they raised above the reach of mortality, according to the superiour model of some ideal nature. (Fusseli, p. 12)

This may mean, as Zeuxis is said to have done, collecting into one image beauties that Nature has scattered (the various charms of five different girls in Zeuxis' case). Raphael did likewise for his Galathea. He says of his working method (in Guys' words): 'je supplée à ce qui me manque par un effort de mon imagination & par une idée sublime qui me saisit' (II, 40) ('I was obliged to supply the defects, by an extraordinary effort of my own imagination, and by a sublime idea which then took possession of me' (Eng. ed., III, 46)).

Guys comes close to suggesting, since everywhere he looks in Greece exciting models abound, that the crucial degree between imitation and idealization, between what the eye sees and what the imagination adds, is not so very mysterious and difficult after all. If the artistic productions of the past are compared with the still existent models in the present (subtracting the latter from the former, so to speak) it will be obvious what the imagination has added. We are left wondering why, by so transparent a process, great art is not produced non-stop, day in, day out, in Greece where the climate is so congenial and where models not inferior to those which Phidias had are everywhere to be contemplated. When Winckelmann wrote that our only way to become great, or inimitable, was to imitate the ancients, he had in mind our modern disadvantaged condition *vis-à-vis* Nature. The Greek statue, being a crystallization, through the idealizing process, of Nature's disparate beauties, would serve us moderns better as model, since Nature herself, particularly human beauty, had fallen off since ancient times; or at least, because of Northern Christianity, had become less available. Though he quotes with apparent approval Caylus saying much the same, Guys in fact operates a reversal of this dictum. The statues are no longer available, at least not in Greece; but, overlooked, Nature's beauties are. Therefore, look to them.

These letters on the arts were obviously important to Guys. They seemed to him perfectly a part of his central purpose. The greatest achievement of the ancient Greeks was artistic, and in his praiseworthy wish to discern survivals of the ancient in the modern world it is natural that he should dwell at length on the arts. Since the artistic achievement of the modern Greeks was negligible he turned his attention from the actual to the potential and discovered in the country a more than sufficient beauty only awaiting its artists. Finding in the ordinary life of the modern people tableaux fit, he believed, to be set beside the ancient works of art is a generous act of connection and continuity.

The Greeks liked the book, and so did Catherine the Great, busy, at the time of its publication, interfering in the affairs of Greece. In the *Avertissement* to the third edition Guys boasts modestly of her approval, and looks forward to her ultimate victory in Greece. He sent Voltaire a copy too, with a poem, and had a poem back in reply, from Fernay, dated 22 December 1776, beginning: 'Le bon Vieillard très-inutile,/Que vous nommez Anacréon...' ('That superannuated gent/You call Anacreon...'). Altogether the greatly augmented third edition gives us a fuller picture of M. Guys the Merchant, Antiquary and Man of Letters. It has a 'Discours sur l'utilité réciproque du Commerce & des Lettres', an essay on Tibullus and translations of his least offensive elegies. And also Guys' own verses. These, it must be said, are uninspired. The longest piece is in the manner of Gresset – 'Les Saisons', composed at Naples in the French Ambassador's house, not far from Virgil's tomb. It is packed with classical allusions, and is as far away in spirit from Greece, ancient or modern, as Gresset himself. But that was the idiom most readily available to a man who, though a classicist and a lover of Greece, was poetically quite unoriginal. It is

unlikely that he felt the Rococo prettiness inappropriate, any more than
Winckelmann felt Geßner out of place at Paestum, or Riedesel Gresset
among the islands. In 'Les Souvenirs' Guys remembers his travels, but
only in a stylized way:

> j'ai vu les bords
> Du Nil, & de la mer d'Icare;
> Je m'en souviendrai chez les morts.
> Danses de Crète, & de Thésée,
> Bois d'Idalie, ombrages fraix,
> J'emporterai dans l'Elisée,
> Et votre Image, & mes regrets.

> (I have seen
> The banks of the Nile and the sea of Icarus;
> I shall remember them among the dead.
> Cretan dances, dances of Theseus,
> Idalian woods, refreshing shade,
> I shall take with me into Elyseum
> Wishful memories of you.)

Of them all I like best his verses celebrating 'La Maison de Campagne
du Marseillois'. This summer retreat of his is only twenty minutes'
walk from the Bourse. He has a view of pines, vines and the sea. 'Sous
un Berceau, réduit champêtre, / Je lis Horace le matin...' ('There in
the arbour, quiet in the country, / I spend my mornings reading
Horace...'). He has around him busts of the poets and a few bits and
pieces picked up on his travels:

> Beaux Arts, c'est pour vos favoris,
> Qu'autour de ma maison rustique,
> De ces Lares que je chéris,
> J'ai rassemblé quelques débris
> De Rome, & de la Grèce antique.

> (Fine arts, for your favourites
> Around my house in the country
> Like beloved household gods
> I have assembled a few fragments
> Of Rome and Ancient Greece.)

Winckelmann said of him that he cared more for books than his
accounts, but really Guys seems to have combined both pursuits
admirably. He was a generous lover of the country he worked and
travelled in, and a man in whom current enthusiasms were very happily
incorporated.

8

THE INSURRECTION OF 1770

The insurrection of 1770 is dealt with very briefly in histories of Greece. It came to nothing and was in any case a Russian rather than a Greek affair. Catherine the Great inherited Czar Peter's desire to have Constantinople from the Turks, to be the metropolis of the Orthodox faith; and Turkey furthermore blocked Russia's egress to the south. Thus it was against Turkey and only incidentally for the benefit of Greece that Catherine began her intrigues in the mid-1760s. Her agents in Greece induced the inhabitants to believe that, were they to rise, Russia, with massive force, would help them to their independence. Catherine's intentions seem to have been generally well understood in Europe. Voltaire, writing to her at the end of 1769, prophesied that Constantinople would be her new capital before very long.[1] Persuaded that her preliminary work had been successful and that Greece, ripe for rebellion, was ready to serve Russian ends in the Bosphorus and the Aegean, she despatched her fleet, in two squadrons, under the high command of Count Alexis Orloff, into Greek waters.

When the Russians arrived, the rising in the Peloponnese began. Successes against the Turks were, however, short-lived and characterized by indiscriminate atrocity. Albanian irregulars, in the service of Turkey, soon put the insurgents down; and when the Russians withdrew the Greeks were left to suffer, for years, terrible reprisals. A great Russian victory was won off Tchesmé, near Chios; two British officers, Dugdale and Mackenzie, led an attack with fire-ships by which the Turkish fleet in harbour was wholly destroyed. But Orloff neglected his advantage thereafter.

Historically the insurrection of 1770 is not very important, only one brief passage in the interminable rivalry and warfare of Russia and Turkey. For the Greeks there was no hope in it. Fifty years later, after the American and the French Revolutions and when Ottoman power had been further eroded, the auspices were much better. At the time however the Russian expedition into the Aegean did excite considerable interest, and Orloff's progress was closely followed in the European press.

The *London Magazine* offered its readers in June 1770 'an accurate map of the Morea and the Islands, with the neighbouring countries in Greece, being the seat of war between the Russians and the Turks'. The *Gentleman's Magazine* in the following month did likewise, and gave besides, quoting Tournefort, 'a description of the Morea and the chief cities'. Readers were thus enabled to follow and visualize the campaign as it was reported, almost daily but after a time-lag of about four weeks, in despatches from Italy and Turkey. They read accounts – as confused, contradictory, exaggerated or downright false as such accounts generally are – of the sieges of Coron and Modon, of the taking and loss of Mistra, the rout at Tripolis and the victory off Tchesmé. And it was repeatedly noted that both sides were conducting the war with great savagery: 'the ravages committed by both armies . . . are dreadful . . . horrid cruelties perpetrated in cold blood, shocking to human nature'; 'the war is carried on with much Bloodshed and Horror'. When the Greeks got the upper hand they settled old scores; when the Turks and Albanians reasserted themselves they were merciless: recapturing Patras, they left scarcely anyone alive. After Tchesmé Greeks were butchered in the streets of Smyrna. The Russians stoked the fires, paying a bounty of two sequins for every Turkish head.[2]

Public interest in these foreign affairs was the greater and was charged with a particular sentiment because the setting of the encounter between Russia and Turkey was Greece; and because, ostensibly at least, one issue in the fighting was the liberation of Greece. Though nothing like so strong and influential as the Philhellenism of the early nineteenth century the feelings aroused in 1769 and sustained throughout 1770 were essentially the same, and they indicate the hopes and expectations that neo-classical Europe was beginning to cherish with respect to the real homeland of their literary, aesthetic, moral and political ideals. The travellers and scholars with whom I have so far concerned myself were all more or less the carriers of such expectations. Guys and Riedesel, in Greece before the insurrection but publishing after it, contributed, in a small way no doubt, to that confidence through which historical change finally comes about.

In 1770 the first glimmering of the idea of Greek independence excited untoward hopes. The press, though well aware that the real issue lay between Russia and Turkey, dreamed, like Byron half a century later, 'that Greece once more was free' – or about to be: 'all Greece is ready to shake off the Turkish yoke', 'the Inhabitants of Lacedemonia wait only the Arrival of the [Russian] Fleet to act in Concert with them against the Porte'. Equally confident reports had been gathered from the north, from Crete, and from the islands: 'upon the first appearance of the Russian fleet in the Archipelago, the Grecian islands will all revolt'. Everywhere, it was asserted, Greeks were ready to lay hold of this favourable opportunity. The Turks were said to be 'under the panic of an ancient prophesy, that their empire shall be overthrown by a power from the North'.[3]

The revival in newspaper reports of the old names – Lacedemonia, Peloponnesus – is a mark of the particular colouring of these hopes for Greece. The inhabitants of those regions were continually measured against their supposed ancestors. They performed on a public stage, and inevitably failed to meet their audience's demands.

This very widespread literary–sentimental view of the war in Greece may be seen at its crassest in Voltaire's letters to Catherine the Great. His hopes were from the start flatteringly excessive. He seems to have taken at face value her statement that she looked upon it as a religious duty to free the Greeks from Turkish slavery. He imagines them (his 'beloved' Greeks) enjoying full liberty under her protection. In a curious flight of fancy he begs her, the champion of Orthodoxy, to give them their old gods again: 'Rendez aux pauvres Grecs leur Jupiter, leur Mars, leur Venus; ils n'ont eu de la réputation que sous ces dieux là' ('give the poor Greeks their Jupiter, Mars and Venus again; they had some standing under those gods, but never since'). She would revive the Isthmian and the Olympian Games, she would rebuild Troy, she would promenade 'en bateau' up the Scamander, and in grateful thanks 'on vous ferait une Catheriniade, les Zeuxis et les Phidias couvriraient la terre de vos images' ('you would have an epic written in your honour, the descendants of Zeuxis and Phidias would cover the earth with your image'). To this doting flattery or facetiousness Catherine replied as she knew he wanted her to: with Hellenist sentiment and statements of altruistic intent: 'Voilà la Grece au point de redevenir libre . . . on entend avec plaisir nomer le lieu dont on nous a tant battu les oreilles dans notre enfance' ('so Greece is about to be free again . . . it is a pleasure to hear that country spoken of whose name we had dinned into our ears as children').[4] She had promised her lover Gregory Orloff a principality in the about-to-be-liberated Ancient World, and several of her officers must indeed have believed the rhetoric and thought of themselves as agents in the revival of Hellas. A young Ukrainian by the name of Tamara, whom she sent on ahead of her forces to prepare the revolt, had already been in Greece as a tourist and was a confirmed enthusiast. Others like him took advantage of their presence in the country to acquire archaeological remains for the ornamentation of their houses and parks at home. (Some inadvertent archaeology was done by the common soldiers digging in at Mistra.[5])

It does not seem likely that Catherine, despite her pandering to Voltaire, really cared very much for the Hellenic Ideal. But scholars and artists and a large part of the educated public in France, Germany and England certainly did; and when their disproportionate hopes were not realized they felt a disappointment mixed with indignation and with contempt for the modern Greeks who had, so to speak, let educated Europe down. Catherine blamed them outright: they had proved themselves unworthy of Russia's generous aid (that is, they had been less useful to Russian purposes than she had hoped):

Les Grecs, les Spartiates, ont bien dégénéré, ils aiment la rapine mieux que la liberté. Ils sont perdu à jamais s'ils ne profitent point des dispositions et des conseils du héros que je leur ai envoyé.

(The Greeks and Spartans are much degenerated, they love pillage more than liberty. They are lost for ever if they will not let themselves be helped by the hero I have sent them and will not heed his advice.)

And Voltaire, aging sycophant, followed suit. The Athenians were, he said, 'les plus pauvres poltrons du continent' ('the vilest cowards in all the Levant'). They had a place in his heart only because of their great ancestors. Finally he cast them out altogether:

Mon ... chagrin c'est que les Grecs soient indignes de la liberté qu'ils auraient recouvrée s'ils avaient eu le courage de vous seconder. Je ne veux plus lire ni Sophocle, ni Homère, ni Démosthène.[6]

(It grieves me that the Greeks are unworthy of the liberty they would have recovered had they had the courage to support you. I shall give up reading Sophocles, Homer and Demosthenes.)

The newspapers and periodicals were not less harsh: 'the Conduct of the Greeks, instead of favouring the Operations of the Russians, throws difficulties in the Way. The Maniotes (the ancient Lacedemonians) have given at Patras a Proof of their pretended Valour.' They abandoned their positions because of heavy rain, the paper claimed, and so let in the Turks. Their cowardice at Tripolis, their selfish rapacity at Modon and Mistra and other occasions of disgrace were indignantly reported. In October, by which time the campaign in the Morea had been fought and lost, the *St James' Chronicle* published a long letter as an eye-witness testimony and indictment of Greek behaviour. They had come aboard the Russian ships, the correspondent writes, 'making Protestations of Friendship; but we have since found them to be the greatest Villains in the World; they wait for our beating the Turks, that they may take the Plunder'.[7] The summary of the year's events published in the *Gentleman's Magazine* is worth quoting at length. The writer's indignation is palpable. He compares the modern Greeks unfavourably both with their ancestors and with their Russian allies:

On the first appearance of the Russian succours, the Greeks, who had long groaned under the tyrannical yoke of the haughty Ottomans, assumed for a moment the appearance of the manly bravery of their renowned ancestors, and fell upon their oppressors with all the violence of vindictive rage; but their first attacks discovered the womanly spirit by which they were inspired; they fell furiously on all the Turks they could master, and massacred without distinction, men, women, and babes at the breast; their boasted victories were the frantic exploits of enraged madness, and not the deliberate enterprizes of men, determined to die or shake off their bondage; but while the panic that had seized the enemy prevailed, they seemed to carry all before them. Town after town was either surprized or abandoned; and all who were so unhappy as to fall into their hands were slaughtered without mercy. The few Russians that accompanied them in their horrible exploits, were unable to restrain their fury, or to establish any regular discipline amongst them. At length, fortune that had favoured their first onset, changed sides; an army of 30,000 Turks, hastily drawn together from the neighbouring isles, appeared on a sudden, and surprized the strong city of Patrasso that had just fallen into the hands of the insurgents, and in which their main body was assembled. In a moment their courage failed them. Unable to make any defence, they abandoned themselves to despair, and whole families slew one another to avoid falling into the hands of their incensed conquerors.

Of all the multitudes who had possest the city, not one of the insurgents were suffered to escape; the carnage was dreadful; and as an example of greater terror, the city was set on fire, and those who had secreted themselves from the sword perished in the flames.

The frightened insurgents every where took the alarm, and fled to the mountains with the greatest precipitation, abandoning their Russian allies to the fate of war. Men accustomed to discipline are seldom dispirited at a reverse of fortune. It is upon such occasions that true courage distinguishes the veteran soldier from the raw undisciplined insurgent. A handful of Russian infantry, supported by a contemptible train of Artillery, but headed by an experienced leader, maintained their ground against the whole army of new-raised Turks. (1770, pp. 619–20)

Into this context of real political events and more or less inappropriate sentiment I should now like to place a particular subject, one by which the times are, to my mind, exactly epitomized. My subject is: le comte Marie-Gabriel-Florent-Auguste Choiseul-Gouffier, his travels in Greece in the years 1776–9, his account of the tour – the *Voyage pittoresque de la Grèce* – its partial translation into German by Heinrich August Ottokar Reichard, and the use Hölderlin made of that translation for his novel *Hyperion*. The insurrection of 1770 is the focal point.

Choiseul-Gouffier, we are told by his biographer, a personal friend and fellow-royalist, in the *Biographie Universelle*, longed to go to Greece from an early age, but was prevented at first by marriage and a necessary spell in the army (where he rose rapidly to the rank of colonel). His main inspiration in classical matters was the abbé Barthélemy, author of *Voyage du jeune Anacharsis*, whom he was fortunate enough to have as a personal tutor. He sailed finally in March 1776, still only twenty-four years old, on board the *Atalante*, captained by Chabert, who was on a mapping-expedition to the Archipelago.

Choiseul's full itinerary need not concern us. He was in Greece for three years and travelled very extensively, especially in Asia Minor. The insurrection was recent enough for him to be able still to observe its terrible consequences at first hand, and in the account of his tour he gives the events of 1769 and 1770 detailed attention. The war in the Morea (the siege of Coron, the battles at Mistra and Tripolis) are dealt with at length, as is the sea-battle off Tchesmé, with careful engravings to support the text. On Paros he recalls that the Russian fleet was stationed there, describes the effects of their stay and the epidemic that decimated their forces. The tone of all these passages is quite even; that is, events are described impartially, but the underlying sympathy is for the Russians and the Greeks. (It will be important to study this carefully in a moment.)

There runs throughout the book, far more overtly than in Chandler but perhaps no more than in Riedesel and Guys, a nostalgia for the ancient days and a lament over the falling-off. The country (the Holy Land of Greece) is under the governance of barbarians, the natives themselves are forgetful, even unworthy of, their heritage. I cite a couple of classic instances of this – the sarcophagus vilely abused, the enslaved Greeks' predilection for dancing – in the chapter on Chandler. When he is hospitably received on Siphanto or Ios, Choiseul imagines himself back in the age before the Fall: ' Je me crûs transporté aux beaux jours de la Grèce ... tout rapelle la simplicité des premiers âges ... un portrait fidéle & touchant de l'antique hospitalité' ('I thought myself back in the Greece of a better age ... everything calls to mind the simplicity of former times ... a faithful and touching image of ancient hospitality').[8] There is everywhere much ignorance and misery – on Ios for example where even Homer is forgotten – but, like Guys, whose primacy in that field he acknowledges, Choiseul discerns here and there traces of the former people. Thus the extraordinary patriotism and independence of the inhabitants of Tenos (noted by Guys too, and, significantly, Hölderlin's Hyperion hails from there), or the fierce Spartan love of freedom still alive among the much-praised Maniotes. These details and others, together with the serious attention given to the recent insurrection, constitute a moral or political tendency that is stronger still in Guys and notably less so in Chandler.

The most explicit political emphasis, however, is not in the text itself but in the *Discours préliminaire* which prefaces the first volume in 1782 but which was also published separately in 1783.[9] In it Choiseul recalls his sentimental expectations on setting off for Greece. His prose here fills with pathos. Though now less idealistic he can still celebrate Greece as the cradle of liberty, the motherland of the arts and sciences etc. etc., and he remembers his profound shock at seeing how ruinous the country was, how barbarous its oppressors, how debased its native people. Like Guys he looked for vestiges of the original character. Then he gives us the crux of the matter, in words which could serve as epitaph for that whole age of European travel in Greece:

Chez un autre peuple, je n'eusse été touché sans doute que d'un sentiment de pitié pour des hommes opprimés par la force, & courbés sous la tyrannie; mais ces esclaves n'étoient pas seulement des hommes, c'étoit la postérité des Grecs, & mon respect pour leur nom aggravoit à mes yeux leur avilissement.

(Among another people I should doubtless have felt no more than the pity due to men forcibly repressed and bowed down under tyranny; but these slaves were not merely ordinary mortals, they were the descendants of the Greeks, and the respect I felt for their great name intensified my sense of their abasement.)

His view of them now, he says, in 1782, is more balanced, less harsh – and the political point of his discourse emerges: Greece might still be free. There are encouraging signs. The love of liberty is not eradicated. He celebrates the courage of the mountain people, the Maniotes, descendants of Lycurgus, and cites instances of their bravery in the last war. They are the true Greeks. Follows a post-mortem on the 1770 revolt – its failure, the punishment visited upon the insurgents. Even despite that there is hope, there are signs of a renaissance of revolutionary feeling. He thinks it the duty of the Great Powers to intervene again. Russia and Greece are natural allies, having religion in common; Turkey grows ever weaker; it would bring stability to the area if an independent Greece were established as a buffer-state. This would be good for trade, especially French trade (if France had freer access there then she could avoid the hated English in the Channel). The discourse ends with much rhetoric on the liberation of Greece for the good of all mankind. But the *Realpolitik* is clear: France would benefit by encouraging another Russian intervention in the Aegean against the Turks and on behalf of the Greeks.

The frontispiece to the volume is a classic of its kind. It shows Greece in chains among the memorials of her famous men. An *avertissement* explains the emblem in detail:

La Grèce, sous la figure d'une femme chargée de fers, est entourée de monumens funèbres, élevés en l'honneur des grands Hommes de la Grèce qui se sont dévoués pour sa liberté; tels que Lycurgue, Miltiade, Thémistocle, Aristide, Epaminondas, Pélopidas, Timoléon, Démosthène, Phocion, Philopoemen. Elle est appuyée sur le tombeau de Léonidas, & derriere elle est le cippe sur lequel fut gravée cette inscription, que Simonide fit pour les trois cents Spartiates tués au combat des Thermopyles.

Passant, va dire à Lacédemone que nous sommes morts ici pour obéir à ses lois.

La Grèce semble évoquer les mânes de ces grands Hommes, & sur le rocher voisin sont écrits ces mots,
   Exoriare aliquis . . .

(Greece, depicted as a woman in chains, is surrounded by sepulchral monuments erected in honour of the great men of Greece who have championed her liberty, as for example Lycurgus, Miltiades, Themistocles, Aristides, Epaminondas, Pelopidas, Timoleon, Demosthenes, Phocion and Philopoemen. She leans on the tomb of Leonidas, and behind her stands the column on which were engraved Simonides' lines for the three hundred Spartans who died at Thermopylae:

> Traveller, tell them in Lacedaemon
> We lie here in obedience to her laws.

Greece seems to be conjuring up the shades of these great men, and on the rock nearby these words are inscribed:
   '*Let someone arise . . .*')

These sentiments are quite unequivocal. Choiseul was twenty-four when he travelled and thirty when he published the first volume of his

8 'Greece in chains'

account. It is worth tracing his subsequent career. Even before he returned home he had made a reputation for himself in academic circles by sending back interim reports on his discoveries and some inscriptions. When he returned he was elected to the two academies – to the Académie des inscriptions and, succeeding d'Alembert, to the Académie française – an extraordinary honour. His sumptuous volume in 1782 made him well known. Two years later he sailed to Constantinople as Louis XVI's ambassador to the Porte, taking with him a whole entourage of scholars and men of letters. He became an extremely able promoter of French interests, and thus automatically a betrayer of Greece. For official French policy was rather the opposite of that adumbrated in the *Discours préliminaire*: it was to keep the Porte strong, against Russia, which meant of course simultaneously keeping the Greeks enslaved. Choiseul-Gouffier, as ambassador, was actually responsible for bringing in French engineers and military experts to improve the fortifications of Constantinople and the Bosphorus. But what really damns him and reveals the practical worthlessness of his Philhellene sentiments, expensively advertised in 1782, is an amusing *contretemps* that his biographer recounts unabashedly as proof of the ambassador's diplomatic astuteness. Rival nations in Constantinople, alarmed at the progress of French interests, brought it to the attention of the sultan that his favourite ambassador, the Turcophile Choiseul, was the author of a book, the *Voyage pittoresque*, whose line in politics was the liberation of Greece from the barbarian Turk. Choiseul's answer to this vile ploy was to print in his private ambassadorial press another version of his work, from which all sentiments offensive to the Turks were expunged, and this he presented to the sultan as the genuine article, denouncing the book his enemies were exhibiting as a wicked counterfeit. The sultan, who in the ordinary way of things never read books, believed him.

As French Ambassador, helping the Turks maintain their hold over the Greeks, Choiseul pursued his scholarly interest in the glorious Greek past. He sent his staff exploring and surveying up and down Asia Minor and among the islands, and found time himself to tramp the Troad with the unscrupulous Lechevalier. At home came the Revolution, which he ignored. Recalled in 1791 he refused to obey, and when an order came for his arrest he fled to Russia, where Catherine, with whom he had Philhellene sentiments in common, protected him, and Paul after her. He came home in 1802 when the laws against the *émigrés* were relaxed, and lived quietly in an academic world working on the second volume of his *Voyage pittoresque* (feeling that others in the meantime, notably Lechevalier, had benefited from the archaeological researches that he had instigated). The first part of his second volume appeared in 1809. It is just as lavish as volume 1, but lacks, of course, the pathos, the call to arms. He lived long enough to become a peer of France, to vote for the death-sentence on Marshal Ney and to profit from the Restoration. The Louvre got his collection of classical remains. At his death in 1817 he was working on a replica of the Theseum at his residence on the Champs Elysées. This was sold – a sign of the times – to some industrialists, who pulled it down.

Heinrich August Ottokar Reichard (1751–1828) was a German hack whose main interest lay in the theatre and in travel-books. He began translating Choiseul's book from the first fascicules as they appeared, before the bound volume of 1782. His aim was the laudable one of making available in cheap form a work that in the original was way beyond the reach of all but the very wealthy. Thus in Reichard's version it ceases to be a *Voyage pittoresque* – that is, a series of magnificent engravings accompanied by a narrative and explanatory text – and becomes all narrative with only a couple of poor prints and a map. It shrinks from a volume in folio to one (in two parts) in duodecimo. Conditions in the two nations are rather epitomized in this. Reichard commends the French (and the English) on having moneyed classes who care about the arts. Germany, he admits, is less well off in that respect.

Even so reduced, shorn of its engravings, the book was still worth making available to the German public, so Reichard believed, for its accuracy in depicting regions 'wo blos Tournefort zeither unser sicherster und neuester Wegweiser war' ('where for trustworthy and up-to-date guidance we previously had only Tournefort to turn to'),[10] and also for its account of the recent insurrection. It was Reichard's announced intention to translate the whole of the first volume. His translation would be in two volumes, each of two parts. The first part of his first volume was done in 1780, the second in 1782; but then he seems to have got no further. That is, he translated only as far as p. 164 of the French original.

Reichard was, according to his autobiography, something of a sentimental Hellenist. As a boy during the Seven Years War he had conceived a powerful enthusiasm for the military glories of Ancient

Greece: 'Aristides war mein Held; auf den Schlachtfeldern von Marathon und Platää war ich zu Hause...[ich] wurde ganz Spartaner, der in den Thermopylen lebte und webte' ('Aristides was my hero; I was at home on the battlefields of Marathon and Plataea...I became a Spartan through and through and had my being at Thermopylae').[11] In that spirit, so he says in the preface to his translation, he enjoyed reading the accounts of travellers in Greece:

Es ist, ich weis nicht welche süße Schwärmerey dabey, sich mit dem Buch in der Hand in die Gegenden und Weltalter zu träumen, die durch die Meisterstücke jeder Kunst, durch die Gesänge der Unsterblichkeit, und die Thaten der Edlen und Heroen geweiht wurden. Gern wandle ich an Chandler's Hand, an den Gräbern des Achilles und Patroklus, durch die Thäler des Ida's bis an die Quellen des Simois und fabelhaften Skamanders, oder weile mit ihm, nach so vielen Jahrhunderten, in Marathons Ebene, auf dem Grabhügel der Wackern Athener, die für den Sold der Freyheit fielen, blicke umsonst nach den Pfeilern, welche die Namen enthielten, und klage mit ihm, daß solche Denkmäler jemals zerstört werden mußten!

(What a sweet indulgence of the sentiments it is to dream oneself back, book in hand, into the localities and the times made sacred by great achievements in all the arts, by immortal song and by the deeds of noble and heroic men. I love to wander with Chandler as my guide past the graves of Achilles and Patroclus, through Ida's valleys to the very springs of Simois and the fabulous Scamander, or to linger with him, after so many centuries, on the plain of Marathon, to climb the mound raised over the brave Athenians who died for the wages of freedom, to search in vain for the pillars that bore their names, and to lament with him the destruction of such monuments.)

And presumably also in that spirit, as a man in love with the past and offended by the present, he falsified Choiseul's account to the greater disparagement of the Greeks.

German translators of English and French travellers quite normally add notes and commentaries on the original, as though to compensate through a display of erudition for not having themselves travelled in the places described. Reichard announces that he will do the same, and that his notes will be distinguished by a letter R. But his systematic mistranslation of the French text in those passages dealing with the insurrection (and only those) is not indicated, and the German reader without the original to hand would suspect nothing.

Among Reichard's worst mistranslations and interpolations are the following.[12]

Choiseul-Gouffier, anchored off Coron, describes the evidence still to be seen of the recent war. The worst sufferings among the local Greeks were caused by Albanian irregulars called in by the Turks and for years after the insurrection still roaming freely and committing atrocities. Reichard simply *adds* this sentence:

Die ausgearteten und durch die lange Knechtschaft entnervte Griechen, wagten es nicht einmal, sich gegen diese Handvoll Räuber zu vertheidigen, und liessen sich metzeln wie eine Schlachtheerde.

(The Greeks, grown degenerate and cowardly during the long years of slavery, did not even dare fight back against this handful of brigands, and let themselves be butchered like a herd of sheep.)

That the Albanians were there in more than a handful Reichard knew full well, since he had just correctly translated Choiseul's 'des Hordes d'Albanois'.

Choiseul explains the failure of the siege of Coron thus:

On ne peut attribuer le peu de vigueur et de succès de cette attaque qu'au trop petit nombre de troupes réglées qui suivoient le Comte Orlow, et sur-tout au mécontentement réciproque des Russes et des Grecs qui s'étoient mutuellement exagéré leurs moyens.

(The reasons for the feebleness and small success of the attack were the insufficient number of regular troops following Count Orloff and above all the dissatisfaction of the Russians and Greeks with one another, each party having overestimated the resources of the other.)

The Maniotes were – he implies understandably – discouraged by the smallness of the Russian force. They were poorly armed and, moreover, 'découragés... par la crainte de ne point combattre pour leur liberté' ('discouraged by the fear that they might not be fighting for their own freedom'). In that mood they took what booty they could and returned to their mountain homes. Choiseul's tone is measured and sympathetic. This is Reichard's version:

Man kann die Fehlschlagung dieses Angriffs allein den Griechen und ihren Excessen von allerley Art zuschreiben, die den Grafen Orlow endlich nöthigten, sie zu verabschieden, und als Räuber wegzujagen, die nicht für die gemeine Freyheit zu streiten, sondern ihre Mitbrüder zu plündern gekommen waren.

(This attack failed solely because of the Greeks and their manifold excesses – by which Count Orloff was finally obliged to dismiss them and to chase them away as brigands who had come not to fight for the freedom of all but to pillage their fellows.)

Choiseul concludes quite simply: 'Le Comte Orlow, se décida enfin à lever le siège de Coron, le 26 Avril 1770' ('Count Orloff finally decided to raise the siege of Coron on 26 April 1770'). Reichard expands thus:

Der Graf Orlow wußte aus der Erfahrung, wie wenig auf die Griechen zu rechnen war, von denen er doch den ganzen Auschlag seiner Unternehmung erwartet hatte; er beschloß also zuletzt die Belagerung von Coron aufzuheben, und that es den 16. April 1770.

The Insurrection of 1770

(Count Orloff knew from experience how little he could rely upon the Greeks, whom he had expected to be the decisive factor in his enterprise; finally he made up his mind to raise the siege of Coron, and did so on 16 April 1770.)

This version, in which Count Orloff cannot rely upon his Greeks, contradicts Reichard's earlier falsification, according to which the Count sent them away and continued the siege, as Reichard put it without any foundation in the French text, 'blos mit seinen Russen' ('with no one but his Russians'). He also gets the day wrong (elsewhere the month: May instead of March) but that is a minor matter.

In Choiseul's description of the taking of Mistra there is nothing that redounds to the discredit of the Greeks. Here Reichard makes no attempt to translate, but simply *replaces* the original with this:

Sie eroberten es [Mistra] durch Capitulation; aber diese Räuber, denen der Verlust einer so reichen Plünderung, des einzigen Zweckes ihrer Heldenzüge, nahe gieng, verbreiteten sich durch die Stadt aller angewandten Mühe der Russen ohngeachtet, tödteten ihre Einwohner, ihre Mitbürger, ihre Freunde, ihre Verwandte zu tausenden, und erneuerten jene Auftritte des Abscheus und Entsetzens, wovon die Jahrbücher der Welt, leider! nur zu voll sind. Schandtaten, wie man sie kaum von den feindseligsten und erbittersten Nationen vermuthen sollte, übten Menschen gegeneinander aus, die Ein Himmel geboren werden sah.

(Mistra capitulated; but these brigands, unwilling to lose such a golden opportunity for pillage – the sole object of their heroic campaigns – spread through the city, despite all the efforts of the Russians to prevent them, and slaughtered the inhabitants – their fellow-citizens, friends, relatives – in thousands: and thus repeated those abominable and horrifying scenes of which the world's annals are, alas, only too full. Atrocities such as one would scarcely expect between the most hostile and embittered nations were perpetrated upon one another by people born under a common sky.)

The battle of Tripolizza is then similarly travestied. Reichard supplies figures (there are none in Choiseul) to make the Greeks appear the more cowardly. In fact he overdoes things and has 15,000 Greeks fleeing before 500 Albanian cavalry (in Choiseul: 'une troupe nombreuse de cavaliers Albanois' – 'a large force of Albanian cavalry'). This cowardice is then set against the outstanding bravery of 40 Russians (Reichard's figure) who fight to the last man.

It is a curious impulse on the part of a self-confessed lover of Ancient Greece so to go out of his way to malign her modern inhabitants. Choiseul, as I have said, is pretty even-handed in his account, but his underlying sympathy is for the Greeks and Russians together, as enemies of the Turks. Reichard actually had to introduce material not even remotely suggested by the French original, material in fact quite contrary to the spirit of the whole book and therefore quite at odds with the rest faithfully translated. His reference to the ' Jahrbücher der Welt' probably indicates the source of his bitter indignation. It is true, as I have shown, that the Greeks in 1770 had a bad press, and what Reichard read then, as a youth of nineteen or twenty, must have so upset him that he remembered his feelings a decade later and used the occasion of the translation from Choiseul's book to take his revenge on the Greeks for letting him, Reichard, a Hellenist, down. It seems unlikely that he invented the scurrilous details himself. He must have had the periodicals by him whilst he worked and grafted their stories on to his text *tant bien que mal*.

It is known that Hölderlin when working on his novel *Hyperion* used Choiseul-Gouffier's *Voyage pittoresque*, but only in Reichard's partial and dishonest translation, not in the original. It is from Reichard, in both detail and *Tendenz*, that the political element in Hölderlin's novel derives. Hyperion's brief and disastrous excursion into the real world of politics is solely the insurrection of 1770 as the *Voyage pittoresque*, through the untrustworthy medium of Reichard's translation, describes it. His more actively revolutionary friend Alabanda writes to him (on Poros with his beloved Diotima) from a village near Coron in the Peloponnese:

Es regt sich, Hyperion... Rußland hat der Pforte den Krieg erklärt; man kommt mit einer Flotte in den Archipelagus; die Griechen sollen frei seyn, wenn sie mit aufstehn, den Sultan an den Euphrat zu treiben. Die Griechen werden das Ihre thun, die Griechen werden frei seyn...

Bist du noch der Alte, so komm! (III, 94)

(Things are stirring, Hyperion... Russia has declared war on the Porte; they are sending a fleet into the Archipelago; the Greeks are to be free, if they will rise with the Russians and drive the Sultan to the Euphrates. The Greeks will do what is required of them, the Greeks will be free...

If you are still what you were, then come!)

Hyperion is easily persuaded. He conjures up the usual great names: Harmodius and Aristogiton, Pheidippides, Agis and Cleomenes. Diotima has grave misgivings. She doubts that the ideal – what *he* calls 'der Olymp des Göttlichschönen, wo aus ewigjungen Quellen das Wahre mit allem Gutem entspringt' ('the Olympus of the divinely beautiful, where truth and all goodness flow from the springs of unending youth') (III, 96) – can ever be realized by violent political means. He replies:

Der neue Geisterbund kann in der Luft nicht leben, die heilige Theokratie des Schönen muß in einem Freistaat wohnen, und der will Plaz auf Erden haben und diesen Plaz erobern wir gewiß. (III, 96)

(Our new confederation of like minds cannot live in thin air, the sacred theocracy of beauty must have its home in a free state, and that needs a place in the world, and we shall win ourselves such a place for sure.)

And her foreboding is that the means will vitiate the end. What follows is then the testing of their different views, and the savage proof of Diotima's rightness. There is a sort of terrible will to failure in *Hyperion*, the idealist's almost vengeful insistence on the unrealizability of his ideals. For that masochistic act of disappointment Reichard's travesty serves very well.

Hyperion crosses from Poros and journeys down through the Peloponnese to join Alabanda and the rebels. *En route* he writes in heroic vein to Diotima:

Ich schreibe dir von einer Spize der Epidaurischen Berge. Da dämmert fern in der Tiefe deine Insel, Diotima! und dorthinaus mein Stadium, wo ich siegen oder fallen muß O Pelopones! o ihr Quellen des Eurotas und Alpheus! Da wird es gelten! Aus den spartanischen Wäldern, da wird, wie ein Adler, der alte Landesgenius stürzen mit unsrem Heere, wie mit rauschenden Fittigen. (III, 103)

(I write to you from a peak among the Epidaurian mountains. I can see your island, Diotima, far below and faint in the distance, and I can see my place of trial and contest ahead of me, where I must win or die. In the Peloponnese, where the Alpheus and the Eurotas rise, there we shall bring our resolution to the test. Out of the woods of Sparta, like an eagle, the old spirit of our country will swoop down with an army as with rushing wings.)

Localities excite him:

Ich wandere durch diß Land, wie durch Dodonas Hain, wo die Eichen tönten von ruhmweissagenden Sprüchen. Ich sehe nur Thaten, vergangene, künftige, wenn ich auch vom Morgen bis zum Abend unter freiem Himmel wandre. Glaube mir, wer dieses Land durchreist, und noch ein Joch auf seinem Halse duldet, kein Pelopidas wird, der ist herzleer, oder ihm fehlt es am Verstande. (III, 104)

(As I travel through this land I seem to be passing through Dodona's holy wood where the oak-trees rustled with glorious prophecies. I see great exploits wherever I look, past and future deeds, as I go my way from morning till evening under the open sky. He must assuredly be without passion or understanding, the man who could travel through this country and still bear the yoke across his neck and not become another Pelopidas.)

He feels in the mountain people 'eine rächerische Kraft' ('an avenging power'); they are 'wie eine schweigende Wolke, die nur des Sturmwinds wartet, der sie treibt' ('like a silent cloud, only awaiting the gale that will drive them') (III, 104). Then the fear that this force, once released, will be uncontrollable, is raised but at once dismissed:

Sie werden so wild nicht seyn. Ich kenne die rohe Natur. Sie höhnt der Vernunft, sie stehet aber im Bunde mit der Begeisterung. Wer nur mit ganzer Seele wirkt, irrt nie. (III, 104)

(They will not be unmanageable. I know what nature unrefined is like. It despises reason but listens to the dictates of the spirit. No one who acts with all his soul can go wrong.)

In fact, the conditions for the most painful débâcle imaginable are being arranged. Once Hyperion and Alabanda meet, the emotional climb, before the fall, becomes rapid and precipitous. Alabanda makes what approximates to a realistic assessment of the Greeks' situation: 'Ich weiß es wohl, die guten Russen möchten uns gerne, wie Schießgewehre, brauchen' ('I know full well that the Russians would like to use us as their muskets'). But it is not difficult for him to overwhelm that worry:

Aber laß das gut seyn! haben nur erst unsere kräftigen Spartaner bei Gelegenheit erfahren, wer sie sind und was sie können, und haben wir so den Pelopones erobert, so lachen wir dem Nordpol ins Angesicht und bilden uns ein eigenes Leben. (III, 107)

(Be that as it may, once our brave Spartans have had occasion to appreciate who they are and what they are capable of, and once their strength has won us the Peloponnese, we shall snap our fingers at the Arctic Power and make a life of our own.)

Essentially their enthusiasm is excited by and really confined within the past – in Ancient Sparta, at Salamis, at Nemea. They excite themselves with these magical names 'zum Ziele... wo der junge Freistaat dämmert und das Pantheon alles Schönen aus griechischer Erde sich hebt' ('onwards... towards the dawning of our Free State, to where the pantheon of everything that is beautiful rises from the soil of Greece') (III, 108).

The tone is more ecstatic and the character who speaks the words is a fictional one, but the expectations and hopes of quite prosaic Europeans watching the real events of 1770 were much the same.

It is in the spring of the year when the campaigns begin; the whole cosmos seems to be enjoying rejuvenation. There is a revolutionary confidence; even Diotima is persuaded and adopts a heroic tone (which contravenes her essential nature). *Total* revolution is demanded:

Es muß sich alles verjüngen, es muß von Grund aus anders seyn; voll Ernsts die Lust und heiter alle Arbeit! nichts, auch das kleinste, das alltäglichste nicht ohne den Geist und die Götter! Lieb' und Haß und jeder Laut von uns muß die gemeinere Welt befremden und auch kein Augenblik darf Einmal noch uns mahnen an die platte Vergangenheit! (III, 111)

(Everything must be made young again, fundamentally changed; a seriousness in all our pleasure and joy in all our work; nothing, nothing however trivial and mundane, to be without the spirit and the gods. Let us in our love and hate and in our every utterance astonish the commonplace world and may never a moment ever again remind us of our former mediocrity.)

With those demands on real life Hyperion and Alabanda in the spring of 1770 begin the campaign: 'Der Vulkan bricht los. In Koron und Modon werden die Türken belagert und wir rüken mit unserem Bergvolk gegen den Pelopones hinauf' ('the eruption has begun. The Turks are besieged in Coron and Modon and we are advancing with our mountain people against the Peloponnese') (III, 111). Everything begins well. Hyperion exercises his men, wins their love and trust, delights in the community of soldiers in a just cause, intensifies his heroic friendship with Alabanda. Meanwhile they are approaching Sparta.

Hölderlin makes nothing of any of the battles until the siege of Mistra. Hyperion reports that they have won three successive skirmishes, have taken Navarino – but the climax is set at Mistra, which Hölderlin calls, inaccurately but for the effect very aptly, 'den Überrest des alten Sparta' ('the remains of ancient Sparta') (III, 114). He throws his turban, symbol of Turkish rule, into the Eurotas, and puts on a Greek helmet. His tent is by the famous river (some distance from Mistra in fact). And at this point, in overweening confidence, he prefers the present to the past: 'der kleinste unsrer Siege ist mir lieber, als Marathon und Thermopylä und Platea' ('the least of our victories is dearer to me than Marathon, Thermopylae and Plataea') (III, 114–15).

For the catastrophe Hölderlin follows Reichard very closely, because that tendentious translation exactly suits his own wish to render the disappointment unbearably bitter. In Sparta, of all places, his men, the Maniotes, of all people, behave like savages:

Es ist aus, Diotima! unsre Leute haben geplündert, gemordet, ohne Unterschied, auch unsre Brüder sind erschlagen, die Griechen in Misistra, die Unschuldigen, oder irren sie hülflos herum und ihre todte Jammermiene ruft Himmel und Erde zur Rache gegen die Barbaren, an deren Spize ich war. (III, 117)

(It is all over, Diotima! Our people have plundered and murdered without discrimination, even our brothers are slaughtered, the Greeks in Mistra, innocents, or they wander helplessly to and fro, a lifeless misery in their faces that cries out to heaven and earth for vengeance against the barbarians whom I led.)

Hyperion's only wound is given him by one of his men, whom he tried to restrain from looting. The Peloponnese falls into anarchy:

An allen Enden brechen wütende Hauffen herein; wie eine Seuche, tobt die Raubgier in Morea und wer nicht auch das Schwert ergreift, wird verjagt, geschlachtet und dabei sagen die Rasenden, sie fechten für unsre Freiheit. Andre des rohen Volks sind von dem Sultan bestellt und treibens, wie jene. (III, 117)

(Savage marauders everywhere; rapine rages in the Morea like the plague and any who do not take up the sword themselves are driven out or butchered. And these madmen profess to be fighting for our freedom! Other brutal elements are in the pay of the Sultan and their conduct is the same.)

Finally the cowardice in Tripolizza, deriving from Reichard:

Eben hör' ich, unser ehrlos Heer sei nun zerstreut. Die Feigen begegneten bei Tripolissa einem Albanischen Hauffen, der um die Hälfte geringer an Zahl war. Weils aber nichts zu plündern gab, so liefen die Elenden alle davon. Die Russen, die mit uns den Feldzug wagten, vierzig brave Männer, hielten allein aus, fanden auch alle den Tod. (III, 117-18)

(News has just reached me that our inglorious army has now been dispersed. Near Tripolizza the cowards met a force of Albanians, only half their number. But since there was no prospect of plunder the wretches all took to their heels. The Russians, our companions in the campaign, forty brave men, alone held their ground and were all killed.)

He concludes – the conclusion that satisfies the bitter will to failure – 'In der That! es war ein außerordentlich Project, durch eine Räuberbande mein Elysium zu pflanzen' ('indeed it was an extraordinary undertaking, to build Elysium with a band of robbers') (III, 117).

Sick of life – 'am Eurotas hat mein Leben sich müde geweint' ('I exhausted my life in tears by the Eurotas') (III, 119) – he joins the Russian fleet in order to end it all, and at the battle of Tchesmé, in the manoeuvres described by Choiseul and faithfully rendered (since the Greeks were not involved) by Reichard, he courts death, but wakes up alive on the island of Paros. Thinking now to return to Diotima, and her view of things, Hyperion is finally crushed by news of her death. Believing him dead, she herself had simply lost the will to live. In a sense he uprooted her, and left her to die in a foreign element. Political failure, failure to establish the ideal state in a real country, is compounded by the failure even to keep alive an ideal love. This compound disaster in reality constitutes the wilful triumph of the book: 'Der ächte Schmerz begeistert. Wer auf sein Elend tritt, steht höher' ('true suffering inspires. The man who ascends his own unhappiness stands one step higher') (III, 119). 'Des Herzens Wooge schäumte nicht so schön empor, und würde Geist, wenn nicht der alte stumme Fels, das Schiksaal, ihr entgegenstände' ('how could the waves of the heart be made to rise so beautifully, how could they be turned to spirit, were they not opposed by the old mute rock of fate') (III, 41). When they first met Diotima said to him 'Dir ist wohl schwer zu helfen' ('perhaps you are scarcely able to be helped') (III, 66).

The question of Hyperion's (and Hölderlin's) 'elegiac character' exceeds the question of what hopes and expectations eighteenth-century Hellenists invested in Greece. Still, Hölderlin – born in that spring of 1770 and even in madness following the progress of liberation fifty years later – fixed on Greece throughout his life as the aptest object of his, and the age's, 'sentimental' longing. In Greek terms he expressed the lament for mankind's lapse from a better state: the real, and abortive, attempt of 1770 exactly epitomized for him the difficulty, the impossibility, of recovering the ideal anywhere but in the spirit. When in his youth, and only across the border, another and far more violent revolution broke out, he put his hopes in that, and depicted it in his poetry in the terms of Greece. France in the subsequent wars was, he said, like democratic Athens fighting for survival against the absolutism of Persia. But reality rejected the image before very long.

Real events, in a real country, both excite the idealist to formulate his idealistic demands, and then, inevitably, disappoint them. In Hölderlin, in his elegiac hero Hyperion, that process is peculiarly intense and painful; but in Reichard too, with no better means of expressing it than crude travesty, we can perhaps detect the same. The real world, to which Alabanda and Hyperion make only passing concessions, the real politics, in which Greece was only the battle-ground and Greeks, all too human despite their ancestry, were only tools in the hands of cynical Great Powers – that world is nicely represented by le comte Choiseul-Gouffier, who doctored his earlier enthusiasms to please a sultan.

9

RICHARD CHANDLER'S EXPEDITION

Chandler's expedition to Asia Minor and Greece, begun in June 1764 and completed in November 1766, was well financed and carefully planned, and its aim was almost exclusively the exploration and description of classical sites. It was a professional classical enterprise, in its organization and purposiveness distinct from any before it, but anticipating many to come. Tournefort's in 1700 was similar in certain respects – the financing, the organization – but differed in emphasis and in its greater variety of purpose. Spon and Wheler, Wood, Dawkins and Riedesel, travelled after their own independent inclinations; Chishull and Guys, on the spot in Smyrna, and Constantinople, did tours for their own amusement, business and edification. Stuart and Revett canvassed support in Rome for their own independent venture, and were not taken up by a sponsoring body until their work was well advanced. Certain French expeditions under the patronage of the Crown, like Fourmont's in 1728–32, perhaps come nearest to Chandler's, but none equals it for completeness. In its organization and execution, and in the ensuing publications, Richard Chandler's journey through Asia Minor and Greece may be thought the classic of the age. His travels have a transparency and integrity all their own; and yet, being of the period in manner and aspirations, they have that pathos which often accompanies the essentially typical.

It is very clear, reading Chandler, that by 1764 a threshold had been reached in the exploration and description of Greece. In no other book is the sense of precedent and collaboration so strong. I do not think we disparage Chandler if we say that his was not a very original nor a particularly adventurous mind; his great aptitude was for clear compilation. By 1764, when he set out, there was indeed already a good deal to sift and assess; and in the years after his return, as he worked on the books deriving from his travels, still more was becoming available or was becoming clear to him, often through that happiest and perhaps characteristically eighteenth-century medium, one's personal acquaintances and friends in the as-yet still small world of classical topography. Back from Greece, the scholarly but previously untravelled Chandler was better able to assimilate what Robert Wood or James Stuart might tell him, and his reading of Spon and Wheler and Pococke took on actuality. What I shall examine mainly in this chapter is Chandler's modest and lucid manner of collaborating with his predecessors and contemporaries in the production of two travel-books that are among the century's very best. Professionalism was still a comparatively light attire in Chandler's day – his sponsors were after all the Dilettanti – and we cannot feel that he minded making available the journals of his travels to the reading public in plain English. He was urged at the outset, by the Committee of the Society of Dilettanti, to keep his diary 'in the plainest Manner, and without any regard to Style or Language, except that of being intelligible' and the published versions too retain that cardinal merit. Of course, he had at his disposal for such plain speaking an English exact without pedantry and of a natural dignity. Never enthusiastic or sentimental (in a pejorative sense) Chandler expressed a true love of Greece and all the excitement, weariness and triumph of the journey in a style that never strains.

The best introduction into the nature of the enterprise is undoubtedly (as Chandler himself realized) the instructions drawn up on behalf of the Society of Dilettanti by Robert Wood and published then as a main part of the preface to *Travels in Asia Minor*. They are dated 17 May 1764. Wood's own travels were by that time far behind him; but despite increasingly pressing commitments in public life he had been elected into the Society of Dilettanti in 1763 and it was he who suggested the expedition and recommended Chandler for leader (as a *quid pro quo* perhaps: Chandler's *Marmora Oxoniensia* (1763) is full of praise for Wood as a collector of inscriptions). Wood by 1764 was an elder statesman among classical travellers. Chandler was a young scholar who had never left the clerical and academic circles of England.

In 1764 the Dilettanti, thirty years old, were in funds. Their decision to send an expedition to Greece reinforced the new seriousness among the members, whose aims to date had been largely convivial. Electing Wood, Dawkins, Charlemont, Stuart and Revett into their membership, the Society was transforming itself into a pioneering force in classical archaeology, since all these men knew Greece; and the financial assistance the Dilettanti gave the latter two, in their work and in the publication of the *Antiquities of Athens* (volume 1 in 1762) was the first important contribution in that sphere. Chandler's expedition followed naturally, and became the Society's greatest single promotion.

This was their resolution: 'that a Person or Persons, properly qualified, be sent with sufficient Appointments to some Parts of the East, in order to collect Informations, and to make Observations, relative to the ancient State of those Countries, and to such Monuments of Antiquity as are still remaining'.

The first of these persons was Richard Chandler, Fellow of Magdalen College, Oxford. His qualifications 'to execute the Classical Part of the Plan' were his edition of *Elegiaca Graeca* in 1759 and, more especially, his *Marmora Oxoniensia*. He was appointed leader of the expedition and its 'Treasurer, Paymaster, and Accomptant'. His companions were Nicholas Revett for 'the Province of Architecture' – 'who had already given a satisfactory Specimen of his Accuracy and Diligence in his Measures of the Remains of Antiquity at Athens'; and William Pars, 'a young Painter of promising Talents', was chosen as 'a Proper Person for taking Views, and copying Bass Reliefs'. Revett was to be paid a salary of £100 per annum, Pars of £80 – which marked their subordination to Chandler. In all £2000 was made available.

They had instructions to proceed to Smyrna (their passage was arranged, on board the *Anglicana*), and to take the advice of the English Consul, a Mr Hayes, on the best courses of action. Smyrna was to be their centre, and from it they were to explore the surrounding region within a radius of eight or ten days' journey. They were required, on their various excursions, to 'procure the exactest Plans and Measures possible' of the buildings they might come across, to make 'accurate Drawings of the Bass-reliefs and Ornaments', to copy inscriptions, to sketch the localities, and to note 'every Circumstance which [could] contribute towards giving the best Idea of the ancient and present State of those Places'. Since a major part of their undertaking was to be the actual discovery and identification of classical sites, they were to be exact in marking distances and directions 'by frequently observing [their] Watches and Pocket Compasses'. Though they were in those parts for the furtherance of classical archaeology, they were besides to report 'whatever can fall within the Notice of curious and observing Travellers' and to 'keep a very minute Journal of every Day's Occurrences and Observations', this and any drawings to be considered the property of the Society. The instructions, precise in their main intentions, wisely leave the travellers leeway to make what practical arrangements might be necessary on the spot. A serious outbreak of plague in Smyrna did in fact cause them to alter their plans, though not very much to the detriment of their purposes. Initially it was envisaged that they would stay abroad for about twelve months, but the tour was extended to include some exploration of the Peloponnese, and it was more than two years before the party returned. In the meantime, as directed, they sent home letters and journals, drawings and inscriptions, which were produced at meetings of the Society and put on display for its members.

Smyrna, but for the plague, was the natural centre from which to explore Greek Asia Minor. Trade and diplomatic links were well established there, so that some of the practical business of travelling – the provision of finance, the acquisition of a firman, the hiring of guides and guards – could be seen-to through the good offices of the local consul and merchants. In fact, put off by the plague, Chandler's party sailed on as far as the Hellespont and landed first in the Troad. When they did arrive in Smyrna (11 September) they left again quite soon (30 September) on a month's tour, spent the relatively safe winter there, and were away again between March and May 1765 (Chandler conflates these two excursions in his account); and returning they found the city too pestilential to enter and sheltered in a village on the outskirts until August, when the plague abated and they sailed for Athens. On tour in Asia Minor they visited, among other places, Miletus, Clazomenae, Teos, Priene, Laodicea, Sardes, Philadelphia and Magnesia. They arrived in Athens on 31 August 1765, via Sunium and Aegina, and that city was their base until June of the following year. Then, having carefully surveyed Athens (supplementing the work done by Stuart and Revett in the 1750s) and made some excursions into Attica, they crossed via Poros to the Peloponnese and made their way via Epidaurus, Nauplion and Tiryns (but missing Mycenae) to Corinth. From there they reached Delphi, crossed to Patras and continued round the coast as far as Olympia, a new site but not, to them, a very revealing one. Their travels in Greece ended with fourteen days' quarantine in the lazaret on Zante.

The practicalities of travelling, though he does not dwell on them at all laboriously, are very evident in Chandler's account. It is as well to remember how inconvenient and sometimes dangerous journeying in Greece and Turkey was. Quite often their classical purposes were hindered or completely thwarted by the unfavourable circumstances in which the travellers happened to find themselves. The plague is the most extreme instance. Returning to Smyrna after their second excursion they were in very real fear of infection and for three months or more, holed up in Sedicui, they did no more than safeguard their lives. They left Delphi abruptly, when Chandler would have been glad to climb Parnassus, for fear of Albanian soldiery in their camp. Where they ventured and how long they lingered on sites in Asia Minor was in large measure determined less by the intrinsic interest of the place than by how safe or unsafe they felt themselves to be from local bandits. The fickle despotism of Turkish governors was a constant worry. Even their firman from Constantinople, carefully procured before they set off, could not assure them safe conduct in remote regions where a local aga did not respect the sultan's name. And all over the place their guides led them astray; they got benighted and hopelessly lost, they were attacked by sheepdogs as fierce as wolves, eaten alive by mosquitoes and vermin. Chandler, Fellow of Magdalen College, was of that breed of adaptable and stoical Englishmen who appeared, strangely attired and about some business deeply mysterious to the natives, in all manner of outlandish places in the eighteenth and nineteenth centuries. Here he is at Mylassa:

Beneath the hill, on the east side of the town, is an arch or gate-way of marble, of the Corinthian order. On the key-stone of the exterior front, which is eastward, we observed a double-hatchet, as on the two marbles near Myûs. It was with difficulty we procured ladders to reach the top; and some were broken, before we could find three sufficiently long and strong for our purpose. The going up, when these were united, was not without danger. The Aga had expressed some wonder at our employment, as described to him; and seeing one of my companions on the arch, from a window of his house, which was opposite, pronounced him, as we were told, a brave fellow, but without brains. We desired him to accept our umbrella, on his sending to purchase it for a present to a lady of his Harám, who was going into the country. By the arch was a fountain, to which women came with earthen pitchers for water, and with their faces muffled. (*Asia Minor*, p. 189)

Short and plump, (or 'round and considerably below the standard', as his biographer puts it[1]) he explored mosquito-infested Elis in a long dress with a towel around his head.

Here he sums up the life of the party on trek in Asia Minor:

Our mode of living in this tour had been more rough, than can well be described. We had endeavoured to avoid, as much as possible, communicating with the people of the country; and had commonly pitched our tent by some well, brook, or fountain near a village; where we could purchase eggs, fowls, fruits, wine, rakí or brandy, and the like necessaries; with bread, which was often gritty and of the most ordinary kind. We had seldom pulled off our clothes at night; sleeping sometimes with our boots and hats on, as by day; a portmanteau or large stone serving instead of pillow or bolster. But one consideration had softened the sensations of fatigue, and sweetened all our hardships. It was the comfortable reflection, that we enjoyed our liberty, and were, as we conceived, at a distance from the plague; but now we were about to lose that satisfaction, and at every stage to approach nearer to the seat of infection. (*Asia Minor*, p. 246)

The publications resulting from or enlarged by Chandler's journey were, in one form or another, rather numerous. When the travellers returned they presented the Society of Dilettanti with their collected journals, drawings, inscriptions and marbles, and a committee sat to decide how best these things should be published. Since Stuart and Revett's *Antiquities of Athens* were continuing, albeit slowly (the second volume did not appear until 1787), it was thought advisable to avoid any publication that might detract from that work; and accordingly the committee turned their attention from Athens to Ionia. The *Ionian Antiquities*, the first part of its first volume published in 1769, consists of views and exact depictions of three important temples: that of Dionysus at Teos, that of Athene at Priene and that of Apollo Didymaeus near Miletus. Chandler visited all these, but Robert Wood had been there some fifteen years before him, and the two journeys contribute to the same book, whose author, Chandler, quotes Wood extensively. Pars and Revett did the drawings, but views by Wood's artist, Borra, were also included. It was published at the expense of the Dilettanti. That collaboration produced a magnificent volume of a kind, as Heyne said, reviewing it, that other nations had come gratefully to expect of the English.

The journals of the expedition and the many inscriptions that the travellers had copied were handed over to Chandler by the Society of Dilettanti, to publish as he saw fit. This leave was given him in 1768, but not until 1774, by then Doctor of Divinity at Oxford, did he publish his *Inscriptiones antiquae, pleraeque nondum editae: in Asia Minori et Graecia, praesertim Athenis, collectae*, a scholarly work like Chishull's *Antiquitates Asiaticae*. The more popular volumes *Travels in Asia Minor* and *Travels in Greece* followed then in 1775 and 1776. Those are our chief concern here, but mention should also be made of a work advertised in the first of them and, although not published until 1802, also deriving ultimately from the same journey. That is Chandler's *History of Ilium or Troy*. A few remarks in the preface are of particular interest. Wood had been dead thirty years by then, but Chandler looks back to their friendship and collaboration:

> The following Work is founded on an extensive research into Antiquity concerning Troy, made, several years ago, in consequence of frequent conversations on the subject with Mr. Wood, the celebrated Editor of the Ruins of Palmyra and Balbec; who honoured the Author with his friendship, and who procured for him an opportunity of visiting the Tröia, as a traveller, under the auspices of the Society of Dilettanti.

Chandler had with him in the Troad a map belonging to Wood, one made, he believed, 'by a Frenchman, in 1726'. His preface continues:

> The Author intended communicating the result of his Enquiries to Mr. Wood, for his use in the *Comparative View of the ancient and present state of the Troas*, which accompanies his Essay on Homer; but was prevented by the unexpected death of that excellent person.

The *Comparative View*, so important to scholars at the time with their new-found fascination with the locality itself and its depiction in Homer, would have benefited from a serious collaboration of the two men. But after 1766 Chandler settled down to the leisure and libraries of Oxford and Italy and Wood became busier and busier in high diplomacy, and his *Comparative View* never got the revision it needed. That was very much in the past when Chandler returned to his *History of Ilium* (advertised in *Travels in Asia Minor* as an *Essay on the Troad; or, a Review of the Geography, History, and Antiquities of the Region of Troy* – in first intention, then, a more descriptive work, perhaps closer to Wood's *Comparative View*). He was prompted to take up his subject again, he says, largely because of the – to his mind – unsatisfactory nature of Lechevalier's work, and by Bryant's notorious assertion that Troy never existed.

There was a second edition of *Asia Minor* in 1776, another of that and *Greece* in 1817, and another of both in 1825. This last is useful in that it contains a memoir of Chandler (who died in 1810) by Ralph Churton and also, as footnotes, Nicholas Revett's comments and corrections in his own copies of the *Travels*. There is more than a little tartness in many of these. Wood, in his instructions, had foreseen the possibility that the party would not always agree and had for that reason made Chandler's position as leader quite unequivocal. Volume IV of the *Antiquities of Athens* contains a list of Observations and Corrections written by Revett in response to the first three volumes. Their tone is the same as that of the comments on Chandler: rather aggrieved. Socially, commercially, Revett remained far less successful than his colleague 'Athenian Stuart'. Their collaboration after the first volume of the *Antiquities of Athens* was unhappy. Revett sold out his share to Stuart in 1782.

The tone of Chandler's book is quite unlike that of Riedesel's, Choiseul-Gouffier's or Guys'; and this is not just a matter of differences natural to the two languages. Chandler writes as it is proper for a man to write who is presenting to the public an account of a professional and sponsored expedition. The enthusiasm for the undertaking can be taken for granted and its too frequent or too vehement expression would be out of place. Chandler has no special thesis to promote; his presentation of what the party observed is as balanced as he can make it. He rather supplies details for the enthusiasm and interpretation of his readers than writes enthusiastically or slantedly about them himself. Even the obvious disparity between past and present excites him to very little indignation and pathos, though of course he was as aware of it and pained by it as all classical travellers were. So he supplies without comment those often noted, naturally symbolic details of degradation: the antique altars or drums of pillars used for bruising corn, the marbles immured higgledy-piggledy in squalid modern dwellings, the sarcophagi used as cisterns. On these last Choiseul-Gouffier provides a classic instance of eighteenth-century sentimental Hellenism. His seventh plate shows a sarcophagus put to such use, and his accompanying text is this:

Fait pour consacrer peut-être, la mémoire d'un héros, la barbarie des habitants l'a dévoué aux usages les plus vils.

Tous les monuments de la Grèce éprouvent le même sort: les étables mêmes sont construites avec les débris les plus riches; ici c'est un entablement, là une frise, une corniche magnifique; souvent des Statues sont maçonnées dans les murailles; enfin on ne peut faire un pas dans cette contrée, sans trouver des chefs-d'oeuvres, vestiges de ce qu'elle a possédé, et témoins de ce qu'elle a perdu.

(What was made perhaps to commemorate a hero is put now by a barbarous population to the vilest use.

That is the fate of all the monuments of Greece: even the stables are built of precious remains; here an entablature, there a frieze or a magnificent cornice; statues are often built into the walls; in short, it is not possible to travel any distance in this country without coming upon masterpieces, traces of what she once possessed and proof of what she has lost.)

Both he and Chandler note the modern Greeks' predilection for singing and dancing, but only Choiseul adds that thus they hope to forget their slavery. In that sense the detail goes into Hölderlin's poetry (in 'Der Main' and 'Der Nekar').

Chandler's concern at the barbarity of the Turks and the ignorance of the Greeks is essentially that of the scholar and archaeologist. He is anxious that beautiful and interesting relics shall be removed from where they are neglected or abused into the safe-keeping of English museums and country houses. Thus his appeal at Sigeum or his justification of the removal of marbles from Athens. His interest is much more antiquarian than moral. Guys certainly, and Choiseul-Gouffier to some extent, may be said to take a moral interest in the predicament of the Greeks themselves. But Chandler's brief was stones, not the people.

His tone throughout, towards ancient and modern alike, is that of the reasonable man. Towards Catholicism, Greek Orthodoxy or the worship of the Ancients he is quite even-handed. True, he rejoiced on a safe arrival 'in the happier regions of Christendom' when the journey was over but, good Anglican though he doubtless was, we see very little of the Wheler in him. It is striking that in his observations at Sardes, Ephesus and Laodicea, there is no hint that these places were once of great Christian significance. He was at those three of the Seven Churches as a classical scholar and not, like Smith or Wheler, as a rather hectoring evangelist for the Church of England. He *was* sensitive on the spot, as any traveller might be, to the ruin of great places, but the pathos is quietly conveyed, there is not the least bombast:

We saw no traces either of houses, churches, or mosques. All was silence and solitude. Several strings of camels passed eastward over the hill; but a fox, which we first discovered by his ears peeping over a brow, was the only inhabitant of Laodicea. (*Asia Minor*, p. 228)

At Ephesus: 'We now seek in vain for the temple; the city is prostrate; and the goddess gone' (*Asia Minor*, p. 141). And here at Athens, near the Dipylon:

The mansions of the illustrious dead, like the bodies which they covered, are consumed, and have disappeared. Time, violence, and the plough have levelled all, without distinction; equally inattentive to the meritorious statesman, the patriot, the orator, and philosopher, the soldier, the artist, and physician. (*Greece*, pp. 109–10)

Chandler never felt the need, as Wheler did, to mock or disparage ancient religious usage. Their myths do not seem to him ridiculous, merely the natural products of a certain stage in human thinking and imagination:

The shepherd-poet of Smyrna, after mentioning a cave in Phrygia sacred to the Nymphs, relates, that there Luna had once descended from the sky to Endymion, while he was sleeping by his herds; that marks of their bed were then extant under the oaks; and that in the thickets around it the milk of cows had been spilt, which men still beheld with admiration; for, such was the appearance, if you saw it very far off; but, that from thence flowed clear or warm water, which in a little while concreted round about the channels, and formed a stone pavement. The writer describes the cliff of Hierapolis, if I mistake not, as in his time; and has added a local story, current when he lived. It was the genius of the people to unite fiction with truth; and, as in this and other instances, to dignify the tales of their mythology with fabulous evidence, taken from the natural wonders, in which their country abounded. (*Asia Minor*, p. 232)

In that rational spirit, observing a rainbow, he explains the invention of Iris, the messenger of the Olympian gods. He discourses briefly and reasonably on nympholepsy – that madness befalling a man who sees the nymphs (Chandler knew his Theocritus but was not a man to see the nymphs); and at Delphi, having washed in the freezing waters of Castalia, he explained thus to his own satisfaction the fine frenzy of the Sybil:

The water is limpid, and exceedingly cold. Returning from the village in the evening, I began to wash my hands in it, but was instantly chilled, and seized with a tremor, which rendered me unable to stand or walk without support. On reaching the monastery, I was wrapped in a garment lined with warm fur, and, drinking freely of wine, fell into a most profuse perspiration. This incident, when Apollo was dreaded, might have been embellished with a superstitious interpretation. Perhaps the Pythia, who bathed in this icy fluid, mistook her shivering for the god. (*Greece*, p. 268)

Chandler was not overawed by the places he visited. He did not reimpose their former glory, nor gild them in any way. In this he felt himself to be more honest than certain contemporary writers and painters who had made of them what they liked. Doubtless it pained him to find the Ilissus so much debased from the days when Socrates sat with Phaedrus on its banks, but he marks the painful contrast plainly. Ilissus was a poor trickle, quite dry in summer, and when flowing used by a currier and 'often offensive'. Chandler writes:

... that the poets who celebrate the Ilissus as a stream laving the fields, cool, lucid and the like, have both conceived and conveyed a false idea of this renowned water-course. They may bestow a willow-fringe on its naked banks, amber waves on the muddy Mæander, and hanging woods on the bare steep of Delphi, if they please; but the foundation in nature will be wanting; nor indeed is it easy for a descriptive writer, when he exceeds the sphere of his own observations, to avoid falling into local absurdities and untruths. (*Greece*, p. 79)

It was Gray who wrote of Ilissus 'laving the fields' and it is rather prosaic of Chandler to put him right. His realism is more properly applied not to poets (whose business is something else) but to predecessors and contemporaries in his own field: classical topography. Here it is quite in order and indeed an important part of the whole undertaking that he should correct previous false reports. In doing so his tone is generally courteous; only towards the Frenchman Leroy is he unfriendly, and for the good reason that he, Leroy, with his *Ruins of Athens*, published in London in 1759, had attempted to upstage Stuart and Revett. He was in Athens after them but published sooner and cheaply. The superiority of their work was evident once the first volume had appeared. In their preface Stuart and Revett condemn Leroy as a mere pirate of their idea, and their text is a running polemic against him. For the most part, they assert, he copied Spon and Wheler (and all their mistakes); where he made observations of his own they were invariably wrong. Chandler continues this demolition, on behalf of his friends and the Society of Dilettanti. The rivalry between the two nations (apparent on the other side in Choiseul's frequent correction of Chandler and Lechevalier's continual disparagement of Wood) sharpens the scholarly traveller's proper wish to get things right. What earlier travellers have reported needs to be tested; and qualified or corrected if necessary. Pococke (*A Description of the East*) is a predecessor whom Chandler cites frequently as a trustworthy authority; but when in Pococke too he discovers 'local absurdities and untruths', he indicates them. Thus, on Chios, concerning the so-called School of Homer, in fact a temple of Cybele: 'Pocock has metamorphosed the goddess and the two lions on the sides of the chair into Homer and a couple of the muses. The three figures, instead of certain parts only, were, I should suppose, *supplied by the fancy of the drawer*' (*Asia Minor*, p. 53).

Chandler offers his own account of places in Greece and Asia Minor to the same free and impartial scrutiny: 'I wish to have my omissions supplied as well as my errors corrected', and to that end he recommends a particularly useful hillock on the plain near Iasus from which topographical observations might be made. Taken together, the various publications resulting from his expedition – the collection of inscriptions, the exact depictions of the three temples, the detailed travel-journals – constitute a large increase in trustworthy knowledge about Greece. And the *Antiquities of Athens* are another cornerstone. These are books of a founding and consolidating kind. They make a firm basis. Obviously the process of addition and correction goes on – indeed, in 1765 it might be said to have barely begun – but we do feel with Chandler, with Stuart and Revett and with the Dilettanti in their serious vein, that Greece, her surviving monuments, had become a discipline. If some of its first effects seem peripheral – that the Right Honourable Lord Le Despencer at his seat near High Wycombe got Revett to erect him an exact replica of a portico of the Temple of Dionysus at Teos – this does not detract from the achievement. Nor do scholarship and enthusiasm here seem at all at odds. Accurate knowledge is not detrimental to a true love. Pars, Stuart and Revett believed they were delineating in their drawings the realization of a supreme ideal; such information substantiates, or in a novice excites, a love of beauty. The minutely accurate drawings of cornices, flutings and capitals are as loving as Aubriet's miniatures of plants. There is the same intensity of perception. A single column is like a basic unit of aesthetic pleasure; it pleases the eye and the imagination in a peculiarly whole and substantial way; and that pleasure is not in the least undermined when its $\mu\eta\chi\alpha\nu\dot{\eta}$, the means of its composition, are made known through exact measurement and delineation.

If Chandler's books may be viewed as cornerstones in the love and knowledge of Greece, they are themselves founded on the work of others and composed of contributions. They could not have been written sooner; they form a first firm step, as Chandler repeatedly acknowledges, only thanks to the work already done. No earlier classical travel-books are so transparent in their debt to authorities. When Spon published his *Voyage . . . du Levant* a hundred years before Chandler's *Travels* he was virtually without modern predecessors. Chandler really ends the line of pioneers, and establishes the exploration of Greece on a sounder footing.

It is not difficult to see how Chandler wrote his books. His method is perfectly clear and is, though not very imaginative, entirely apt, if tradition and collaboration be thought truly important. He invariably begins his account of a site with a more or less extended history of it and a reported description of its former state. That is work that he will have done beforehand, in preparation for the journey, and again when he sat down to write his account. It is simply a matter of compiling extracts from ancient authors in the study. His *History of Ilium* is only an extended equivalent of the account with which, in his travel-books, he prefaces his remarks on all the classical sites. The former state followed by an account of the present state makes for some pathos of the *sic transit* kind, but this is so obvious and so repeated that Chandler most often leaves it to us to feel or not, as we like. In the field the ancient authorities, Strabo, Pausanias, Pliny, may enable a traveller actually to identify a classical site under its modern Turkish name or in its absolute namelessness. The ancient geographers and guides may perhaps be substantiated by the researches of renaissance and seventeenth-century scholars interested, in an exclusively bookish way, in classical topography. So Chandler cites Peutinger and Cellarius (Spon often turns to Meursius); but since these authorities never visited Greece – Christoph Cellarius indeed was known to have taken only one short walk throughout the fourteen years of his professorship in Halle – the modern traveller on the spot will always prefer Strabo and Pausanias, real travellers themselves, if ever the sedentary bookmen are in disagreement with them. Chandler was a very enthusiastic admirer of both Strabo and Pausanias. 'It is a matter of regret', he says

... that travellers too commonly hasten along in the beaten road, uninformed of the objects on the way; when by consulting and following those invaluable guides, they might increase their own pleasure, and at the same time greatly advance the general knowledge of antient geography. (*Greece*, p. 278)

The natives themselves, ignorant of their heritage, may be less helpful in their own country than the ancient texts. Thus Chandler, searching for Clazomenae: 'Finding our guide ignorant and at a loss which way to go, we adopted the surer direction of ancient history.' Especially in his account of Athens and Attica Chandler quotes *at length* from Pausanias, several pages at a time, to convey what the tourist could see in the fourth century A.D. On that then follows what remained for the traveller in 1765.

Next in line after the ancient geographers (occasionally aided by their cloistered descendants in the Renaissance) come the travellers to Greece from 1675 onwards, and their published accounts. With most of those whom Chandler cites we are by now more or less familiar: Vernon, Wheler, Tournefort, Chishull, Pococke, Lebrun, Leroy. These are his chief authorities, to whom he refers approvingly or critically. Others are Smith, Sandys, Rycaut (see pp. 24–5), Randolph, Paul Lucas and Lady Montagu. As he compiles his account of a particular site he will turn to a modern immediately after Strabo or Pausanias. Thus at the Corycian Cave on Parnassus:

All Parnassus was renowned for sanctity, but Corycium was the most noted among the hallowed caves and places. 'On the way to the summits of Parnassus', says Pausanias, 'as much as sixty stadia beyond Delphi, is a brazen image; and from thence the ascent to Corycium is easier for a man on foot and for mules and horses. – Of all the caves, in which I have been, this appeared to me the best worth seeing. On the coasts and by the sea-side are more than can be numbered; but some are very famous both in Greece and in other countries. – The Corycian cave exceeds in magnitude those I have mentioned, and for the most part may be passed through without a light. It is sufficiently high; and has water, some springing up, and yet more from the roof, which petrifies; so that the bottom of the whole cave is covered with sparry icicles. The inhabitants of Parnassus esteem it sacred to the Corycian Nymphs and particularly to Pan. From the cave to reach the summits of the mountain is difficult even to a man on foot. The summits are above the clouds, and the women called Thyades madden on them in the rites of Bacchus and Apollo.' Their frantic orgies were performed yearly.

Wheler and his company ascended Parnassus from Delphi, some on horses, by a track between the Stadium and the clefts of the mountain. Stairs were cut in the rock with a strait chanel, perhaps a water-duct. In a long hour, after many traverses, they gained the top, and entering a plain turned to the right, toward the summits of Castalia, which are divided by deep precipices. From this eminence, they had a fine prospect of the gulf of Corinth and of the coast; mount Cirphis appearing beneath them as a plain, bounded on the east by the bay of Asprospitia and on the west by that of Salona. A few shepherds had huts there. They returned to the way, which they had quitted, and crossed a hill covered with pines and snow. On their left was a lake, and beyond it a pike, exceedingly high, white with snow. They travelled to the foot of it through a valley four or five miles in compass; and rested by a plentiful fountain called Drosonigo, the stream boiling up, a foot in diameter, and nearly as much above the surface of the ground. It runs into the lake, which is about a quarter of a mile distant to the south-east. They did not discover Corycium, or proceed farther on, but keeping the lake on their right came again to the brink of the mountain, and descended by a steep and dangerous track to Racovi, a village four or five miles eastward from Delphi. (*Greece*, pp. 269–70)

This is a translation of Pausanias (x, 32) and a paraphrase of pp. 316–19 of Wheler's *Journey into Greece*, and those two authors between them constitute four fifths of a chapter that then concludes with Chandler's admission that he was in fact prevented from climbing Parnassus himself. The same editorial procedure is adopted to compile an account of Marathon. He abstracts from Wheler an itinerary to nearby Rhamnus, where he himself, because of local Turks 'bearing a very bad character', did not venture; then cites Pausanias' description of the battlefield and adds to this, concluding the chapter, his own firsthand observations.

To an astonishing degree – certainly more than any other traveller – Chandler uses his predecessors both to corroborate his own account and to extend it into areas where he himself for one reason or another did not go. This means that quite a large proportion of each of his books consists of extracts or summaries of accounts written by other men. He translates two or three pages of Pausanias, he summarizes, barely in his own words, Chishull's journey, in 1699, from Sardes to Ephesus

(*Asia Minor*, pp. 260–1); or Pococke's into Caria from Guzel-hissar (*ibid.* pp. 203–5); or Wheler's from Sunium to Athens (*Greece*, p. 148). There are in the two books dozens of such extracts from previously published accounts, especially Wheler's *Journey into Greece* and Pococke's *A Description of the East*. They may be paraphrased or cited verbatim; they may be commentated and qualified, or left to stand as the reliable truth; and they occur so frequently in *Travels in Greece* and are accompanied by such sizeable extracts from Pausanias, that a reader might suppose Chandler to be wearying of his author's task and to be pursuing the easiest means of composition. It is difficult to say. On the whole I prefer to think of Chandler's method of compilation as both modest and apt. I should say that he himself realized that his own expedition to Greece was the consolidation of a century's previous effort, and in composing his account he wished to give his predecessors their due. He is a judicious compiler, and only uncritical where he believes there is nothing to criticize.

Chandler *did* go to Greece and even when he includes in his books reports on places he did not himself visit he can do so with some personal confidence and authority; but it will be recognized that his method of putting together a travel-book is one that the armchair traveller could equally well adopt. In essence that is what Guillet de Saint-George did, whom Spon denounced indignantly as an impostor; and in Chandler's own time the deservedly famous *Voyage du jeune Anacharsis* was composed in the same fashion. Barthélemy, who got no nearer to Greece than Rome, used for his imaginary journey through the Greek world of the fourth century B.C. the ancient and the Renaissance geographers and the seventeenth- and eighteenth-century travellers, Chandler among them. And since travel-books generally were a popular genre in the seventeenth and eighteenth centuries the temptation to compose one without travelling must have been quite strong, and bibliographies of Greek travel-literature do contain works cobbled together by hacks and charlatans who, with so many genuine accounts at their disposal, had very little to invent. Chandler's working method, apt and effective though it is, would be very imitable by a counterfeiter.

Chandler had also, for the compilation of his account, certain sources more personal to himself. He cites several unpublished reports that had been made available to him in person, some even by word of mouth.

This is in the best tradition of Greek travel-literature. Wheler included in his account a report given him by Pickering and Salter of their excursion to the Maeander (Chandler takes it up again, so does Choiseul-Gouffier). Spon quotes Babin at length on the Euripus tides. The outstanding authority of this kind in Chandler's book is the otherwise very obscure Anton Picenini. Of him it is known only that he was a Swiss, a doctor of medicine, and a friend of Leibniz. He visited the Seven Churches in 1705 in the company of John Tisser, the English Chaplain to the Turkey Factory, and two merchants, Cutts Lockwood and John Lethieullier. His diary of that trip, written in Latin, was found among Edmund Chishull's papers. It came into the possession of John Loveday, who was married to a Lethieullier. Loveday was Chandler's friend from Magdalen – he did the index for the *Marmora Oxoniensia* – and it was natural that he should lend him the diary. In *Travels in Asia Minor* Chandler cites Picenini frequently, on four occasions at some length to summarize his journeys to Ephesus, Magnesia, Laodicea and Chonos. Elsewhere he refers to him more briefly as a reliable authority: 'Magnesia, according to Strabo and Pliny, was only fifteen hours from Ephesus, but Picenini makes it eleven hours from Aiasalúck' (*Asia Minor*, p. 208). There is a pleasing sense in this reference to an obscure source, seventy years old when Chandler published, of effort acknowledged, information preserved and the tradition continued. The connection between the author and his dead predecessor in remote places is alive in the journal written in Latin, their language in common.

Another such contact was the French Consul in Smyrna, Charles Peysonnel (the younger) whom Chandler and his party doubtless met. Peysonnel was, like his father before him (his predecessor as consul in Smyrna) an amateur archaeologist whose work Guys in particular frequently commends. Chandler refers to the father's researches at Sardes: 'See a view and a plan of the ruins in Peysonnell's Travels' (*Asia Minor*, p. 252). Whether these Travels were published or not is unclear. The work is said to have been left among his papers. But Chandler must have been shown it, probably by Charles the son during the long winter period in Smyrna, 1764–5. The meeting, in an interlude from travelling, will have informed and inspired them as did that of Wheler and Spon with the Marquis de Nointel in 1675, when they were shown the drawings of the Acropolis.

During their fourteen days in quarantine on the island of Zante, in

July and August 1766, Chandler's party were visited in the lazaret by a Mr Joachim Bocher. Chandler reports:

> This gentleman in November, 1765, from Pyrgo crossed the Alpheus, and passing by Agolinizza traversed a wood of pines to Esidero, where is a Turkish Khan. An hour beyond, leaving the plain by the sea, he began to ascend the mountains, and passing by some villages arrived at Vervizza at night. This was a long journey. His design was to examine an antient building near Caritena. He was still remote from that place, when he perceived a ruin, two hours from Vervizza, which prevented his going any farther. (*Greece*, pp. 295–6)

This ruin was the Temple of Apollo Epicurius at Bassae. Chandler relates what Bocher saw:

> The ruin called *the Columns* stands on an eminence sheltered by lofty mountains. The temple, it is supposed, was that of Apollo Epicurius, near Phigalia, a city of Arcadia. It was of the Doric order, and had six columns in front. The number, which ranged round the cell, was thirty eight. Two at the angles are fallen; the rest are entire, in good preservation, and support their architraves. Within them lies a confused heap. The stone inclines to gray with reddish veins. To its beauty is added great precision of execution in the workmanship. These remains had their effect, striking equally the mind and the eyes of the beholder. (*Greece*, p. 296)

And to that he appends Pausanias' account.

Joachim Bocher, the rediscoverer of Bassae, was a French architect employed by the Venetians on Zante 'which island', Chandler says, 'he had adorned with several elegant villas' (*Greece*, p. 295). By the time Chandler published his discovery Bocher was dead. On a second visit to the site he had been murdered, apparently for the silver buttons of his coat.

The community of early explorers of Greece is not a very large one and it is possible to become quite well acquainted with a majority of its members in the pages of the published accounts. Chandler himself seems keenly aware that he is one of a community, of the living and the dead. He shows some piety towards the tradition in which he belongs, particularly towards those in the line who died on their travels. He had a warm admiration for Vernon. In the Theseum he distinguished his autograph on the south wall. Vernon was killed a hundred years before the publication of *Travels in Greece*. Closer in time, and closer too through personal friends, was the death of John Bouverie. Chandler's party visited the English burial-ground in Smyrna:

> Mr. Bouverie, the friend and companion of Mr. Dawkins and Mr. Wood, is interred there, and has over him a plain marble with a long Latin inscription. He died at Guzelhissar or Magnesia by the Maeander. (*Asia Minor*, p. 68)

At Magnesia:

We were visited soon after our arrival at the khan by a Frenchman, a practitioner in physic; who told us that he had attended Mr. Bouverie in a pleurisy at Sanderli. He conducted us about the town. (*Asia Minor*, p. 267)

Shortly afterwards the plague, spreading from Smyrna, reached Magnesia 'and the civil Frenchman, our guide, perished among the first victims' (*ibid.* p. 269).

Robert Wood, as the friend of Bouverie, the mentor of Richard Chandler, and the party's precursor in Greece and Asia Minor, must have been very present in their thoughts at many sites. When they explored the Troad they had his map with them (a less than perfect one). At Priene, Miletus and Teos they combined their observations with his. On the Pactolus, at the Temple of Cybele, they recognized a pillar whose base Wood had cleared for inspection some fifteen years before. And at various sites in Attica, and at Delphi, they did research with which he must have commissioned them when they set off: 'At the village we searched for a piece of wall . . . from which Mr. Wood had copied several inscriptions' (*Greece*, p. 267).

Similar reference is made to Wheler. They searched at Corinth for a marble he had copied: unsuccessfully – it had been removed in the interim to Verona museum. After one hundred years a balance could be taken of the state of certain monuments – of the Acropolis before and after Morosini (Chandler actually met a man in Athens who could remember the bombardment);[2] of the pillars still standing of the Olympeium: 'Seventeen were standing in 1676; but, a few years before we arrived, one was overturned' (*Greece*, p. 76). Revett in his notes supplies a date for this: 1754; he was probably still in Athens when it happened. The sense of loss is heightened when the images are transmitted thus through a line of familiar predecessors and personal friends.

In conclusion I want to quote two paragraphs in which, so it seems to me, the essence of Chandler's books, and indeed much of the whole experience of travelling in Greece in the 1760s, is contained. The first is his brief account of Segigeck, an insignificant site near Teos:

Segigeck was antiently called Geræ, and was the port of the city Teos toward the north. It was peopled with Chalcidensians, who had arrived under Geres. In the wall of the fortification next to the sea are several inscribed marbles, the colour a blue-gray, which have been transported from Teos. One is fixed in a fountain without the south gate. In the hot bath are two large fragments placed upside down, and serving for seats, which

In the Footsteps of the Gods

I examined, but hastily, fearing some infection, as the plague was known to be near. All these have been published by the learned Chishull. By a mosque and in the burying-grounds are some scattered fragments, and a sepulchral inscription or two. This place is reckoned eight hours from Smyrna. (*Asia Minor*, p. 96)

This holds *in nuce* much of what I have been indicating as typical of the spirit and method of Chandler's book: the former history of the place, its present remains (somewhat abused), a previous modern publication, the inconvenient circumstances (plague) of the latest visit. It is a plain and minimal account. The next, from the same volume, is more evocative. Though Chandler writes without any straining after effect the site seems luminous with beauty and interest. It seems to hold in solution a long human preoccupation, from the time of its habitation and proper use (and celebration as a living place) to the time of its revival as an object of antiquarian and sentimental attraction. The site is the Temple of Cybele by the golden River Pactolus:

After resting awhile, we were conducted toward the mountain, and suddenly struck with the view of a ruin of a temple, near us, in a most retired situation, beyond the Pactolus, and between the hill of the Acropolis and mount Tmolus. Five columns are standing, one without the capital; and one with the capital awry to the south. The architrave was of two stones. A piece remains on one column, but moved southward; the other part, with the column, which contributed to its support, has fallen since the year 1699. One capital was then distorted, as was imagined, by an earthquake; and over the entrance of the Naos was a vast stone, which occasioned wonder by what art or power it could be raised. That fair and magnificent portal, as it is stiled by the relater[1], has since been destroyed; and in the heap lies that most huge and ponderous marble. Part of one of the antæ is seen about four feet high. The soil has accumulated round the ruin; and the bases, with a moiety of each column, are concealed; except one, which was cleared by Mr. Wood. This was probably the temple dedicated to the local goddess Cybebe or Cybele[2], and which was damaged in the conflagration of Sardes by the Milesians. It was of the Ionic order, and had eight columns in front. The reader, who recollects the embarrassment of Metagenes in building the temple of Diana at Ephesus, where a similar mass of marble was placed over the entrance, will be inclined to pronounce, that both fabrics were planned by the same bold and enterprizing architects. The shafts are fluted, and the capitals designed and carved with exquisite taste and skill. It is impossible to behold, without deep regret, this imperfect remnant of so beautiful and glorious an edifice. (*Asia Minor*, pp. 255–6)

1 Chishull.

2 See Sophocles. Philoctet. 390.

She is the goddess celebrated by Sophocles, in the line to which Chandler learnedly refers, as 'Queen of the Mighty River / Pactolus of the golden sands'. Her temple has been visited by three modern travellers: the clergyman Chishull, the Homeric enthusiast Wood and the Oxford scholar Chandler. The further passing of her shrine is marked, as usual one might almost say, by the prostration of another column. When Hölderlin came across this passage, reading Chandler in German for his novel *Hyperion*, the image became his own and he composed a scene of those details in the light of a longing and a love of beauty that is there, but muted, in Chandler:

Ich hatt' am Fuße des Bergs übernachtet in einer freundlichen Hütte, unter Myrthen, unter den Düften des Ladanstrauchs, wo in der goldnen Fluth des Pactolus die Schwäne mir zur Seite spielten, wo ein alter Tempel der Cybele aus den Ulmen hervor, wie ein schüchterner Geist, in's helle Mondlicht blikte. Fünf liebliche Säulen trauerten über dem Schutt, und ein königlich Portal lag niedergestürzt zu ihren Füßen. (III, 20)

(I had spent the night at the foot of the mountain in simple but agreeable shelter among myrtles and the scent of ladanum where swans idled beside me on the golden waters of the Pactolus, and where an ancient temple of Cybele peeped like a shy ghost into the moonlight from among the elms. Five beautiful columns stood in mourning over the rubble and a majestic gateway lay in pieces at their feet.)

Hölderlin's debt to Chandler, both in the novel and in the poems, is well known. I have discussed it elsewhere.[3] The images in Chandler – jackals howling on Mount Ida, the barrows of the heroes above the Hellespont, the terrific debris below the Acropolis – stand out from his plain narrative in peculiar clarity, and attracted the attention of imaginations such as Hölderlin's. In Chandler the surviving physical beauty of Greece is very apparent. Details that Hölderlin used again and again – the snow on the high mountains, the scents of lentisc, ladanum and *lauriers-roses*, the flight of cranes, the sporting of dolphins, the innumerable geese and swans on Homer's Asian Meadow, the vines, the lemons and the olives, and the great beauty of watering-places in the heat – these all occur *passim* in Chandler. And it is in such a landscape that the surviving pillars of beautiful temples still stand, that fragments of sculpture may be turned up by the plough, and worked pieces of marble found abused or casually immured or lying overlooked. To the scholar and the poet Chandler's *Travels* set out in peculiar lucidity images of Greece that satisfy the mind like archetypes. We may be grateful to Providence, or to Hermes, patron of travellers, that Chandler's party, on leaving quarantine, boarded the brig *Diligence* with Captain Long and not, as they had intended, the *Seahorse* with Captain James, since the latter ship went down off Scilly in a gale.

Chandler married in 1785 and for the next four years or so travelled abroad, in France, Switzerland and Italy. He worked in the libraries of Florence and Rome collating manuscripts of his favourite poet Pindar;

but before and after that he and his wife lived at fashionable places on Lake Geneva and moved in the circles frequented by Edward Gibbon. Gibbon and Chandler had an important acquaintance in common: the late Robert Wood – he had bought the Gibbons' family house in Putney in 1769. Gibbon had a low opinion of him: he was, he said, 'an author who in general seems to have disappointed the expectation of the public as a critic, and still more as a traveller'.[4] Chandler's own estimation of Wood (his patron in classical archaeology) was quite the reverse. He thought the *Essay* by far the best thing ever written on Homer and a necessary correction of the (in his view) quite false image of the poet given currency by Pope. He conceded that Wood had 'little sensibility to beauty', but he was, Chandler insisted, a man of high moral character who embraced the Great and the Good 'with unequalled warmth'. Perhaps Wood was a topic at table when Chandler and his wife dined with Gibbon in December 1789. For Chandler himself Gibbon seems to have had a high regard; at least, he made good use of him in the composition of his *Decline and Fall*.

Chandler's remarks on Wood, cited above, were made in conversation with the German poet Friedrich von Matthisson. Matthisson, a sentimental and classicistic poet who befriended and encouraged the young Hölderlin, met Chandler in the salon society of Rolle in May 1789 and wrote an enthusiastic account of the meeting to his Swiss friend Bonstetten.[5] He knew Chandler's books and was delighted to meet him. He describes him as 'short, but somewhat robust . . . with a fine colour, and very animated eyes'. Chandler was flattered to be recognized and willingly answered Matthisson's questions. 'In a few minutes', Matthisson says, 'we were transported from Rolle to Athens.' And he goes on:

You know how often it has been my wish to meet with one who had actually trodden that sacred ground. In order to give me a more clear and precise idea of the situation and circumference of Athens, he carried me to the banks of the lake, and pointed out the distances of such and such things by near and remote houses, by trees, and rising grounds. A tree on a distant eminence was Acropolis, and a promontory running into the lake the Piraeus. He accurately defined also the distance at which Salamine would appear from hence, and described the prospect from Hymettus, which he pronounced to be one of the most charming and varied in the world, with the utmost glow of animation.

Chandler spoke particularly warmly of the Temple of Cybele at Sardes and of the 'stupendous ruins of the temple of Apollo at Ura, near Miletus, the description of which', Matthisson writes

. . . has perfectly transported me. Chandler saw them towards evening when a herd of goats had spread themselves over the majestic reliques, climbing among blocks of marble and massy pillars, while the whole was illumined with the richest tints of the setting sun, and the still sea glistened in the offing.

Thus it was depicted by the artist Borra in Part 1 of the *Ionian Antiquities*.

The meeting of the English explorer of Greece with the German poet who had never been remotely near 'that sacred ground' may serve as a final small instance of the transmission between nations of the century's most powerful enthusiasm.

Ralph Churton, Chandler's memorialist, noted as Matthisson had done, that he glowed with delight whenever he spoke of his travels. Whilst still in Oxford (before he became Vicar of Tilehurst) he was wont to compare the Castle Hill 'in form and magnitude' to the *Soros* on the Plain of Marathon in which the Athenians buried their 192 glorious dead.

CONCLUSION

I am tempted to finish there, with that image: Richard Chandler in Oxford remembering his travels in Greece. The world I have looked at, the eighteenth-century world of enthusiasm for Greece, contains both Chandler comparing the mound of Oxford castle to the *Soros* at Marathon, and Hölderlin thinking of the Alps as Olympus and Frankfurt as 'the navel of the earth'; Chandler recounting his adventures to fashionable company in Rolle or to his colleagues in Magdalen, and Hölderlin composing 'Pindaric' hymns for an audience beyond his grave.

After 1800 there was a great expansion of travel to Greece; after Independence ever more so. It becomes difficult then, among the innumerable accounts, to distinguish travellers as I hope I have distinguished Spon, Wheler, Tournefort and the rest; nor are the connections of so personal and immediate a kind. The sense of a small community of amateurs is inevitably lost. There are still good and bad accounts, of course, and those that can stand with Spon and Chandler are only a handful; but what interested me most in the men I have studied was their being at once individual and typical – each distinct in himself, but each also representative of one or more possibilities in the Hellenic Ideal; and I have not yet been able to discern that dual quality in many writers of the nineteenth century. Or perhaps it is rather that for one reason or another – after Independence and under the tonnage of archaeological and scholarly information – some of the imaginative urgency goes out of the preoccupation with Greece. It is especially agreeable to be in at the beginning of new enthusiasms and ideas; and almost everyone I have read in that century or so from Spon to Hölderlin seemed possessed of novelty. People expressing their material, intellectual and imaginative discoveries are invariably good company.

Still, certain topics that I have discussed with reference to writers of the eighteenth century might profitably be continued into the nineteenth. It is a facile convenience to think of Classical and Romantic as opposites. The eighteenth-century cult of Greece was, in many important aspects, a central part of the Romantic revolution that shaped the nineteenth century and our own.

I have been particularly interested in the tension, ideally a creative one, between facts and the idea, scholarship and imagination. In the course of the nineteenth century that tension becomes a division. Greater professionalism sorts out fact from fancy, and despite their name the Dilettanti, once they had adopted Stuart and Revett, were the first professionals. Leroy's work looked foolish once the *Antiquities of Athens* appeared; but in the second edition of his *Ruins of Athens* (1770) he answers Stuart's criticisms of him thus: 'When publishing . . . the Ruins of ancient edifices . . . one could aim . . . at presenting servilely the measurements; and the most scrupulous exactness, when measuring them, constitutes, according to Mr. Stuart, almost the only merit that a book of this kind may possess. I confess that I have very different views on the subject.' His own intention, he said, had been by no means to depict the ruins with servile accuracy, but to draw them and present them in such a way that they would 'affect the spectator more vividly, and succeed in passing on to his soul all the admiration by which one is stricken when looking at the Monuments themselves'.

Though this is a legitimate intention we should probably think that Leroy with his jumbled rococo settings did not achieve it. Furthermore, the intention itself looks increasingly odd, after Stuart and Revett, in a book on the ruins of Athens. The scrupulous will be bound to find such a book, as Francis Vernon found Guillet's, 'wide from truth'. Leroy was attempting, in what had become the wrong place, something that poets and landscape painters might properly do. It was rather in the manner of Leroy that Hölderlin evoked localities in *Hyperion* and that nineteenth-century artists painted the landscapes of Greece. In their pictures mood and sentiment are dominant, and classical 'props' – ruins, shepherds, a sarcophagus – are assembled from here and there. The collecting and presenting of factual knowledge in the manner of Stuart and Revett continued, ever more exhaustively, throughout the century; and so did, as a separate enterprise, attempts to answer imaginative and sentimental needs. Schliemann looks monstrous in the late nineteenth-century scholarly world; but he would have been fit company for Pasch van Krienen.

Some tension between the two ways of knowledge is inevitable and beneficial, but not a polarization into flat opposites. Exactness as achieved by Stuart and Revett is anything but soulless – why should not the imagination love precision? – and Thomas Allason on discovering *entasis* in 1814 will have felt what poets feel when a line of verse is 'given'.[1]

Hellenism was many-faceted and capable of change, as any living enthusiasm is. I have tried to indicate shifts in taste, understanding and imaginative grasp to which travellers, scholars and poets contributed and sometimes, as it were representationally, felt themselves. During the nineteenth century's continued preoccupation with Ancient Greece further such shifts occurred. They were occasioned by, among other things, the discovery that Greek statuary was polychromatic; by excavations at Mycenae, Troy and, around 1900, on Crete; by Nietzsche's insistence on Dionysus. Each of these adjustments collides with the notion that the Greeks in their art were chiefly characterized by 'eine edle Einfalt und eine stille Größe'. At the first publication of the phrase Lessing observed that it might serve for the plastic arts and to describe the effect that the French at least *intended* in their statuesque, classicistic tragedy, but that it did not suit either Homer or Sophocles. Lessing was afraid that under Winckelmann's imprimatur a general blandness and emotional frigidity might set in. Certainly the rage and passion of Greece, the sense of tragic cruelty that lies in the heart of her culture, was something many eighteenth-century writers were shy of approaching. Goethe was appalled by it: his *Iphigenie* is, as Schiller remarked, 'erstaunlich modern und ungriechisch' ('astonishingly modern and un-Greek'), modern in its determinedly optimistic humanism; and his *Achilleis*, conceived as a continuation of the tragic *Iliad*, he could not finish. Hölderlin came nearer to the truth perhaps, or nearer to the idea of the Greeks we have had since Nietzsche, giving great offence to colleagues still politely adhering to 'noble simplicity and quiet grandeur', published *Die Geburt der Tragödie* in 1871. Hölderlin feared Apollo as the god who flayed Marsyas alive; and he feared the temptation to ecstatic unrestraint embodied in Dionysus.

The appreciation of Greek landscape seems analogous to and may even be a part of the gradual realization that the spirit of Greece was tragic, and of the shying away from or facing up to that fact. Chandler, in the interests of a certain kind of truth, reprimands Gray for lending woods to Delphi's bare slopes and fields and cool water to the dry

Ilissus. Chandler notes, dispassionately, that Greece is not as Gray imagined it. Riedesel, a reader of Gresset, preferred his author's rococo fancies to the real thing. Stuart at Delphi shows a developing Romantic taste for the picturesque and the sublime. But Fani-Maria Tsigakou, in her *The Rediscovery of Greece*, notes how Romantic painters insisted on painting Greek landscapes in the manner of Poussin or Claude, in a haze of golden light, despite being in the country itself and seeing its characteristic clarity of atmosphere and sharpness of detail with their own eyes. That softening and toning down and envelopment in a vague nostalgia derives from a sentimental need; and it is as though empirical reality can only be seen through a haze of predisposition. To see Greece as harsh with treeless rock, bitter with salt, exposed under a pitiless light and brilliant with flowering thorns, would require a shift in the direction of Nietzsche and her twentieth-century poets.

The intense Philhellenism of the 1820s has been well documented. There never was a cause, as Byron said, 'which . . . had such strong and commanding claims on the sympathy of all the people of Europe'. By drawing attention to Guys, Hölderlin, Reichard and Choiseul-Gouffier, I hope to have indicated its first upsurge half a century previously. Between 1770 and 1820 there occurred two successful and world-altering revolutions, the American and the French, whose rhetoric, the language in which they conceived and expressed their ideals, derived in large measure from the democratic tradition of Ancient Greece. Those two successes then materially aided the cause of revolution in the surviving homeland itself.

Altogether, it would be interesting to study the reintroduction into Greece of a style, rhetoric and idealism originally her own. From the early nineteenth century onwards, beginning with Bartholdy in 1803, Germans went to Greece in increasing numbers. The first King of Greece was a German; Ludwig Ross, as Director of the Archaeological Department, began a systematic survey of all the sites; German architects began the redesigning of Athens in neo-classical style. Schliemann, in his monomania, attempted a personal appropriation of Homeric Greece. It would be worthwhile, I think, to study the predilections and prejudices of the latter-day German Hellenists in Greece. They were, after all, men brought up on Goethe, Schiller, Winckelmann, Humboldt and Hölderlin; they derived their Hellenism from poets and scholars who had never been to Greece but whose enthusiasm was coloured and substantiated by reading the accounts of travellers who had. How many Germans read Hölderlin in the land itself, in Friedrich Beißner's *Feldauswahl* of 1940? It was a tenet of National Socialist ideology that only the Germans had properly grasped the spirit of Ancient Greece – and grasped it ever more firmly after rather feeble beginnings in the humanism and cosmopolitanism of Goethe's Weimar. Excellence and helotry – for the SS state as for Athens and Sparta. The physical occupation of Greece was thus only the culmination of a long process of ever more radical *Aneignung*.

Appropriation in a simple sense meant for the early travellers taking home what inscriptions and bits of statuary one could carry. George Wheler's souvenirs, which he donated to the University when he took holy orders, are marbles of a modest size, not much bigger than a carriage clock most of them; they have a curious innocence when one thinks of the entire friezes, altars and temple porticos reconstructed and displayed in the museums of London, Munich and Berlin. Doubtless the earliest travellers would have carried off more had they been able to; plausible justification was there from the outset. Simply, the nineteenth-century professionals employed more powerful means. So Hallerstein got the friezes from Aegina for Germany, and Cockerell those from Bassae for Great Britain. The brutality accompanying such acts of rape or salvage still makes one wince. How Elgin proceeded on the Acropolis is well known; and when in the same year, 1801, Professor Clarke of Cambridge stole the last cult image of Demeter from Eleusis the villagers were terrified, for they still venerated her; an ox ran up and butted repeatedly at the statue, then fled bellowing; Clarke's ship sank, as the villagers had prophesied, but he and his booty still got back to Cambridge. After Independence there was much talk of 'returning the Muses to Greece', but by this was meant commissions for German neo-classicists, and not the return of her stolen statues.

APPENDIX: HOMER'S TOMB

Places connected in legend with the life of Homer were eagerly visited by early travellers in Greece. I have already mentioned Chishull and Chandler (and the fictional Hyperion) on the banks of the River Meles at Smyrna where, according to some accounts, Homer was born, and the grotto there in which he composed his verses. Another site was the so-called School of Homer on Chios. There he was supposed to have lived and taught in the latter part of his life, and the seats in the rock on which he and his disciples sat were still being shown to travellers in modern times. The chief source for such particularities of place was the *Life of Homer* ascribed to Herodotus; but another seven such Lives were in circulation in antiquity. And deductions were made from the works themselves; the 'Hymn to Apollo', for example, speaks (line 172) of 'a blind poet of Chios', and it was assumed this must be Homer himself.

Seven cities (and not always the same ones at that) disputed the honour of being his birthplace, but the place of his death was more generally agreed upon. He was said to have been brought ashore on the island of Ios whilst voyaging from Samos to Athens, and to have died there. In Pausanias' day tourists were shown Homer's tomb and that of his mother (reputed to be a native of Ios) by the islanders. But, says Choiseul-Gouffier, 'le tems l'a détruit, & l'ignorance plus destructive encore, a effacé chez les habitans jusqu'au souvenir d'Homère' ('time has destroyed it, and ignorance, yet more destructive, has obliterated among the inhabitants even the memory of Homer') (*Voyage pittoresque*, p. 19). That was doubtless his own experience, in 1776 ; but he adds a disparaging reference to one Pasch van Krienen who claimed, four years earlier, to have discovered and opened the tomb. Choiseul seems not to have known about his eccentric predecessor on Ios until he came to write up his own account. He must have missed, when they appeared, the two very full reports of the discovery in the

Appendix

Gazette de France of 3 February and 13 April 1772 (to which he himself refers). Had he known beforehand or learned of van Krienen from the islanders when he arrived, he would surely have made some inquiries after the truth of this sensational matter. He concludes that since nothing more has been heard of the discoverer the whole story must be quite without foundation.

At this point Heinrich Reichard, Choiseul-Gouffier's translator, does his German readers a real service by quoting at length, in German, van Krienen's own account of the discovery as it is contained in his extremely rare *Breve Descrizione dell' Arcipelago* (Livorno, 1773), adding that a translation of the whole work was being undertaken by a certain Galletti in Gotha.

Who was Pasch van Krienen? Ludwig Ross, doubting whether any copies of the *Breve Descrizione* had ever reached Germany (he was wrong in this: Reichard had one) and thinking that the book, for all its extravagances, had real merit (he calls it the best account of the islands between Tournefort and Choiseul), prepared an edition of it before his death with an account of the author. This was published in Halle in 1860. The story is certainly odd and worth the telling. It exactly characterizes the times in several amusing respects.

Almost all that is known of the Count Pasch van Krienen derives from his own book. He was born in Prussia of Dutch parentage. He served with the Russian fleet in the Archipelago, as a recruiting officer, from the spring until the autumn of 1771. But he had been among the islands and in Smyrna for years before that. When he left the service he undertook a little amateur archaeology – his book contains an angry denial of an accusation in the English press that he had financed his excavations with Russian money – and it was at the end of 1771 that he made his great discovery. The war favoured the transmission of news of it to Europe. The Russians, in control of the Cyclades, had a base on Paros; and French and Italian clergy on the islands, and consuls of the western nations, would all have taken an interest in van Krienen's claims and sent word home. There were reports in the French and English press as early as February, March and April 1772, in such detail, some of them, that they must have derived from the excavator himself. The correspondent for the *Gazette de France* who published the discovery on 13 April 1772 was very likely Charles de Peysonnel, the French Consul in Smyrna, himself an amateur archaeologist.

The Swedish scholar Björnstähl wrote from Livorno on 2 June 1772 that he had met van Krienen there and had seen the supposed tomb of Homer packed in crates. Van Krienen was then trying to sell it to Frederick the Great. Björnstähl also saw copies that van Krienen claimed he had made of the famous distich ἐνθάδε τὴν ἱεράν κεφαλήν... ('here within, the sacred head...') which, according to the Herodotean *Life*, was inscribed on the tomb. When van Krienen's book came out (perhaps in the last weeks of 1772, since a copy had certainly reached Constantinople by 18 January 1773) it received some attention in the literary press. An article in the *Mercure de France* (April 1773) concludes with the customary demand that this valuable relic should be removed out of the hands of the ignorant and brought into enlightened safekeeping:

... notre siécle doit par sentiment de reconnoissance, placer ses cendres honorablement ... L'Europe peut donc s'approprier ce monument, & placer dans son sein les précieux restes du plus grand des Poëtes.

(... we ought, in gratitude, to give his ashes an honourable resting-place. Let Europe then appropriate this monument and lay in her bosom the precious remains of the greatest of poets.)

Ross assumes that the very controversial count must have died soon after the publication of his book.

Pasch van Krienen rather discredited himself by his tales, in the *Breve Descrizione*, of quite fantastic adventures and discoveries underground at Ephesus. But his account of what happened on Ios is full and coherent at least. Of course, he knew what he was looking for. Like Schliemann, he knew the story. He was, he says, towards the end of 1771, on the island of Ios for the second time, pursuing certain clues as to the whereabouts of Homer's tomb that had been given him on the previous occasion. He persisted, getting warmer, through a series of bribes and encouraging signs until he was eventually directed to Plakotos on the northern tip of the island and there, having hired men and obtained permission from the owner of the ground, he dug for a month and at last uncovered three sarcophagi, one on top of the other. In each of the first two lay a huge skeleton, which turned to dust when touched. But the third was the jackpot. As his workmen prised up the heavy lid, van Krienen, peering inside, saw a figure seated on a marble slab. Unfortunately his men, unable to hold the weight, let the lid drop, and when it was raised again they saw in the tomb no seated figure any more but only a heap of dust. Other finds in the tomb itself convinced van Krienen that the dust was Homer's. These were a copper medallion inscribed OMIROS (an unusual spelling and one causing scepticism among scholars when the news broke), the inscription ἐνθάδε τὴν ἱεράν etc. (cut in the slab on which the figure was sitting) and things resembling an inkwell, pen, stylus and stylus-sharpener. These last were of particular interest in view of contemporary controversy in scholarly circles on the antiquity of the art of writing. Ferret's view that it was practised in Homer's day seemed proved if this was indeed Homer's tomb.

Van Krienen himself was in no doubt at all that he had seen the skeleton of the Prince of Poets sitting upright in his final dwelling-place with the tools of his trade around him. What happened to the tomb itself, with its inscription and marvellous contents, is a mystery. Björnstähl saw it in Livorno, ready to be despatched to the King of Prussia (who did not want it). Years later Heyne in Göttingen was induced by Lechevalier to publish drawings and write a learned commentary on a sarcophagus that he, Lechevalier, had seen in St Petersburg, in the grounds of the Stroganoff summer palace, on the banks of a small artificial lake, overshadowed by cypresses. This was known in the city as the Tomb of Homer, and was one of various remains that had come to Russia through the agency of the Russian army and navy during the war of 1770. Heyne supposed it to be van Krienen's find, and expended a good deal of learning and rather heavy sarcasm demolishing the suggestion that it might be Homer's tomb. Certainly it wasn't Homer's tomb; but there was enough circumstantial evidence – that it came from Andros, not Ios; that there was no inscription; that the measurements did not tally – to indicate that it wasn't van Krienen's discovery either. Heyne's *Das vermeinte Grabmal Homers*, published in Leipzig in 1794, then in London the following year (translated into English by Lechevalier), is a very heavy frivolity. What the untravelled Heyne saw was Lechevalier's sketch of a relic from Andros set up in Petersburg as a sentimental ornament. Using Winckelmann as an authority he easily interpreted the relief on the sarcophagus as being a depiction of Achilles among the women on Scyros. He quotes at some length from van Krienen's own account, in order to deride him.

What happened to van Krienen after he had written his *Breve Descrizione* nobody knows, nor what happened to his beloved find. Ross tracked down some of his collection to the vaults of the British Museum. He deserves to be remembered perhaps – at that precise moment when his workmen levered up the lid of the third and lowest sarcophagus – as one who looked on Homer a hundred years before Schliemann looked on Agamemnon.

1 *Travels in Turkey and back to England* (London, 1747), p. vi. But cp. Thomas Smith, *Remarks upon the Manners, Religion and Government of the Turks. Together with a Survey of the Seven Churches* (London, 1678) in his preface, 'To the Reader': 'An incredible number of marbles still remain behind in those parts, and others are continually dug up... and what might be purchased on no very hard terms, if some excellent persons would be at the expence of enriching their Country with the spoils of the East.'

2 Adolf Michaelis, *Ancient Marbles in Great Britain* (Cambridge, 1882), pp. 10ff, also pp. 185–204; Mary Hervey, *The Life, Correspondence and Collections of Thomas Howard* (Cambridge, 1921), ch. 20; Terence Spencer, *Fair Greece Sad Relic* (London, 1954), ch. 4; Warner G. Rice, 'Early English Travellers to Greece and the Levant', in *Essays and Studies in English and Comparative Literature*, University of Michigan Publications, x (1933), pp. 205–60.

3 Jacques Paul Babin, *Relation de l'état présent de la ville d'Athènes* (Lyons, 1674), p. 17.

4 Chishull, *Travels in Turkey*, p. 20. And cf. p. 61; also Tournefort, *Relation d'un voyage du Levant fait par ordre du roy* (Paris, 1717), 1, 61.

5 'Relation abrégée du voyage littéraire que M. l'Abbé Fourmont a fait dans le Levant par ordre du Roy, dans les années 1729 & 1730', in *Histoire de l'Académie Royale des Inscriptions et des Belles Lettres*, VII (Paris, 1733), 344–58. Also Pausanias, *Guide to Greece*, trans. Peter Levi (Penguin, 1979), 1, 37n.

6 A *boustrophedon* or 'ox-turn' inscription runs from left to right and right to left alternately, like an ox pulling a plough.

7 Spon, *Voyage d'Italie, de Dalmatie, de Grèce et du Levant* (3 vols., Lyons, 1678; 2 vols., Amsterdam, 1679), II, 143, speaks of some fragments of a frieze 'que Monsieur le Comte de Vvinchelseay fit enlever il y a quelques mois, qu'il passa à Athenes; pour les envoyer par mer en Angleterre' ('which were removed for Lord Winchelsea as he passed through Athens a few months ago, to be sent to England by sea'). The date (1675) cannot be right – Spon is elsewhere rather wild in his dates – but, on his authority, the error was perpetuated by Laborde (*Athènes aux xve, xvie et xviie siècles* (Paris, 1854), 1, 178) and Michaelis (*Ancient Marbles*, p. 48). John Heneage Finch, third Earl of Winchelsea, was Ambassador to the Porte from 1660 to 1669. Probably he passed through Athens on his way home, late in 1668. Michaelis records that his collection was sold after his death in 1689. The ambassador whom Spon and Wheler got to know in Constantinople was Sir John Finch (1626–82). He was

never in Athens. Spon confuses things by referring to both men as Winchelsea, though only the former was in fact of that title. (Spon's *Voyage* is referred to throughout in the two-volume Amsterdam edition of 1679.)

8 Quoted by Laborde in *Athènes*, I, 124–5. Cf. Albert Vandal, *Les Voyages du Marquis de Nointel, 1670–1680* (Paris, 1900).

9 Laborde, *Athènes*, II, 279.

10 Vandal, *Voyages de Nointel*, pp. 280ff. Cornelio Magni, *Relazione della citta d'Athene* (Parma, 1688), p. 65, says quite definitely that it was 'un Pittore *Fiamingo* Giovane' ('a young Flemish painter') who drew the frieze.

11 Babin, *Relation*, p. 12 and pp. 5–6.

12 On Transfeldt see Adolf Michaelis 'Ein Verschollener', *Im neuen Reich*, 6. Jahrgang (1876), i, 950–67 and 981–94. Also Michaelis, 'J. G. Transfeldts *Examen reliquarum antiquitatum Atheniensium*', *Mittheilungen des deutschen archaeologischen Institutes in Athen*, 1. Jahrgang (1876), 102–26. Being the first known literate German there is treated with some respect and sentiment by Michaelis (and later by Walther Rehm, in *Götterstille und Göttertrauer. Aufsätze zur Deutsch-Antiken Begegnung* (Bern, 1951), pp. 204–5). Transfeldt was still in Athens when Spon and Wheler arrived; he became Spon's numismatic agent in Aleppo.

13 Guillet de Saint-George, *Athenes ancienne et nouvelle* (Paris, 1675); Jacob Spon, *Voyage d'Italie*... (Lyons, 1678); Guillet, *Lettres écrites sur une dissertation d'un voyage de Grèce publié par M. Spon* (Paris, 1679); Spon, *Réponse à la critique publiée par M. Guillet sur le voyage de Grèce de Jacob Spon* (Lyons, 1679). According to Spencer (*Fair Greece Sad Relic*, p. 137), Spon's own copy of the *Lettres*, with notes in his hand, is in the library of London University. Goethe read Guillet's book on Sparta when he was working on the Helena tragedy in *Faust*. Cf. H. Trevelyan, *Goethe and the Greeks* (Cambridge, 1942), p. 244.

14 *Athenes ancienne et nouvelle*, preface (omitted in the English ed.).

15 *Ibid.* pp. 128–9; English ed., pp. 123–4.

16 B. D. Meritt, 'Epigraphic Notes of Francis Vernon', *Hesperia*, supplement VIII (1949), 213–27. Cf. also Meritt's 'The Persians at Delphi', *Hesperia*, XVI (1947), 58–62. Vernon's notes came via Richard Mead into the possession of Edmund Chishull on 15 July 1709. For Wheler at Delphi see *Hesperia*, XII (1943), 43.

17 Bernard Randolph, *The Present State of the Morea* (London, 1686), p. 14. Anthony à Wood in *Athenae Oxoniensis*, ed. P. Bliss (London, 1813–20), III, 1134, apparently quoting Vernon's letters to James Crawford, has them travelling *to* Lepanto when Sir Giles died after three days of fever. But Vernon's journal is quite unequivocal and agrees, as to the direction, with Randolph's account.

18 A letter in *Philosophical Transactions of the Royal Society*, CXXIV (24 April 1676), 577.

19 *Les Voyages du sieur Duloir* (Paris, 1654), p. 312.

20 Spon, *Voyage*, II, 124.

21 Wood, *Athenae Oxoniensis*, III, 1134.

22 *Early Voyages and Travels in the Levant*, ed. J. T. Bent, Hakluyt Society, LXXXVII (London, 1893), pp. 278–9.

23 Wood, *Athenae Oxoniensis*, III, 1133.

24 Smith, *Manners of the Turks*, To the Reader. Smith was John Covel's predecessor in Constantinople. Pp. 205–76 of his book are entitled: 'A Survey of the Seven Churches of Asia as they now lye in their Ruines.'

25 Sir George Wheler, *A Journey into Greece* (London, 1682), p. 482. In his *Notitia* (the

Autobiography of Sir George Wheler, edited with Notes, Appendices, and Genealogies by E. E. Wheler (Birmingham, 1911), also published in the *Genealogist*, n.s., II (1885) and III (1886)) Wheler speaks of his fear, when going abroad, of 'imbibeing ill Principles of Religion and Morals'. A contributor to the *Gentleman's Magazine* of August 1833 concludes his remarks on Wheler thus: 'Nor ought it to be forgotten, that whilst he benefited science and literature by his travels, he returned uncorrupted by the superstitions, and uncontaminated by the vices, of the countries which he visited.' Indeed, he got back safe and sound.

26 *The Antiquities of Athens*, I (London, 1762), 51. Stuart's own copy of Wheler's *Journey into Greece*, dated 1755 (the year of his return to England) is in the University Library at Durham. Book 5, the description of Athens, has numerous marginal notes in which Stuart corrects his predecessor's observations.

27 Vernon, in his letter to the Royal Society. Nointel in his dispatch of 17 December 1674. Quoted by Laborde, *Athènes*, I, 123.

28 *Ibid.* II, 49.

29 *Réponse*, p. 87: 'C'est que j'avois prié M. Wheler, qui promettoit de le traduire en Anglois, de mettre alors son nom le premier' ('since I had asked Mr Wheler, who promised to translate it into English, in that case to put his name first').

30 In the Preface to his *Journey into Greece*. Cf. Smith, *Manners of the Turks*, To the Reader: 'If the thread of a *Church-man* be perceived to run through the whole Relation ...'

31 *Réponse*, p. 87: 'dans tout le temps que nous avons demeuré ensemble à Rome & dans tout nostre voyage, il n'a esté que mon Eleve en Antiquité' ('throughout the time of our residence together in Rome and throughout our journey he remained my pupil in matters of Antiquity').

32 And cf., on the present insignificance of Attica's celebrated rivers, *Voyage*, II, 93.

33 'La legere connoissance que j'en avois [of the antiquities of Athens] alors m'inspira le dessein d'aller voir ce qui me restoit à apprendre' ('the slight knowledge I had of these things prompted me to go and see what I still had to learn') (*ibid.* II, 77).

34 Quoted by R. W. Ramsey in his 'Sir George Wheler and his Travels in Greece, 1650–1724', *Transactions of the Royal Society of Literature*, n.s. XIX (1942), 25.

2 CHISHULL AND TOURNEFORT

1 For a prose account of the voyage see Chishull's 'Letter to Dr. Turner', *Travels*, pp. 170–7.

2 George Sandys, *A Relation of a Journey begun An. Dom. 1610*, 3rd ed. (London, 1627), p. 3.

3 *Manners of the Turks*, p. 261. Smith went to Ephesus in 1671, Spon and Wheler in 1675. Spon offers two interpretations of the reliefs, the Christian and the Homeric; Wheler thinks neither very likely, and suggests a Roman Triumph instead (Spon, *Voyage*, I, 246; Wheler, *Journey into Greece*, pp. 253–4). There is little sentiment in either description.

4 In the second edition of *Travels in Asia Minor* (London, 1776 – the year after the publication of Wood's *Essay*) Chandler advertises Pars' drawings and describes the 'corpse extended' as 'likely that of Hector' (p. 114). Choiseul-Gouffier, who was at Ephesus in 1776 and published his account in 1782, opts definitely for the Homeric interpretation, but adds that locally the reliefs were thought to depict a

Christian martyrdom (*Voyage pittoresque de la Grèce*, vol. 1 (Paris, 1782), pp. 196–7). He places an engraving of the central one, 'The Dragging of Hector' as he calls it, at the head of his book, above the *Discours préliminaire*. As a composition it excels the sketch in Tournefort but is much inferior to Pars'. But his Plate 21, of the whole gate, the engraving of a drawing done by himself, is a very typical eighteenth-century piece: goats and their herdsmen at the foot of a massive and crumbling ruin.

5 For Picenini see ch. 9, p. 203.

6 There is a folder of ninety paintings by Aubriet of rare foreign plants in the University Library, Göttingen. They are marvellously exact and delicate in line and colour.

7 Volcanic Thera was a popular topic. There were many accounts of the eruption of 1707 and the emergence of the new island in the press and in the learned journals, among them a note by Sherard himself (*Philosophical Transactions of the Royal Society*, xxvi, 67).

8 Cf. *The Negotiations of Sir Thomas Roe* (London, 1740), p. 344:

'I hope I am now fallen into a good way by the help of the patriarch of this citty [Constantinople] who hath enformed mee of a small, despised, uninhabited island, in the Arches, a place antiently esteemed sacred, the buriall of all the Greekes, as yett unbroken upp; where, hee tells me, are like to bee found many rare things. Your grace may please to give order to some shipping, that comes for this place … to take directions of mee, and a guide from hence, and to anchor there 5 or 6 dayes, to search it; where they may take, without trouble or prohibition, whatsoever they please.' (Letter of 24 January 1624, to Buckingham)

9 Choiseul-Gouffier, in his *Voyage pittoresque* (pp. 49–58), goes one better and evokes the Glory that was Greece on Delos by quoting at length from the abbé Barthélemy's scholarly–fictitious account of a festival of Apollo supposed to have been celebrated on the island about the year 350 BC.

10 *The Antiquities of Athens*, vol. III, ed. Willey Reveley (London, 1794), p. 57. Reveley was in Greece with Richard Worsley in 1785–7.

11 Ludwig Ross, *Reisen auf den griechischen Inseln des ägäischen Meeres* (Stuttgart and Tübingen, 1840), p. 21.

12 Wheler is almost certainly wrong in his assertion that the statue was still upright on its pedestal until about three years before their visit. Bondelmonte saw it whole but prone at the beginning of the fifteenth century (Ross, *ibid.* p. 34); Jean de Thévenot heard more or less the same of it in 1655: that it lay on the ground, intact but for one broken arm. But his account (*Relation d'un voyage fait au Levant* (Paris, 1665), p. 200) is contradicted by Duloir, who was told, in 1640, that on Delos there remained 'la moitié d'une statuë haute de dix pieds, representant Apollon, & que les Anglois ont sciée en deux, de haut en bas, pour en emporter une partie' ('half of a statue of Apollo ten feet high which the English sawed in two from top to bottom, to take part away') (*Voyages*, p. 8). 'From top to bottom' sounds most unlikely. Perhaps he means they cut through the head. If Spon has the same atrocity in mind then the perpetrator of it in his version was a Venetian. This is his account. He says they found the statue

'… couchée par terre, & presque reduite à un tronc sans forme. Ce sont des suites inévitables de sa vieillesse, ou des mauvais traitemens qu'elle a receus par diverses personnes qui ont abordé à Delos. Les unes luy ont emporté un pied, les autres une main, sans respect ni consideration de l'estime qu'on en faisoit anciennement. Il n'y a pas même long-temps qu'un Provediteur de Tiné luy fit scier le visage, voyant que la tête étoit une trop lourde masse pour la pouvoir enlever dans son Vaisseau.' (*Voyage*, 1, 137)

('... lying on the ground and reduced to little more than a shapeless trunk – the inevitable consequence of his great age or of the maltreatment he has suffered from various people who have landed on Delos. Some took a foot, some a hand, showing him no respect and having no thought for the reverence he was held in anciently. Not long ago a Proveditor from Tenos had some of the face sawn off since the whole head was too heavy to take away by boat.')

Tournefort (*Voyage du Levant*, I, 301) says that not even the oldest inhabitants of Myconos could remember ever seeing the statue whole.

3 ROBERT WOOD

1 Robert Wood, *The Ruins of Palmyra* (London, 1753), the preface.

2 Hölderlin seems to have had Wood's books, and especially the engravings, in mind when he wrote, very late in his sane life, the poem 'Lebensalter': 'Ihr Städte des Euphrats! / Ihr Gassen von Palmyra! / Ihr Säulenwälder in der Eb'ne der Wüste...' ('Euphrates' cities! / Streets of Palmyra! / Forests of columns in the level desert...')

3 *Antiquities of Athens*, vol. IV (London, 1816), p. vii.

4 Robert Wood, *An Essay on the Original Genius and Writings of Homer with a Comparative View of the Ancient and Present State of the Troade* (London, 1775), p. vi. All subsequent references to the work are incorporated in the text.

5 Matthew Arnold, *Essays Literary and Critical*, Everyman Edition (London, 1911), p. 220.

6 J. G. Buhle (ed.), *Literarischer Briefwechsel von Johann David Michaelis* (Leipzig, 1795), II, 238.

7 Wood's letters to Michaelis are in the University Library, Göttingen (Cod. Mi. 330). Hans Hecht quotes from them in his *T. Percy, R. Wood und J. D. Michaelis. Ein Beitrag zur Literaturgeschichte der Geniezeit* (Stuttgart, 1933), pp. 25–6.

8 Cf. Buhle, *Michaelis*, II, 506–7 (Bryant to Michaelis, 28 June 1775): 'The world would think me the least proper person of any, to publish a Treatise concerning *Troy*, and its history, if they were apprised of my private opinion. For I doubt very much about the Trojan war: and am confident, that the city Troy of Homer never existed.'

9 In summarizing and discussing the arguments of Wood's book I have quoted from the English edition of 1775; but everything quoted will be found, most often word for word, in the provisional version of 1769 – which Germans read in the translation of 1773. I have carefully checked that translation: it is exact and stylish throughout.

10 Aeschines: *Monthly Review*, LIII (1775), 369. Guys: see ch. 7. Lady Montagu: 'While I view'd these celebrated Fields and Rivers, I admir'd the exact Geography of Homer, whom I had in my hand. Allmost every Epithet he gives to a Mountain or plain is still just for it' (*The Complete Letters of Lady Mary Wortley Montagu*, ed. Robert Halsband (Oxford, 1965), I, 420).

11 Cf. Sterne on the eloquence of Corporal Trim: 'going straight forwards as nature could lead him, to the heart' (*Tristram Shandy*, Book V, ch. 6).

12 In Goethe, *Sämtliche Werke* (*Sophienausgabe*), (Weimar, 1887–1919), XXXVII, 204–6.

13 J. G. Herder, *Sämtliche Werke*, ed. Bernhard Suphan (repr. Hildesheim, 1967), V, 330, 167, 169. Homer and Ossian were not the only authors who, it began to be thought, should be read for the greatest pleasure and profit in their own localities. Rousseau recommended himself particularly in this respect. Cf. Friedrich Matthisson, *Letters written from various parts of the Continent between 1785 and 1794*, trans. Anne Plumptre (London, 1799), pp. 291–2:

'With what different emotions would the *Iliad* be read on the fields watered by the Scamander from what are experienced in poring over it amid the gloomy walls of an academic study? By a like difference of emotions was my breast inspired on reading *La Nouvelle Heloise* upon the banks of the Leman Lake.'

Rousseau is then praised for his exactness in topographical depiction and compared with Theocritus himself 'who, according to the testimony of a very learned and sensible traveller, in the descriptions introduced into his pastoral world, absolutely places before his reader's eyes the fine and rich valleys of the fertile island of Sicily'.

4 HEYNE AND WINCKELMANN

1 J. E. Sandys, *A History of Classical Scholarship*, 2nd ed. (Cambridge, 1906), III, 51 and 52.

2 A. H. L. Heeren, *Christian Gottlob Heyne biographisch dargestellt* (Göttingen, 1813), pp. 210–12.

3 Heyne, in his introduction to J. B. Lechevalier's *Beschreibung der Ebene von Troja* (Leipzig, 1792), p. xiii.

4 In Heyne's review of Wood's book, reprinted as a foreword to the translation *Versuch über das Originalgenie des Homers* (Frankfurt, 1773), p. 14.

5 *Beschreibung* pp. 246–7.

6 *Ibid.* pp. 206ff. In the English edition, *Description of the Plain of Troy*, trans. A. Dalzel (Edinburgh, 1791), Lechevalier's assertion and Dalzel's more sceptical note are pp. 135–41. Choiseul-Gouffier, with Lechevalier in the Troad, came to the same conclusion about the circumference of Troy and thus about the meaning of the word περί. Cf. C. G. Lenz, *Die Ebene von Troja nach dem Grafen Choiseul-Gouffier und andern neuern Reisenden* (Neu-Stretlitz, 1798), pp. 33 and 41.

7 *Odyssey*, XXIV. 71–84. For Achilles' instructions on the raising of the mounds see *Iliad*, XXIII. 236–48.

8 Many interesting anecdotes concerning these tombs are retailed by Chandler in his *History of Ilium or Troy* (London, 1802), especially pp. 40, 70–3, 132–9. My favourite (p. 40) relates that Homer 'keeping some sheep by the barrow of Achilles, he prevailed upon him by supplication and offerings to *appear*; when the insufferable glory which surrounded the hero deprived him of his eye-sight'.

9 Cf. *Briefe*, ed. Walther Rehm (Berlin, 1952–7), I, 151 and II, 232–3, where to Berendis in 1754 and to Berg in 1762 he expounds his ideal of heroic friendship such as Achilles and Patroclus enjoyed – an un-Christian, a pagan–Greek ideal, as he explicitly asserts.

10 *Asia Minor*, p. 42. In the preface (pp. xiii–xiv) he promises to expand on his simple assertion in the forthcoming *History of Ilium*.

11 Lechevalier, *Plain of Troy*, p. 148.

12 William Borlase, *The Antiquities of Cornwall* (Oxford, 1754), Book II, ch. 8, 'Of Barrows'. This admirable antiquary would have been in his element among the tumuli on the Sigean promontory; but his situation in life (Rector of Ludgvan in West Penwith) confined him, as he says in his preface, to 'the ruder products of Ancient Britain'.

13 Lechevalier, *Plain of Troy*, p. 149.

14 *Achilleis*, lines 432–40. In 1798, at work on his epic, Goethe was reading Wood, Lechevalier and C. G. Lenz. Lenz actually supplies diagrams of the supposed tomb of Achilles.

15 Lechevalier, *Plain of Troy*, p. 150. And cf. Guys, *Voyage littéraire de la Grèce*, 3rd ed. (Paris, 1783), II, 240–1:

'Mais j'ai senti la joie de voir ce mont Ida couvert de pins, comme Homère le représente, de suivre les bords du Scamandre, & du Simoïs, de trouver dans un champ inculte, mais agréable de la Phrygie, un vieux javelot que j'aurois baisé avec respect, & que je conserverois avec soin, si j'avois pu imaginer tenir celui d'Hector, ou même celui de Priam, *telum imbelle sine ictu*. Enfin, *juvat ire, desertosque videre locos*. Et de pouvoir dire: *Hic saevus tendebat Achilles.*'

('But I have had the joy of seeing Mount Ida covered with pines as Homer describes it, of following the Scamander and the Simois, and of finding in an untilled but pleasant field in Phrygia an ancient spear which I would have kissed respectfully and kept had I been able to imagine that it was Hector's weapon I was holding or even Priam's, "unwarlike and unused". In a word, "it pleased me to go and see the deserted places". And to be able to say "here fierce Achilles was laid low".')

16 Heeren, *Heyne*, pp. 220–1.

17 'The Life of Heyne', in *The Works of Thomas Carlyle* (London, 1899), XXVI, 353.

18 *Gedancken über die Nachahmung der Griechischen Werke in der Mahlerey und Bildhauer-Kunst*, in J. J. Winckelmann, *Kleinere Schriften*, ed. Walther Rehm (Berlin, 1968), p. 29.

5 WINCKELMANN AND GREECE

1 Winckelmann, *Kleinere Schriften*, p. 29.

2 'Brief eines reisenden Dänen', in *Werke*, ed. J. Petersen and H. Schneider (Weimar, 1949–), XX, 101–2. Goethe visited the collection in October 1769 and described his visit in the eleventh book of *Dichtung und Wahrheit*. There were casts of all the best-known and highest esteemed works of classical sculpture – the Laocoön, the Apollo Belvedere, the Dying Gladiator, the Farnese Hercules, the Antinous, the Torso Belvedere, the Medici Venus etc. etc. – 'ein Wald von Statuen', Goethe calls them, 'durch den man sich durchwinden, eine große ideale Volksgesellschaft, zwischen der man sich durchdrängen mußte' ('a forest of statues, a great concourse of ideal forms, through which one wound or pushed one's way') (*Werke*, ed. Erich Trunz *et al.* (Hamburg, 1949–66), IX, 501).

3 Among the items were a few fragments from the Acropolis picked up by Hessian mercenaries after the bombardment of 1685. Friedrich Matthisson records that the Minerva had been brought up into the museum 'from among some rubbish in a cellar, where she had long served as a stand to an oil cask'. And he adds: 'As the cask once burst, she became so impregnated with oil, that even now, in warm weather, drops are emitted from various parts of her body' (*Letters written from various parts of the Continent*, trans. Anne Plumptre (London, 1799), p. 46).

4 Wilhelm Heinse, *Ardinghello und die glückseligen Inseln* (Insel edition), p. 176. If this is not a tenable theory, it does have some polemical point.

5 *Briefe*, III, 195: 'Italien ... hat derselbe [Lessing] nur im Traume, wie ich Griechenland und Elis gesehen ... und dieses muß ihm vorgerücket werden' ('Lessing has only seen Italy in his dreams (just as I have only seen Greece and Elis in mine) and this must count against him').

6 Riedesel, *Remarques d'un voyageur moderne au Levant* (Amsterdam and Stuttgart, 1773), p. 98. His *Reise durch Sicilien und Großgriechenland* (Zurich, 1771) has for frontispiece an engraving drawn by Geßner in wholly rococo style.

7 In a letter of July 1758 to Bianconi. It may be that Dawkins, who saw Stuart at work in Athens in May 1751, had obtained such a drawing and circulated it among

interested persons in Rome, perhaps as an advertisement for the intended publication. Winckelmann could not have seen it before December 1755, of course.

8 On Winckelmann's reading of and excerpting from the travellers see André Tibal, *Inventaire des manuscrits de Winckelmann déposés à la Bibliothèque nationale* (Paris, 1911). How he made use of them in practice may be seen in the following passage taken from his polemical expansion of the *Gedancken* (here in Henry Fusseli's translation (London, 1765), pp. 162–4):

'The modern Greeks, though composed of various mingled metals, still betray the chief mass. Barbarism has destroyed the very elements of science, and ignorance overclouds the whole country; education, courage, manners are sunk beneath an iron sway, and even the shadow of liberty is lost. Time, in its course, dissipates the remains of antiquity: pillars of Apollo's temple at Delos, are now the ornaments of English gardens: the nature of the country itself is changed. In days of yore the plants of Crete were famous over all the world; but now the streams and rivers, where you would go in quest of them, are mantled with wild luxuriant weeds, and trivial vegetables.

Unhappy country! How could it avoid being changed into a wilderness, when such populous tracts of land as Samos, once mighty enough to balance the Athenian power at sea, are reduced to hideous desarts!

Notwithstanding all these devastations, the forlorn prospect of the soil, the free passage of the winds, stopped by the inextricable windings of entangled shores, and the want of almost all other commodities; yet have the modern Greeks preserved many of the prerogatives of their ancestors. The inhabitants of several islands, (the Greek race being chiefly preserved in the islands), near the Natolian shore, especially the females, are, by the unanimous account of travellers, the most beautiful of the human race.

Attica still preserves its air of philanthropy: all the shepherds and clowns welcomed the two travellers, Spon and Wheeler; nay, prevented them with their salutations: neither have they lost the Attick salt, or the enterprising spirit of the former inhabitants.'

The authorities cited are, for the ancient state, Theophrastus and Galen (on plants), and for the modern: Stukely, Tournefort, Belon, Lebrun, Spon and Wheler. (For the same thesis – continuity – and a similar working method see Guys, in ch. 7.)

9 *Boswell on the Grand Tour: Italy, Corsica and France 1765–1766*, ed. F. Brady and F. A. Pottle (London, 1955), p. 255.

6   WINCKELMANN AND RIEDESEL

1 Walther Rehm, 'Johann Hermann von Riedesel. Freund Winckelmanns, Mentor Goethes, Diplomat Friedrich des Großen', in *Götterstille und Göttertrauer*, p. 209; cf. p. 207.

2 For example, awaiting Riedesel in Rome:

'Ich wollte Ihnen viel mehr schreiben, weil mich Ihre nahe Gegenwart belebet; es soll aber mit Geist und Leibe und mit der ausgelassensten Vertraulichkeit mündlich geschehen.' (*Briefe*, III, 142)

('I had much more to write to you, I am filled with new life by the thought that you are so close now. But let it be in spoken words, body and soul, in an intimacy without the least restraint.')

And cf. III, 50, 96, 157, 233–4.

3 *Reise*, p. 20 (Eng. ed. (1773), pp. 14–15). Cf. Winckelmann, *Briefe*, III, 268 and *Sämtliche Werke* (Donaueschingen, 1825), XI, 352.

4 *Briefe*, III, 268; and cf. II, 161. On the advantages of being born an aristocrat, Rehm refers to Goethe's Wilhelm Meister, who says:

'... in Deutschland ist nur dem Edelmann eine gewisse, wenn ich sagen darf, personelle Ausbildung möglich. Ein Bürger kann sich Verdienst erwerben und zur höchsten Not seinen Geist ausbilden, seine Persönlichkeit geht aber verloren, er mag sich stellen, wie er will.' (*Werke*, VII, 290)

('... *Personal* development, if I may call it that, is possible in Germany only for the nobly born. A man of the middle classes may win a good name for himself and may, at a pinch, develop his mental powers; but his personality will suffer fatally whatever course he takes.')

5 Both quotations from 'Von der Fähigkeit der Empfindung des Schönen', addressed to Berg.

6 The *Reise* was translated into English by J. R. Forster in 1773; the *Remarques* rather disgruntledly into German (why did a German have to write in French?) by C. W. Dohm in 1774. There was a nice edition of both, in French, in 1802; a reissue of both, with a biographical essay by E. E. Becker, in 1942; the *Reise* was reissued by the Winckelmann Gesellschaft (Berlin, 1965), edited by A. Schulz, with a portrait of Riedesel.

7 Rehm, *Götterstille und Göttertrauer*, p. 207.

8 *Briefe*, III, 288, 291, 311.

9 And cf. p. 16. In the German translation see especially the long note on p. 216.

7 PIERRE AUGUSTIN GUYS

1 *Biographie Universelle*, XIX, 259.

2 And cf. *Briefe*, III, 254 and 273.

3 *Voyage littéraire de la Grèce* (Paris, 1771), I, 3. References are to this, the first edition, unless otherwise stated and are hereafter incorporated in the text.

4 *Complete Letters*, I, 332–3; Pope, *Correspondence*, ed. George Sherburn (Oxford, 1956), I, 406 and 493.

5 *Athenes ancienne et nouvelle*, p. 238. English ed. (1676), p. 226.

6 *Decline and Fall of the Roman Empire*, ed. J. B. Bury (London, 1898), VI, 486.

7 Cf. the letter to Guys written by his son in the third edition of the *Voyage littéraire*, III, 2:

'... vous qui avez vengé les Grecs modernes du mépris avec lequel on voit des Républicains devenus esclaves. Vivement excité comme Racine par l'enthousiasme que vous avez puisé dans les écrits anciens, vous avez cherché à discerner leurs traits dans leurs descendants, vous les avez saisis, vous avez écarté les ombres qui les voiloient à leurs propres yeux, vous les avez même fait revivre.'

('... you who avenged the modern Greeks for the contempt bestowed on them as republicans enslaved. Fired, like Racine, with an enthusiasm deriving from the ancient authors, you sought to discern their features in their descendants, you saw the likeness, you dispelled the shadows concealing them from themselves: indeed, you made them live again.')

Also Mme Chénier's tribute to him, in the name of the modern Greeks, 3rd ed., I, 188.

8 Guys, 1st ed., I, 24. Montesquieu, *Esprit des Lois*, XIV, 4. In the preface to the English edition this view is emphasized: 'nature is invariable in her operations... the

principles of a polished people will influence even their latest posterity' (*A Sentimental Journey through Greece* (London, 1772)). And Riedesel (*Reise*, p. 271), though he was not quite so convinced of continuity as Guys, quotes Horace as if he were: 'Naturam expellas furca, tamen usque recurret' ('you may drive out nature with a pitchfork, yet she will always come running back again').

9 Cf. Riedesel, *Remarques*, pp. 200–1.

10 *Gedancken*, in *Kleinere Schriften*, p. 29.

11 *Ibid.* p. 34.

12 *Ardinghello*, p. 181.

13 *Gedancken*, in *Kleinere Schriften*, p. 34.

8 THE INSURRECTION OF 1770

1 Voltaire, *Correspondance*, ed. T. Besterman (Geneva and Toronto, 1968–77), xxxiv, 136. And cf. xxxvi, 423.

2 *Gentleman's Magazine* (1770), 343; *St James' Chronicle* (25 May), vol. 1443; (2 June), vol. 1447.

3 *Gentleman's Magazine* (1770), 620 and 137; *St James' Chronicle*, (22 February), vol. 1404. And cf. Chandler, *Travels in Greece*, (Oxford, 1776), pp. 137–8:

'In the first year of our residence in the Levant [that is, 1764–5], a rumour was current, that a cross of shining light had been seen at Constantinople pendant in the air over the grand mosque once a church dedicated to St. Sophia; and that the Turks were in consternation at the prodigy, and had endeavoured in vain to dissipate the vapour. The sign was interpreted to portend the exaltation of the Christians above the Mahometans; and this many surmised was speedily to be effected; disgust and jealousy then subsisting between the Russians and the Porte, and the Georgians contending with success against the Turkish armies. By such arts as these are the wretched Greeks preserved from despondency, roused to expectation, and consoled beneath the yoke of bondage.'

4 Voltaire, *Correspondance*, xxxvi, 328, 341, 442; xxxviii, 40; xxxvi, 237.

5 Pausanias, *Guide to Greece*, trans. Peter Levi (Penguin, 1979), i, 37n.

6 Voltaire, *Correspondance*, xxxvii, 38; xxxviii, 122, 279.

7 *St James' Chronicle* (1770), vols. 1449 and 1500.

8 *Voyage pittoresque*, p. 14.

9 The *Discours* is sometimes attributed to another author, but the consensus of opinion is that Choiseul wrote it. Certainly he sanctioned its use as the preface to his book.

10 *Reise des Grafen von Choiseul-Gouffier durch Griechenland*, vol. i, part i (Gotha, 1780), preface.

11 The autobiography of H. A. O. Reichard, ed. Hermann Uhde (Stuttgart, 1877), p. 12.

12 Friedrich Beißner exposes Reichard's mistranslations with great thoroughness and clarity in the third volume of Hölderlin's *Sämtliche Werke*, ed. Friedrich Beißner and Adolf Beck (Stuttgart, 1946–77).

9 RICHARD CHANDLER'S EXPEDITION

1 Ralph Churton's *Memoir* in the 1825 edition.

2 *Greece*, p. 88: 'This event was remembered by a little old man living at Athens, who conducted me to a ruined windmill above Pnyx as standing on or near the spot from which the bomb was thrown.'

3 *The Significance of Locality in the Poetry of Friedrich Hölderlin*, MHRA (London, 1979). Goethe read Chandler too, of course, as did Heinse.

4 *Decline and Fall of the Roman Empire*, ed. J. B. Bury (London, 1898), II, 145. But see V, 431 where Wood is praised for his *Palmyra* and *Balbec*. Lechevalier quotes the disparaging comment with some self-satisfaction in his *Description of the Plain of Troy*, p. 75.

5 Friedrich Matthisson, *Letters written from various parts of the Continent*, trans. Anne Plumptre (London, 1799), pp. 136–41. I am grateful to Professor W. P. Bridgwater of the University of Durham for drawing my attention to these interesting letters.

CONCLUSION

1 *Entasis* is a slight swelling in the shaft of a column that corrects the optical illusion by which a perfectly symmetrical column looks slightly concave.

BIBLIOGRAPHY OF WORKS USED

(1) ACCOUNTS OF GREECE

Babin, le père Jacques Paul, *Relation de l'état présent de la ville d'Athènes* (Lyons, 1674); reprinted by Ross in *Hellenika* (Halle, 1846), pp. 75–92, and by Laborde in his *Athènes* (Paris, 1854)

Barthélemy, abbé Jean Jacques, *Voyage du jeune Anacharsis en Grèce* (5 vols., Paris, 1788)
  (English ed.: *Travels of Anacharsis the Younger in Greece* (London, 1791)
  German ed.: *Reise des jungen Anacharsis durch Griechenland* (Berlin, 1789))

Chandler, Richard, *Marmora Oxoniensia* (Oxford, 1763)
  Inscriptiones antiquae, pleraeque nondum editae: in Asia Minori et Graecia, praesertim Athenis, collectae (Oxford, 1774)
  Travels in Asia Minor (Oxford, 1775; 2nd ed. London, 1776)
  (German ed.: *Reisen in Klein Asien* (Leipzig, 1776))
  Travels in Greece (Oxford, 1776)
  (German ed.: *Reisen in Griechenland* (Leipzig, 1777))
  Both *Travels* reissued 1817 and 1825
  History of Ilium or Troy (London, 1802)
  with Nicholas Revett and William Pars, *Ionian Antiquities*, Part 1 (London, 1769), published by order of the Society of Dilettanti

Chishull, Edmund, *Antiquitates Asiaticae* (London, 1728)
  Travels in Turkey and back to England (London, 1747)

Choiseul-Gouffier, Marie Gabriel Auguste Florent, le comte, *Voyage pittoresque de la Grèce*, vol. 1 (Paris, 1782)
  (German ed.: *Reise des Grafen von Choiseul-Gouffier durch Griechenland*, trans. (probably only as far as p. 164) by H. A. O. Reichard (Gotha, 1780 and 1782)
  Choiseul's description of the Troad trans. into German by C. G. Lenz in his *Die Ebene von Troja* (Neu-Strelitz, 1798))

Covel, John, Extracts from his diary in *Early Voyages and Travels in the Levant*, ed. J. T. Bent, Hakluyt Society, LXXXVII (London, 1893)

des Hayes, Louis Baron de Courmenin, *Voiage de Leuant fait par le commandement du Roy en l'année 1621* (Paris, 1624)

Duloir, le Sieur, *Les Voyages du sieur Duloir* (Paris, 1654)

Fourmont, Michel, 'Relation abrégée du voyage littéraire que L'Abbé Fourmont a fait dans le Levant par ordre du Roy, dans les années 1729 & 1730', in *Histoire de l'Académie Royale des Inscriptions et des Belles Lettres*, VII (Paris, 1733), 344–58

Galland, Antoine, *Journal d'Antoine Galland pendant son séjour à Constantinople 1672–73*, ed. and published in Paris in 1881

Guillet de St-George, George, *Athènes ancienne et nouvelle* (Paris, 1675 and 1676 – three eds.)
  (English ed.: *An Account of a late Voyage to Athens* (London, 1676))

Bibliography

Lacédémone ancienne et nouvelle (Paris, 1676)

Lettres écrites sur une dissertation d'un voyage de Grèce publié par M. Spon (Paris, 1679)

Guys, Pierre Augustin, *Voyage littéraire de la Grèce ou Lettres sur les Grecs anciens et modernes, Avec un Parallele de leurs Moeurs* (2 vols.) (Paris, 1771; 2nd ed. 1776; 3rd ed. 1783)

(English ed.: *A Sentimental Journey through Greece* (London, 1772))

van Krienen, Graf Pasch, *Breve Descrizione dell'Arcipelago* (Livorno, 1773); reissued by Ludwig Ross (Halle, 1860)

Lechevalier, Jean Baptiste, *Description of the Plain of Troy*, a paper delivered in French to the Royal Society in Edinburgh and trans. by A. Dalzel (Edinburgh, 1791)

(German ed.: *Beschreibung der Ebene von Troja*, ed. C. G. Heyne (Leipzig, 1792))

Leroy, Julien David, *Les Ruines des plus beaux monuments de la Grèce* (Paris, 1758)

(English ed.: *The Ruins of Athens* (London, 1759))

Magni, Cornelio, *Relazione della città d'Athene* (Parma, 1688)

Montagu, Lady Mary Wortley, *The Complete Letters of Lady Mary Wortley Montagu*, ed. Robert Halsband (Oxford, 1965)

Pococke, Richard, *A Description of the East* (2 vols., London, 1743–5)

Randolph, Bernard, *The Present State of the Morea* (London, 1686)

The Present State of the Islands in the Archipelago (Oxford, 1687)

Riedesel, Johann Hermann von, *Reise durch Sicilien und Großgriechenland* (Zurich, 1771)

(English ed.: *Travels through Sicily and that part of Italy formerly called Magna Graecia*, trans. J. R. Forster (London, 1773)

French ed.: *Voyage en Sicile et dans la Grande Grèce* (Lausanne, 1773))

Remarques d'un voyageur moderne au Levant (Amsterdam and Stuttgart, 1773)

(German ed.: *Bemerkungen auf einer Reise nach der Levante*, trans. C. W. Dohm (Leipzig, 1774))

Reise and *Remarques* reissued together in French (Paris, 1802) and again, in German, with an introduction by K. Edschmid and a biographical essay by E. E. Becker (Darmstadt, 1942); the *Reise* reissued by the Winckelmann Gesellschaft (Berlin, (1965), ed. A. Schulz

Ross, Ludwig, *Reisen auf den griechischen Inseln des ägäischen Meeres* (Stuttgart and Tübingen, 1840)

Sandys, George, *A Relation of a Journey begun An. Dom. 1610*, 3rd ed. (London, 1627)

Smith, Thomas, *Remarks upon the Manners, Religion and Government of the Turks, Together with a Survey of the Seven Churches* (London, 1678)

Spon, Jacob, *Voyage d'Italie, de Dalmatie, de Grèce et du Levant* (3 vols., Lyons, 1678; 2 vols., Amsterdam, 1679)

Réponse à la critique publiée par M. Guillet sur le voyage de Grèce de Jacob Spon (Lyons, 1679)

Stuart, James, and Revett, Nicholas, *The Antiquities of Athens*, vol. I (London, 1762); vol. II (1787); vol. III, ed. Willey Reveley (1794); vol. IV (1816)

Thévenot, Jean de, *Relation d'un voyage fait au Levant* (Paris, 1665)

Tournefort, Joseph Pitton de, *Relation d'un voyage du Levant fait par ordre du roy* (Paris, 1717)

(English ed.: *A Voyage into the Levant* (London, 1718 and 1741))

Vernon, Francis, A letter in *Philosophical Transactions of the Royal Society*, CXXIV (24 April 1676)

Extracts from his journal published in *Hesperia* (1947 and 1949)

Wheler, Sir George, *A Journey into Greece* (London, 1682)

Bibliography

Wood, Robert, *The Ruins of Palmyra* (London, 1753)

　An Essay on the Original Genius of Homer (London, 1769)

　(German trans. of that ed.: *Robert Woods Versuch über das Originalgenie des Homers*, trans. C. F. Michaelis (Frankfurt am Main, 1773))

　An Essay on the Original Genius and Writings of Homer with a Comparative View of the Ancient and Present State of the Troade (London, 1775)

(II) GERMAN SCHOLARS AND POETS

J. W. von Goethe, *Werke*, ed. Erich Trunz and others (Hamburg, 1949–66)

　Briefe, ed. Karl Robert Mandelkow (Hamburg, 1962–7)

Wilhelm Heinse, *Ardinghello und die glückseligen Inseln* (Insel edition)

J. G. Herder, *Sämtliche werke*, ed. Bernhard Suphan (repr. Hildesheim, 1967)

C. G. Heyne, *Einleitung in das Studium der Antike* (Göttingen and Gotha, 1772)

　Lobschrift auf Winckelmann (Kassel, 1778)

　Das vermeinte Grabmal Homers (Leipzig, 1794) (Eng. ed., trans. Lechevalier, 1795)

　A review of Wood's *Homer* in the *Göttinger Anzeigen von Gelehrten Sachen*, XXXII (15 March 1770) repr. as the foreword to the 1773 trans.

　A review of Chandler, Revett and Pars, *Ionian Antiquities* in the *Göttinger Anzeigen*, LIV (5 May 1770)

　'Über das Local in der Iliade': an essay contained in his ed. of Lechevalier's *Beschreibung der Ebene von Troja* (Leipzig, 1792)

Friedrich Hölderlin, *Sämtliche Werke*, ed. Friedrich Beißner and Adolf Beck (Stuttgart, 1946–77)

J. J. Winckelmann, *Kleinere Schriften*, ed. Walther Rehm (Berlin, 1968)

　Gedancken über die Nachahmung der Griechischen Werke in der Mahlerey und Bildhauer-Kunst, trans. as *Reflections on the Painting and Sculptures of the Greeks* by Henry Fusseli (London, 1765)

　Briefe, ed. Walther Rehm (Berlin, 1952–7)

(III) SECONDARY LITERATURE

Abbott, G. F., *Under the Turk in Constantinople* (London, 1920)

Buhle, J. G. (ed.), *Literarischer Briefwechsel von Johann David Michaelis* (Leipzig, 1795)

Carlyle, T., 'The Life of Heyne', in *The Works of Thomas Carlyle* (London, 1899), XXVI

Collignon, M., 'Le Consul Jean Giraud et sa relation de l'Attique au xviiᵉ siècle', *Mémoires de l'Académie des Inscriptions et des Belles Lettres*, XXXIX (1913)

Colvin, Sir Sidney, and Cust, L., *History of the Society of Dilettanti* (London, 1914)

Eliot, C. W. J., 'George Wheler, Christian Traveler and Philosopher', *Echos du monde classique*, XXII, no. 1 (January 1978), 13–24 (Classical Association of Canada, Guelph)

Foerster, D. M., *Homer in English Criticism* (New Haven, 1947)

Haskell, F., and Penny, N., *Taste and the Antique* (Yale, 1981)

Hatfield, H. C., *Winckelmann and his German Critics* (New York, 1943)

Hecht, Hans, *T. Percy, R. Wood und J. D. Michaelis. Ein Beitrag zur Literaturgeschichte der Geniezeit* (Stuttgart, 1933)

Heeren, A. H. L., *Christian Gottlob Heyne biographisch dargestellt* (Göttingen, 1813)

Hervey, Mary, *The Life, Correspondence and Collections of Thomas Howard* (Cambridge, 1921)

Justi, C., *Winckelmann*, 3rd ed. (Leipzig, 1923)

Laborde, le comte Léon de, *Athènes aux xvᵉ, xviᵉ et xviiᵉ siècles* (Paris, 1854)

Bibliography

Leppmann, W., *Winckelmann* (London, 1971)

Malakis, E., *French Travellers in Greece (1770–1820). An early Phase in French Philhellenism* (Philadelphia, 1925)

Meritt, B. D., 'The Persians at Delphi', *Hesperia*, XVI (1947), 58–62
  'Epigraphic Notes of Francis Vernon', *Hesperia*, supplement VIII (1949), 213–27

Michaelis, Adolf, 'Ein Verschollener', *Im neuen Reich*, 6. Jahrgang (1876), I, 950–67 and 981–94
  Ancient Marbles in Great Britain (Cambridge, 1882)

Miller, W., *The English in Athens before 1821. A Lecture delivered before the Anglo-Hellenic League in Athens 10 February 1926* (London, 1926)

Omont, H., 'Athènes au XVIIᵉ siècle', *Revue des études grecques*, XIV (1901), 270–94

Osborn, J. M., 'Travel Literature and the Rise of Neo-Hellenism in England', *Bulletin of the New York Public Library*, LXV, no. 5 (May 1963), 279–300

Pearson, J. B., *Chaplains to the Levant Company, 1611–1706* (Cambridge, 1883)

Ramsey, R. W., 'Sir George Wheler and his Travels in Greece, 1650–1724', *Transactions of the Royal Society of Literature*, n.s., XIX (1942), 1–38

Rehm, Walther, 'Johann Hermann von Riedesel. Freund Winckelmanns, Mentor Goethes, Diplomat Friedrich des Großen', in *Götterstille und Göttertrauer. Aufsätze zur Deutsch-Antiken Begegnung* (Bern, 1951)

Rice, Warner G., 'Early English Travellers to Greece and the Levant', in *Essays and Studies in English and Comparative Literature*, University of Michigan Publications, X (1933), pp. 205–60

Sandys, J. E., *A History of Classical Scholarship*, 2nd ed. (Cambridge, 1906)

Spencer, Terence, *Fair Greece Sad Relic* (London, 1954)

Stern, B. H., *The Rise of Romantic Hellenism in English Literature, 1732–1786* (Wisconsin, 1940)

Tibal, André, *Inventaire des manuscrits de Winckelmann déposés à la Bibliothèque nationale* (Paris, 1911)

Trevelyan, H., *Goethe and the Greeks* (Cambridge, 1942)

Tsigakou, F.-M., *The Rediscovery of Greece* (London, 1981)

Vandal, Albert, *Les Voyages du Marquis de Nointel, 1670–1680* (Paris, 1900)

Wegner, M. (ed.), *Land der Griechen*, 2nd ed. (Berlin, 1943)

Wood, A. C., *A History of the Levant Company* (London, 1946)

Zimmermann, K. (ed.), *Die Dresdener Antiken und Winckelmann*, Schriften der Winckelmann-Gesellschaft, IV (Berlin, 1977)

INDEX